www.ingramcontent.com/pod-product-compliance
Lightning Source LLC
Chambersburg PA
CBHW060756100426
42813CB00004B/844

The

PRACTICAL

TANYA

Also by Chaim Miller

The Kol Menachem Chumash – Gutnick Edition

The Kol Menachem Chumash (Hebrew) – Leviev Edition

Rambam: Principles of Faith – Slager Edition

The Kol Menachem Haggadah – Slager Edition

The Kol Menachem Megillah – Slager Edition

The Five Books of Moses, Lifestyle Books – Slager Edition

Prayers for Friday Night, Lifestyle Books – Slager Edition

The Kol Menachem Tehillim – Schottenstein Edition

Turning Judaism Outward: A Biography of Rabbi Menachem Mendel Schneerson

The Practical Tanya Part One: The Book for Inbetweeners

THE SLAGER EDITION

The

PRACTICAL TANYA

PART TWO
GATEWAY TO UNITY AND FAITH

RABBI
SHNEUR
ZALMAN *of* LIADI

ADAPTED BY

CHAIM MILLER

GUTNICK LIBRARY
OF JEWISH CLASSICS

ISBN-13: 978-1934152638 I ISBN-10: 1934152633

Published and distributed by: Kol Menachem, 827 Montgomery Street, Brooklyn, NY 11213.

1-888-580-1900 I 1-718-951-6328 I 1-718-953-3346 (Fax)

www.kolmenachem.com   I   orders@kolmenachem.com

Contact the author at: chaimmiller@gmail.com   I rabbichaimmiller.com

First Edition — 2017.

Praise for *The Practical Tanya*

"An astonishing accomplishment... and suitable for anyone... even those who do not read in Hebrew and are not familiar with esoteric texts."

—Rabbi Moshe Wolfson, *Mashgiach Ruchani Yeshivas Torah Ve-Da'as.*

"It is wonderful that this sacred text has now been clarified in a way that anyone can benefit from it."

—Rabbi Gavriel Zinner, author *Nitei Gavriel,* Rav of Congregation *Nitei Gavriel.*

"An important contribution... makes the flow of the *Tanya* very clear for all who study.

—Rabbi Yehuda Leib Schapiro, *Yeshiva Gedola* Rabbinical College of Greater Miami.

"With a masterful command of the English language, Rabbi Miller has managed to open up the *Tanya* to the wider public... not an easy task!"

—Rabbi Nochum Kaplan, Director, *Merkos* Office of Education.

"A lucid and scholarly translation... will undoubtedly assist multitudes."

—Rabbi Moshe Bogomilsky, *halachic* authority, author of *Vedibarta Bam* series.

"Brings the warmth, genius, and inspiration of the *Tanya* to life.... This work will certainly help inspire souls."

—Rabbi Zev Reichman, Director, Mechina Program, Yeshiva University.

"Rabbi Chaim Miller has made it accessible to everyone.... This book will awaken, inspire, and challenge you."

—Daniel Matt, translator of *The Zohar: Pritzker Edition.*

"Quite simply the best version in the English language."

—Rabbi Dov Greenberg, Chabad of Stanford University.

"A wonderful work which makes the *Tanya* accessible and understandable to a whole new generation of spiritual explorers... beautifully written."

—Rabbi Mark Wildes, Director, *Manhattan Jewish Experience.*

"A new classic.... Practical and relevant in the fast-moving, rapidly-changing technological era in which we live."

—Rabbi Mendel Lew, Stanmore & Canons Park Synagogue, U.K.

"Rabbi Chaim Miller's crisp, lucid and contemporary translation promises... concrete strategies for personal spiritual growth."

—Henry Abramson, Dean, Touro College, Brooklyn.

THE UNITY WITHIN G-D

TRANSLATOR'S INTRODUCTION

THE SECOND BOOK OF TANYA

The *Tanya* was first published in 1796 as a single volume containing two separate works. The first work, *The Book for Inbetweeners* (*Sefer shel Beinonim*), consisting of fifty-three chapters and an introduction, has been translated and elucidated in volume one of this series.[1] The second section was a shorter treatise of just twelve chapters and a separate introduction, entitled *Gateway to Unity and Faith* (*Sha'ar Ha-Yichud ve-Ha-Emunah*),[2] which is translated and elucidated here in volume two of *The Practical Tanya*.

While they share a similar literary style, the two books are very different in content. *The Book for Inbetweeners* is written with a strong practical emphasis, to guide the reader in "worshiping G-d with the heart and the mind."[3] *Gateway to Unity and Faith,* by contrast, is abstract and theosophi-

---

1. Rabbi Chaim Miller, *The Practical Tanya, Part One: The Book for Inbetweeners* (Brooklyn: Kol Menachem, 2016). For biographical information on the *Tanya's* author, a history of its composition and printing, the origin of the *Tanya's* teachings and its methodology, see my "Translator's Introduction" in volume one. I will only add here additional information pertinent to this volume.

2. For bibliographic details see Rabbi Yehoshua Mondshine, *Torath Habad: Bibliographies of Habad Hasiduth Books,* volume 1, (Brooklyn: Kehos, 1981, Hebrew), pp. 15-16. The date of composition of *Sha'ar Ha-Yichud ve-Ha-Emunah* is unclear. For conflicting views, see Rabbi Nachum Greenwald (ed.) *Ha-Rav* (2015), pp. 361-375.

3. See Miller, *The Practical Tanya, Part One,* p. xxxi. *Sefer shel Beinonim* is by no means an exclusively practical guide, and contains much theosophical material.

    It is interesting that Rabbi Shneur Zalman chose to prioritize practice over theory by placing the more practical *Book for Inbetweeners* as Part One, before the philosophy that underpins it, in Part Two. Apparently, this was a late editorial move, and the author had originally intended to situate the more theoretical *Sha'ar Ha-Yichud* as Part One. See below pp. 1, 5. For a discussion of this decision see Rabbi Menachem Mendel Schneerson, *Likutei Sichos* (Brooklyn: Kehos, 2006), pp. 199-203. For a suggestion as to how the themes from the second book form the basis of Chasidic worship, see *On The Essence of Chasidus* (Herschel Greenberg and Susan Handelman trans.), pp. 84-6. See also: *The Practical Tanya, Part One,* p. 233.

cal; through its twelve chapters, the author rarely, if ever, suggests a practical implication in daily worship.[4]

CENTRAL THEMES OF THE SECOND BOOK

The second part of *Tanya* is a sustained discourse on the unity of G-d. While apparently never completed by its author,[5] its twelve chapters represent one of the clearest, most popular and most enduring treatments of the topic from a Kabbalistic/Chasidic point of view.[6]

The belief in Divine unity is expressed in the standard Biblical declaration, *"G-d is one"* (*Deuteronomy* 6:4). The *Talmud* generally understood this as a statement of G-d's singular authority over the world, *"to declare G-d is King above and below, and over the four directions of the earth."*[7] The Sages also described G-d's unity in terms of *exclusivity,* that there are no other gods besides the one G-d.[8]

Gateway to Unity and Faith takes for granted that the reader is familiar with these concepts and does not elaborate upon them. Rather, our author has two different concerns in the discussion of Divine unity.

The first half of the book, up to and including chapter seven, is a radical re-reading of "Divine immanentism," the way in which G-d is deeply present in our world. We learn that the world's separate existence from G-d, as

---

4.   There is some overlap in the themes discussed by both books. The core theme of chapters 1-7 of *Sha'ar Ha-Yichud ve-Ha-Emunah* (the voiding of the world's identity in G-d) receives a fairly detailed treatment in chapters 20-22 of *Sefer Shel Beinonim;* and the central argument of chapters 8-12 of *Sha'ar Ha-Yichud ve-Ha-Emunah* (the unity of Divine attributes), is articulated a number of times in *Sefer Shel Beinonim* (see *Practical Tanya,* volume one, pp. 46-48; pp. 526-7; 537-9; 623-4). In Part Four of the *Tanya,* (*Igeres Ha-Kodesh* sec. 11), the author offers some suggestions how to implement the central theme of *Sha'ar Ha-Yichud ve-Ha-Emunah* in a practical way.

5.   See below, p. 171.

6.   Important treatments of this topic in the earlier Kabbalistic tradition include: Rabbi Meir Ibn Gabbai, *Avodas Ha-Kodesh* (Warsaw 1883), *Chelek Ha-Yichud* (p. 8b-25b); comments scattered throughout the works of Rabbi Moshe Cordovero, collected in Shmuel Yudaikin (ed.), *Ha-Melech Hakadosh* (Bnei Brak: 2001). See also sources cited from early Kabbalists, below xiv-xvii. For a contemporary analysis, drawing principally from the works of Rabbi Azriel of Gerona, Rabbi Isaac Luria and Rabbi Shalom Sharabi, see Gilad ben Shoshan, *Dorshey Yichudcha* (Jerusalem 2016).

7.   *Talmud, Berachos* 13b.

8.   *Mechilta, Bachodesh* sec.5. For a collection of sources see Norman Lamm, *The Shema: Spirituality and Law in Judaism* (Philadelphia: Jewish Publication Society, 1998), chapters 5-6.

our senses perceive it, is not real, and there is a path to transcend this sensory consciousness through contemplation and meditation. This approach is attributed by the *Tanya* to Rabbi Yisra'el *Ba'al Shem Tov,* upon whose teachings the Chasidic movement was founded.[9]

The second part of *Gateway to Unity and Faith,* from chapters 8-12, builds on a discussion that features extensively in Jewish philosophical and Kabbalistic works from the 12th/13th centuries onwards: the problem of Divine attributes and their unity *within* G-d.[10] The discussion seeks to clarify: How does the notion of multiple Divine attributes, which are often indicated throughout the Biblical and Rabbinic writings, not compromise the unity of G-d?[11]

Placed side by side, the two core sets of teachings in *Gateway to Unity and Faith* complement each other. In chapters 1-7 we learn that *outside G-d there is no (true) existence.* In chapters 8-12 we learn that *inside G-d, everything is unified with Him.* These two concepts *together* clarify how "G-d is one"—inside Him all is one; outside Him there is nothing. The sum total: All that exists, in reality, is the One.

UNITY OF THE DIVINE ATTRIBUTES

Since the issue discussed in chapters 8-12, the unity of Divine attributes, has a richer historical precedent, I will discuss it first, seeking to place the *Tanya's* discussion in the context of earlier sources.

9.   See below, p. 20. A similar emphasis on Divine immanentism (Panentheism) can be found in fragments of the immense corpus of Rabbi Moshe Cordovero (*Ramak, 16th* century), but the concept does not feature prominently. For a collection of these passages see Yudaikin, *Ha-Melech Hakadosh,* sections 58-60.

There are also some hints to the position in earlier Kabbalistic works. See "The Kabbalah and Pantheism" in *Encyclopedia Judaica,* (Macmillan Reference: 2nd edition, 2007), volume 11, pp. 648-651.

10. Throughout Rabbinic literature, G-d is described as acting through the mediation of Divine attributes, such as the "attribute of judgment" or the "attribute of compassion." See, for example, the *Tanya's* citation below on p. 59.

11. The *Tanya* does not comment on the dispute among the medieval Kabbalists (Rabbi Menachem Recanati and the anonymous author of *Mareches Ha-Elokus*) whether the attributes (in Kabbalistic terminology, *sefiros*) are instruments made by G-d (*kelim*) or are of His essence (*atsmus*). In later Chabad discourses this topic is elaborated upon considerably. For an exhaustive treatment, which brilliantly showcases some of the attention to detail and nuanced thinking of Chabad Chasidus, see Rabbi Yoel Kahn, *Sefer Ha-Arachim Chabad,* volume 4 (Brooklyn: Kehos, 1976), entry *Oros De-Sefiros, Peshitusam ve-Tziuryam,* pp. 56-207.

In his discussion of the Thirteen Principles of Faith, Maimonides writes:

> "The Second Principle is G-d's unity. Namely, that we are to believe that He who is the cause of everything, is one. He is not like one of a pair, or one of a species, or like one person who is comprised of many parts. And He is not one like a plain item which is one in number but can be divided and subdivided endlessly. Rather He—May He be exalted!—is one with a unity that has no parallel whatsoever. This is the Second Principle of faith, taught by the verse, 'Hear, O Israel! G-d is our G-d. G-d is one' (Deuteronomy 6:4)."[12]

If G-d's unity is absolute, how are we to understand the notion of His many attributes?

Maimonides answer is very simple: The attributes do not exist! They are nothing more than metaphorical, literary devices, and should not be taken literally. To do so, in fact, would violate the most basic foundation of monotheism.

Maimonides devotes a long section of his *Guide for the Perplexed* to this issue.[13] He opens with the following argument.

> "You must know that He, may He be exalted, has in no way and in no mode any essential attribute. Just as it is impossible that He should have a body, it is also impossible that He should possess an essential attribute."

> "If, however, someone believes that He is one, but possesses a certain number of essential attributes, he says in his words that He is one, but believes Him in his thought to be many. This resembles what the Christians say: namely, that He is one but also three, and that the three are one"[14]

Later, Maimonides goes so far as to say:

> "He who affirms that G-d, may He be exalted, has a positive attribute... has abolished his belief in the existence of G-d without being aware of it."[15]

12. *Rambam, Commentary to the Mishnah, Sanhedrin,* beginning of *Perek Chelek*. See also his *Mishneh Torah, Laws of Foundations of the Torah,* 1:6-7.

13. *Guide for the Perplexed* (part one, chapters 50-60). The best English translation is by Shlomo Pines (Chicago University Press 1974), 2 volumes.

14. *Ibid.* p. 111.

15. *Ibid.* p. 145.

While Maimonides' position may seem extreme, it is clear-cut and logical. As a philosopher, he was not working with any received truth about G-d, and followed a rational argument: If G-d is truly one, He cannot contain multiple components.

In those instances where received tradition appeared to contradict logic, Maimonides often reconciled the two through the approach of *allegorization*. The text which appears to contradict logic, he would argue, is not to be taken literally. That was his way of dealing with the many Scriptural and Rabbinic references to Divine attributes: they are all metaphorical and not literal.

> *"When you encounter a word of the Sages which seems to conflict with reason, you will pause, consider it, and realize that this utterance must be a riddle or a parable. You will sleep on it, trying anxiously to grasp its logic and its expression, so that you may find its genuine intellectual intention.'"*[16]

The Sages chose to speak in allegories, Maimonides argues, because:

> *"It is the method of truly great thinkers. Since the words of the Sages all deal with supernatural matters which are ultimate, they must be expressed in riddles and analogies."*[17]

All this seems fairly straightforward and consistent. If G-d is one, He must be simple and non-composite. Therefore He is devoid of any attributes. Any textual indication to the contrary must be read as an allegory.

Maimonides, however, then confuses us by stating an outright exception to the above rule. There *are*, it turns out, some things we can confidently and accurately say of G-d, that He is: *"living, possessing power, possessing knowledge, possessing will."*[18]

After Maimonides' confident and uncompromising dismissal of the notion of Divine attributes, this is a perplexing about-turn. The characterization of G-d "possessing knowledge" is particularly challenging since the process of acquiring knowledge implies change and duality—a thinker is

---

16.   *Commentary to the Mishnah*, ibid.; see *Guide* 1:53.

17.   *Ibid.*

18.   *Guide* ibid. The contradictory nature of Maimonides discussion is noted in Pines' "Translators introduction," p. xcvii. See also: Howard Kreisel, "Moses Maimonides," in Daniel Frank and Oliver Leaman (eds.), *History of Jewish Philosophy* (London and New York: Routledge, 1997), p. 200-201.

not the same after learning a new insight. How would we understand that process in relation to the perfect and unchanging G-d?

Maimonides answers that G-d's intellect is simply different to ours.

> *"He is the power to know as well as the knower and the known... those three notions form in Him, may He be exalted, one single notion in which there is no multiplicity."*[19]

While Maimonides offers an elaborate proof of this point, ultimately he confesses that, *"the mouth has no power to express this idea, nor the ear to hear it, nor the heart of man to recognize it properly."*[20]

We will now examine how Maimonides' views on this matter were received by the Kabbalistic thinkers that followed him. Since Maimonides' literary activity preceded any public discourse of the Kabbalah, his position became the standard which had to be either accepted or rejected by later authors. As we shall see, the position of the Kabbalah was at odds with Maimonides, resulting in either complete or partial rejection by later Kabbalists.

Rabbi Azriel of Gerona (c. 1160 – c. 1238), discusses the issue of Divine attributes in his *Explanation of the Ten Sefiros*,[21] a short work that aims to clarify the status of the Divine attributes in a series of questions and answers.[22] In his sixth question, the inquirer asks, *"How can we possibly say that He is One and the multiplicity of ten (sefiros) unites within Him?"*

---

19.   *Guide* 1:68. This principle is also codified in his *Mishneh Torah, Laws of Foundations of the Torah* 2:10 (cited below p. 94, 137) and echoes Aristotle's *Metaphysics*. See "Translators Introduction" ibid.

     While such a stance may seem out of character for a rationalist such as Maimonides, he was forced to accept that G-d possesses intellect on the purely logical grounds that anything immaterial must be an intellect, as Aristotle reasons in *De Anima* III.4. For an extensive discussion see Peter Adamson, "Avicenna and his Commentators on Human and Divine Self-Intellection" in Dag Nikolaus Hasse and Amos Bertolacci (eds.), *The Arabic, Hebrew and Latin Reception of Avicenna's Metaphysics* (Berlin: De Gruyter, 2012), pp. 97-122.

20.   *Laws of Foundations of the Torah* ibid.; cited below p. 121. See *The Practical Tanya* volume 1, p. 56.

21.   *Sefiros* (sing. *sefirah*) is the term used by Kabbalists to refer to the Divine attributes.

22.   Printed in Meir ibn Gabbai, *Derech Emunah* (Warsaw, 1890), p. 2a-5b. The work is composed as a series of logical and clear questions and answers about the *sefiros*. For a partial English translation see *The Early Kabbalah*, trans. Ronald Kiener, ed. Josef Dan (Mahwah, N.J., 1986), pp. 89-96. For a discussion of this work as a reaction to Maimonides see: Jonathan Dauber, "Competing Approaches to Maimonides in Early Kabbalah" in James T. Robinson (ed.), *The Cultures of Maimonideanism: New*

Rabbi Azriel responds:

"I have already informed you that the One is the foundation of the many (sefiros) and that no new power is introduced in them, other than from Him."

"He is more than them. Each one of the (sefiros) is superior to the next one below. The power of one is in the other."

"Therefore, the first is the power of them all. (Conversely), the power of them all is nothing other than the first power."

"And while the first is the power of them all, there is nothing in the particular (powers) that is not in the (first) general (power)."

"A metaphor for this is: a fire, with its flame, sparks, and hues. They are all of one essence, even though they differ from each other and are divided into separate components."[23]

The Kabbalah is unequivocal that ten Divine attributes *actually exist* and cannot be dismissed as a mere allegory.[24] Rabbi Azriel therefore cannot accept Maimonides' teaching that G-d is a single, non composite substance. The origin ("first power") is certainly one, but that first power has emanated other Divine powers (*sefiros*) which are now integrated within the G-dhead.

Rabbi Azriel argues that this does not contradict the monotheistic faith of Judaism since, *"there is nothing in the particular (powers) that is not in the (first) general (power)."* All the attributes stem from the One and are powered by the One. Therefore the lower *sefiros* are not separate from their source; they simply express it in a more "particular" way.

This is a very different approach from Maimonides who understood Divine unity more literally, as absolute simplicity, *i.e.*, the absence of any composite qualities.

Approaches to the History of Jewish Thought (Leiden: Brill, 2009), pp. 57-88.

23. ...ועל זה יוסיף השואל לשאול היאך נוכל לומר כי הוא אחד והמספר עשר המתאחדים בו
תשובה. כבר הודעתיך כי האחד יסוד הרבים ואין כח מתחדש בהם אלא ממנו והוא יתר מהם
וכל אחד מהם יתר על חבירו שלמטה ממנו וכח זה בזה א״כ הראשון הוא כח כולם וכח כולם
אינם [אלא] כח ראשון אע״פ שהראשון כח כולם שאין בפרט אלא מה שבכלל והמשל על
זה האש והשלהבת והזיקים והגונין שהם עקר אחד (ו)אע״פ שהם משתנים זה מזה בהתחלק
חלקיהם (*Explanation of the Ten Sefiros* p. 2b-3a).

24. *Sefer Yetzirah*, which is the source of the term *sefiros*, speaks of *"ten ineffable sefiros... like a flame in a burning coal"* (1:7), suggesting that the *sefiros* are real and present.

Rabbi Azriel does not respond directly to Maimonides' concerns of attributing multiple powers to the one G-d. Since the attributes are deeply integrated, and each expresses the other, Rabbi Azriel sees no real multiplicity. There may be ten different energies, but it is all one "fire."

Rabbi Asher ben David, a Kabbalist operating during the same period as Rabbi Azriel, took a different approach, attempting a synthesis with Maimonides' position, while not accepting it fully.

In his *Sefer Ha-Yichud* ("Book of Unity"), a work written to defend the Kabbalah against its critics,[25] Rabbi Asher ben David frames the problem of Divine attributes in very similar terms to Maimonides.

> *"How could (G-d) be ascribed limited and defined attributes, even if they remain bound with the Cause-of-causes?*
>
> *"For, in truth, every limited thing must have a beginning and an end; every form must have a body. Every limited thing can be displaced and every composite thing can be decomposed....*
>
> *"Heaven forbid for us to speak in such a way of (G-d), the 'Rider of the heavens,' or even of His attributes! For how could it possibly be said that they are limited or bound with Him (in a composite way)?"*
>
> *"Therefore, every intelligent person ought to understand and know that (the description of) each attribute is 'to calm the listening ear,' and it is impossible for Him to contain any limited or defined attribute."*[26]

This passage reads as if it were taken right out of one of Maimonides' works. The notion of attributes, the author argues, would impose limitation and is therefore utterly inappropriate for G-d. "Heaven forbid" to say that G-d's attributes are bound with Him in a composite way, (as was argued by Rabbi Azriel). Rabbi Asher ben David even intimates that the whole discussion of attributes is merely, "to calm the listening ear."

25. *Rabbi Asher ben David: His Complete Works and Studies in his Kabbalistic Thought,* ed. Daniel Abrams (Los Angeles, 1996), [Hebrew]. For the polemical nature of the work, see p. 120.

26. איך יתכן לתת מדות קצובות וחלוטות ואף כי מחוברות בעלת העלות וסבת הסיבות כי אמת כל מוגבל יש לו ראש וסוף וכל צורה יש לו גוף וכל מוגבל נטרד וכל מחובר יפרד.... וחלילה לנו מלדבר כזאת על רוכב ערבות גם מדותיו הנאמרות כי מי יאמר שהם מוגבלות או להיותם בו מחוברות. לכן ראוי לכל משכיל להבין ולדעת שכל מדה לשכך אוזן שומעת וחלוטה קצובה מדה בו להיות אפשר ואי (*ibid.* p. 119).

The phrase "to calm the listening ear" is based on *Mechilta* to Exodus 19:18, cited by the *Tanya* below p. 141 and 147,

But, unlike Maimonides, Rabbi Asher ben David *did* maintain that G-d possesses ten intellectual and emotional attributes (*sefiros*). In a brief passage, *Sefer Ha-Yichud* resolves how this is to be reconciled with the Maimonidean doctrine of Divine simplicity and non-compositeness.

> *"They are called 'attributes,' not from G-d's perspective, but according to their effect on us, from our perspective. For He is one from every angle; He is kindness, He is judgment, He is mercy."*[27]

The differentiation into distinct attributes, we are told, is only "from our perspective." From G-d's perspective, there is just simple, non-composite oneness.

The implication here is that there are two states of consciousness or reality. From our lower, worldly point of view, the ten Divine attributes exist and function as modes of expression. But if we were able to see things from G-d's point of view, we would appreciate that "He is one from every angle," and devoid of any multiplicity implied by the attributes.[28]

Rabbi Asher ben David's position is certainly not identical with Maimonides, who maintained that the attributes (other than intellect) are purely metaphorical. But, *Sefer Ha-Yichud*'s higher state of consciousness does closely resemble Maimonides' description of the Divine intellect (the unity is wondrous and not fathomable by man). This has led one scholar to describe Rabbi Asher ben David as a "non-Maimonidean Maimonidean," meaning to say that he has a similar approach to Maimonides to the problem of Divine attributes, although he reaches different conclusions. (Maimonides would not accept *Sefer Ha-Yichud's* position that at a lower consciousness/reality the attributes do exist). Rabbi Asher ben David reconciles the Kabbalistic view of the attributes with the view of Maimonides to the greatest extent possible.[29]

---

27. ולפי פעולותיו בנו נקראו מדות לא מצד לעצמו וכי אם מצד שלנו לפי שהוא אחד בכל צד
הוא החסד הוא הדין הרחמים (*ibid.*).

28. This is not too dissimilar from Maimonides' position that it is acceptable to speak of Divine attributes, not as qualities within G-d, but in relation to *actions* that G-d performs: *"Every attribute that we predicate of Him is an attribute of action"* (*Guide* 1:58, p. 136).

    Even the phrase *"one from every angle"* is identical to the language used by Maimonides in *Laws of Foundations of the Torah* 1:10, (cited by the *Tanya* below, p. 94). See also *Sefer Ha-Yichud* p. 82: *"one from every angle, and in all His attributes from every angle, without any separation and without any conjoining"* (אחד בכל צד ובכל מדותיו מכל צד בלא שום פירוד ובלא שום חיבור), which is almost identical to the language used by Maimonides ibid.

29. For all the above see Dauber, "Competing Approaches."

The *Tanya* follows in the "non-Maimonidean Maimonidean" path. In his discussion of Divine Knowledge in chapter 7, Rabbi Shneur Zalman cites Maimonides' treatment almost verbatim.[30] In a similar fashion to Rabbi Asher ben David, the *Tanya* extends the Maimonidean model of Divine intellect to all the *sefiros* described in the Kabbalah: *"Now as for what Rambam of blessed memory, wrote that G-d is totally one with His essence, being and knowledge in an absolute and non-composite unity, the same is true, literally, of all G-d's attributes."*[31]

In Maimonidean fashion, Rabbi Shneur Zalman concedes that the unity of G-d with His many attributes is ultimately something we cannot fathom: *"This unity, how He is one with the attributes which He emanated from Himself, is also not possible to be understood... their unity with Him is a matter of supra-rational faith."*[32] The *Tanya* also draws a distinction, similar to Rabbi Asher Ben David, between G-d's perception of the attributes and ours: *"It is only from the perspective of the creations (celestial or terrestrial), that G-d's attributes/will/wisdom are designated by the specific names which we use."*[33] This is in contrast to the way each attribute exists from G-d's perspective where *"it cannot be given its own name."*[34]

THE BA'AL SHEM TOV'S MYSTICAL CONSCIOUSNESS

While the *Tanya* draws on the concepts, terms and sources of the Kabbalah in general, the current work seeks to clarify the approach of a particular teacher who worked within this tradition, Rabbi Yisra'el *Ba'al Shem Tov.*

Let us first examine the core values and teachings which emerged from the mystical consciousness of the *Ba'al Shem Tov,* and then we will turn to the *Tanya's* adaptation of them.[35]

---

30. Below pp. 92-97.

31. p. 119. See also p. 121.

32. p. 138-9. See also p, 146. Chapters 8-9 offer the reader a prolonged "meditation" to contemplate how G-d's essence transcends His attributes.

33. p. 148. According to the *Tanya*, G-d's names are synonymous with His attributes (p. 71).

34. p. 147.

35. The author of *Tanya*, Rabbi Shneur Zalman was not a direct disciple of the *Ba'al Shem Tov*, whom he never met (in adulthood). All the Chasidic teachings Rabbi Shneur Zalman received came to him through the filter of the Magid of Mezritch. See "Translator's Introduction" to *The Practical Tanya*, volume 1, p. xvii-xxi.

"Consider yourself a child of the higher world," the *Ba'al Shem Tov* instructed his followers, *"for the whole of this world is like a mustard seed when compared with the higher world."*[36]

Our goal is to inhabit a higher consciousness. To do this we must retreat from the sensory experience of this world, transcending its allure and arresting demand for our attention. The tool which facilitates this shift is *human thought.* As the *Ba'al Shem Tov* teaches, *"When you will think of the upper world, you will be in the upper world. Wherever a person's thoughts are, there he is found."*[37] Thought, in particular, has this unique power: *"The reason why thought enables a person to endlessly grasp great ideas is because thought, too, is infinite."*[38]

Since it is abundant and unlimited, thought provides us with a tool to overcome the barriers which distance us from G-d. Thought enables us to be fully immersed in a perception which is beyond the limits of the senses.

What are we to contemplate in order to reach higher consciousness? The *Ba'al Shem Tov's* most often repeated quotes were, *"The whole earth is filled with His glory,"*[39] and *"There is no place devoid of Him."*[40] We are to look at the world as saturated with the Divine. G-d is the energy which animates all physical forms. He is present in every object, every act, every word. There is no reality that is separate from G-d.

To illustrate the real possibility of reaching such a consciousness, the *Ba'al Shem Tov* taught the "parable of the barriers."

> *"There was once a very wise king who created a magical illusion of walls, towers and gates. He gave orders that people should come to him through the gates and towers, and instructed that some of his royal treasures be scattered at each gate."*
>
> *"Some people made it to the first gate, and then, (happy with the treasure they had found), returned. Others (made it further, but still returned home before reaching the king)."*

36   *Tzava'as Ha-Ribash* (Brooklyn: Kehos, 1998), par. 6.

37   *Ibid.* par. 68.

38   Rabbi Elimelech of Lyzhshank, *Noam Elimelech,* (ed. Gedaliah Nigal, Jerusalem 1978), 25a (vol. 1, p. 132).

39   *Psalms* 72:19.

40   *Tikunei Zohar, tikun* 57, p. 91b; see, for example, *Magid Devarav Le-Ya'akov* (Brooklyn: Kehos, 2004), p 39a.

"But the king's loving son made a great effort to reach his father, and he saw that there was really no barrier separating him from his father, because it was all an illusion."

"And the meaning of the parable is obvious.... When a person knows that 'The whole earth is filled with His glory,' and that every motion and thought comes from Him, then... there is no barrier or curtain separating man from G-d."[41]

Despite its robust appearance, the barrier between us and G-d which the physical world poses, is insubstantial. With the appropriate determination, we can lift our consciousness to penetrate this "illusion" and be united with G-d ("the king").

We do this, not by withdrawing from bodily activity, but by modifying our perception of it. We attune ourselves to the Divine energy which powers every sensory experience. No aspect of reality should be taken at face value; *everything* is a manifestation of G-d. We reach G-d through the world, not around it.

Physical consciousness is "illusory" in that it tends to hide this truth, obscuring the Divine presence which animates the universe.[42] Through the appropriate dedication to contemplative work, physical consciousness can be elevated to mystical consciousness, as our sensory experience becomes filled with the intuitive awareness of the Divine in all things.

Gateway to Unity and Faith is essentially a guide to succeed in this task. It offers us, in rich detail, ideas we can contemplate in order to reach the kind of consciousness the *Ba'al Shem Tov* had exemplified.

To achieve this goal of "deconstructing" physical awareness, the first seven chapters of our work focus on a radical, new way of understanding the creation process. In the traditional paradigm, creation is a process where G-d brings a new, non-Divine substance into being; He makes something that is not Himself. In the Chasidic paradigm, the Creator undergoes a kind of metamorphosis until some of His own energy *becomes* the creation. This is a very significant point and is the key to understanding *Gateway to Unity*

---

41   Rabbi Ya'akov Yosef of Polonnoye, *Ben Poras Yosef,* (Petrikau/Piotrków 1884), p. 70c.

42   Chasidic thought does not maintain that the world is *actually* an illusion, a conclusion which would undermine the notion of Divine commandments performed in this world; only the world's apparent independence from G-d is illusory. For an often-cited proof of this point from a *Talmudic* law, see Rabbi Shmuel Schneersohn, *Toras Shmuel* 5629 (Brooklyn: Kehos, new edition 1992), pp.161-2.

and Faith. This book is essentially an answer to the question: How, exactly does G-d become the world?[43]

Once we have a convincing explanation of this point, we can begin to transcend the sensory illusion. We become aware that the world is really a Divine energy that has been cloaked or "dressed" as something else. Every creation remains Divine at its core.

Perceiving the world as something G-d has *become* is the secret to attaining the *Ba'al Shem Tov's* mystical ethos, that *"the whole earth is filled with His glory* and *"there is no place devoid of Him."*[44]

THE ROLE OF LANGUAGE

How does G-d become the world? The *Tanya* illustrates this point using the symbolism of *Divine language,* which was a significant point of disagreement between Maimonides and the Kabbalists.

Maimonides saw creation as utterly removed from Creator, and argued that there is nothing that the former can adequately say of the latter.[45] As a result, Maimonides perceived language itself as a mere convention, a set of labels for objects and ideas, and saw nothing intrinsically sacred about words themselves, even when articulated in Hebrew.[46]

The Kabbalists differed sharply on this point.[47] The system of *sefiros* teaches us *similarities* between G-d and ourselves. The same ten attributes

---

43   In the Chasidic paradigm, G-d does not "become" the world in the pantheistic sense that He is nothing more than the world. Rather, He emanates energy ("light") which morphs into the world, through various diminishments. G-d always transcends the world at the same time that he energizes and "becomes" it. See below p. xxv.

44   The Lurianic teaching of *Tzimtum*—that G-d vacated a space in which to create the universe, rendering it devoid of the Divine—is therefore interpreted non-literally in Chasidic thought, as discussed below in the "addendum" to Chapter 7, p. 99*ff.* For a more extended discussion see Rabbi Zvi Einfeld, *Toras Ha-Gra u-Mishnas Ha-Chasidus* (Jerusalem: Mosad Harav Kook, 2009) [Hebrew].

For a re-evaluation of the Chabad position see Rabbi Menachem Mendel Schneerson, *Hisva'aduyos* 5743 (Brooklyn: Va'ad Hanachos Lahak, 1984), volume 3, 1599-1601. See also the Rebbe's comments printed in Rabbi Aharon Chitrik (ed.), *Likutei Amarim Tanya, Sha'ar Ha-Yichud ve-ha-Emunah, Be-Tziruf Ma'arei Mekomos, Likut Perushim, Shinui Nuscha'os,* (Brooklyn: Kehos 1989), pp. 178-180.

45.   *Guide* 1:58-59.

46.   ibid. 2:30; 3:8.

47.   See Nachmanides' criticism of Maimonides' view of language in his commentary to Exodus 30:13.

found within G-d, the Kabbalah teaches, are also present in our souls, and throughout every layer of the universe. A separation between Creator and creations is, of course, preserved, but it is significantly blurred as all existence is looked upon as the embodiment or "clothing" of Divine energies that lie below the surface. From this perspective, language is both sacred and Divine. Creation occurs through G-d *investing Himself* in the language of Hebrew, the letters acting as a luminous bridge from the Divine to our mundane world.

The letters and words which G-d "utters" in Genesis 1, are now perceived as Divine "packets" of energy. With a little more "repackaging" of this energy, our diverse universe soon emerges.

The *Tanya* returns to this issue repeatedly. What is the nature of Divine speech energy? Is it the same as the energy of ten *sefiros?* If not, what is its relationship with the *sefiros?* Why is the symbolism of speech, in particular, used? How, exactly, are the "packets" of energy in Divine speech rearranged to power the universe? What is the relationship between any given created entity and the Divine speech which powers it? Is Divine speech something of the past or is it "uttered" in the present too?

It is through clarifying the answers to these questions, the author of *Tanya* maintained, that we can truly internalize the notion that G-d has "become" the universe and that *"there is no barrier or curtain separating man from G-d."*

To appreciate the *Tanya's* use of the Divine speech metaphor, it would be helpful to briefly examine how earlier sources treated the subject.

The narrative of Genesis 1, of course, introduces the notion of Divine language causing creation; but from a simple reading of the text, G-d's, "creative statements" read more like instructions for something else to take place later on, rather than the actual medium of creation itself. In fact it is very difficult to find in the *Talmudic/Midrashic* corpus a clear indication that the letters of Divine speech are the "raw material" from which the universe is formed.

One Midrashic tradition teaches that creation was powered by a Divine name,[48] but this is quite different from the *Tanya's* teaching that the world was formed from Divine language *in general,* from all twenty-two letters of the Hebrew alphabet.

---

48. *Genesis Rabah* 12:10. The role of Divine names in emanation and creation features extensively in Kabbalah, and dominates the teachings of Rabbi Isaac Luria and Rabbi Moshe Cordovero.

In another *Midrash* we are taught that G-d created the world after "looking into" the Torah.[49] However, even if we presume that this primordial Torah had already assumed its current, linguistic form, the *Midrash* does not actually imply that Divine language became the *material* of creation. It suggests that G-d consulted the Torah, deriving the form of the universe from it, but the world's substance seems to have emerged from elsewhere.

The only source we have from the *Talmud/Midrash* which at all resembles the *Tanya's* model of creation is the phrase, *"Betzalel knew how to combine the letters through which heaven and earth were created"*[50] This, as *Rashi* points out, means that Betzalel was adept in the techniques described in *Sefer Yetzirah* (Book of Creation).[51]

(*Sefer Yetzirah* is a short but very important book of cosmogony and is probably the oldest speculative treatise in Hebrew. The book has greatly influenced Kabbalistic discourse due to the many mystical commentaries written on it.[52] *Sefer Yetzirah's* teachings are traditionally attributed to our patriarch Abraham, though in its current textual form, the book probably emerged some time in late antiquity.[53])

Sefer Yetzirah details the mechanism through which the universe was created by means of *all* twenty-two letters of the alphabet,[54] not just the letters of G-d's name. G-d "carved" these Hebrew letters out of Himself,

49.   Ibid. 1:1; *Zohar* 2, 161a.

50.   *Berachos* 55a; *Zohar* 2, 152a. This is the reason why he was chosen to construct the Tabernacle, G-d's "home" on earth.

51.   *Rashi* ibid connects this with the *Talmud's* account that *"Rav Chanina and Rav Oshaya would sit every Sabbath eve and engage in the study of Sefer Yetzirah, and a third-born calf would be created for them, and they would eat it"* (*Sanhedrin* 65b). Even if this is not precisely the same text of *Sefer Yetzirah* in our possession, it is likely to have contained similar material.
      The Zohar weaves together the two narratives (the creative power of letters and of the Divine name): *"When the blessed Holy One created the world, He created it by the mystery of letters, and letters revolved and created the world by engravings of the Holy Name"* (*Zohar* 2, 151b). The *Tanya* addresses the role of Divine names in creation below in chapters 4-6.

52.   For a list of commentaries on *Sefer Yeztirah* see Rabbi Aryeh Kaplan (trans.), *Sefer Yetzirah: The Book of Creation in Theory and in Practice* (Weiser Books, 1997) p. 325-334.

53.   Traditional authors who attribute the text to the Patriarch Abraham include Saadia Gaon, Hai Gaon, Shabbatai Donnelo, Donash ibn Tamim, Judah Halevi and Moshe Cordovero. For references see Kaplan, p. 342, notes 14-15.

54.   And the ten *sefiros*, a term that the book never actually defines.

and they were combined in a variety of ways to create time, space and all existence.

While *Sefer Yetzirah* makes no explicit connection to G-d forming the universe through spoken word, it is the primary source for the *Tanya's* model of creation, that the letters of the Hebrew alphabet are not only a creative force but part of the universe's structure.[55]

The metaphor of speech remains important from a philosophical perspective because it makes clear that not all of G-d becomes the world. The universe is formed from just a few words uttered by G-d, which we interpret to mean: a small amount of energy which emanated from Him. A person can speak almost endlessly, rendering the value and effort invested in any given sentence negligible; and the same is true of the Divine energy which formed the substance of the universe: it is negligible to G-d.

The metaphor of speech therefore teaches us two very important truths about G-d's relationship with the world. The world is made from Divine energy, so G-d is *immanent*. But it was also made from a negligible amount of Divine energy, so He is still *beyond* the universe and in no way limited by it.

CHASIDIC PANENTHEISM

This philosophical position, of simultaneous Divine immanence and transcendence has been described by scholars as *panentheism*. The term is derived from the Greek *pan-en-theos* which means "all-in-God."

Panentheism represents a maturation of our understanding of G-d, that incorporates some advantages of earlier positions, and sheds some of their disadvantages.

The view of G-d which dominated pre-modern and early modern thought was *theism*. This sees G-d as the perfect being (necessarily existent, eternal, changeless, almighty, all-knowing, supremely good), who is the creator of everything distinct from Himself. The salient point here is that G-d is absolutely separate from the world.

A popular trend among subsequent modern thinkers was to reject theism in favor of *pantheism,* the view that G-d is identical with the universe, and no more than it. The appeal of this position is that it leads to a deep

55. *Sefer Yetzirah* is cited by the *Tanya* on pp. 24-25, 164. This model of language also transforms our understanding of prophecy, which is not merely the hearing of an external Divine speech but rather an actual experience of the Divine as "encapsulated" in language. See p. 36.

reverence for the world in which we find ourselves and it helps us to look at G-d as something which can be encountered directly. Pantheism also sat well with the modern skeptical outlook which was uncomfortable with the supernatural theistic G-d and preferred a more naturalistic approach that would be compatible with science.

Most thought systems are reactionary; they develop out of a dissatisfaction with the preceding model. Therefore they usually *transcend and reject:* they deem it necessary to eschew the prior thought system in order to embrace a new one. The disadvantage of this is a proverbial "throwing out the baby with the bathwater." In rejecting the disadvantages of the previous paradigm, they reject all of it, including its virtues.

This was pantheism's relationship to theism. The drive to perceive G-d as immanent and associated with nature resulted in an unnecessary rejection of the all-powerful G-d.

A more mature development from one paradigm to the next is to *transcend and include.* We progress to a higher way of thinking, but not in a reactionary way, hostile to the paradigm that preceded. On the contrary, we appreciate the virtues of the old paradigm, and try to carry them forward with us into the new.[56]

Chasidic panentheism took this approach. We gain the immanence and sense of G-d-within-nature which was appealing to the adherents of pantheism; but we do not feel compelled to reject the sacred tenets of theism and are able to carry them with us into the new paradigm. In panentheism, G-d is *also* distant, supernatural and utterly transcendent, as in theistic thinking. The world finds itself *in* (the *en* of pan-en-theism) a much greater, transcendent Divine matrix.[57]

With this approach the *Tanya* brings us a new paradigm of elevated mystical consciousness, typified by a radically new immanentism, and yet it does do so within the bounds of traditional Jewish religious belief and practices (*theism*).[58]

---

56. I have borrowed the model of "transcending and including" from the writings of Ken Wilber. For an example see his *A Theory of Everything: An Integral Vision for Business, Politics, Science and Spirituality* (Shambhala, 2001), p. 25.

57. For a discussion of panentheism and the postmodern turn, see David Ray Griffin: *G-d and Religion in the Postmodern World: Essays in Postmodern Theology* (State University of New York Press, 1989), p. 90-91.

58. For more on panentheism see below p. 41. The precise form of panentheism articulated here in the *Tanya* would be best described as *apophatic panentheism,* ("apophatic" meaning "negation"), since the *Tanya* argues that the separate existence of the universe

COMMENTARIES ON THE SECOND BOOK OF TANYA

The second book of *Tanya, Gateway to Unity and Faith,* has been the subject of significant commentary and analysis. Some of the commentaries on book one, *Sefer Shel Beinonim,* also discuss book two, so I will recap these first. Since they have already been described in the "Translator's Introduction" to book one, I will mention them just briefly here.

The Lubavitcher Rebbe, Rabbi Menachem Mendel Schneerson, *Notes on Tanya.*[59]

Rabbi Aharon Chitrik ed., *Likutei Amarim Tanya, Sha'ar Ha-Yichud ve-ha-Emunah, Be-Tziruf Ma'arei Mekomos, Likut Perushim, Shinui Nuscha'os,* (Brooklyn: Kehos 1989), an anthology of comments on the *Tanya* found in the discourses of Chabad Rebbeim. This material is complex, and is, generally speaking, not aimed at clarifying the literal meaning of the text.

Rabbi Alexander Sender Yudasin (d. 1982), *Ha-Lekach Ve-Ha-Libuv* (Kfar Chabad, 1968), the second volume of this series contains commentary on *Sha'ar Ha-Yichud ve-ha-Emunah.*

Rabbi Yehoshua Korf (1905-2007), *Likutei Biurim Be-Sefer Ha-Tanya* (Brooklyn, 1968-1980), 2 vols.

Rabbi Yosef Wineberg (1917-2012), *Shiurim Be-Sefer Ha-Tanya, Sha'ar Ha-Yichud Ve-Ha-Emunah* (Brooklyn: Kehos, 1984, Yiddish); Rabbis Levy Wineberg and Shalom B. Wineberg (trans.), *Lessons in Tanya,* volume 3 (Brooklyn: Kehos, 1989, English).

Rabbi Yoel Kahn (b. 1930), (Rabbis Avraham Kirshenbaum and Menachem Mendel Feldman eds.), *Sha'ar Ha-Yichud Ve-Ha-Emunah im biurei Ha-Rav Yoel Kahn* (Jerusalem: Mayanosecha, 2012). This is the best in-depth Hebrew commentary available.[60]

---

is voided and negated within G-d's presence. This classification was suggested by Elliot Wolfson in his *Open Secret* (Columbia University Press, 2009), p. 91. See below p. 79.

For a panentheistic reading of Maimonides see Rabbi Menachem Mendel Schneerson, *Hadran al Ha-Rambam* 5735 (Brooklyn: Kehos, 1984).

59. Rabbi Menachem Mendel Schneerson, *Notes and brief comments to Sefer Shel Beinonim* (Brooklyn: Kehos, 2014). I refer to this work here as *"Notes on Tanya."*

60 Rabbi Kahn's commentary on *Sha'ar Ha-Yichud Ve-Ha-Emunah* has also been adapted by Rabbi Moshe Link in his series, *Likutei Amarim Tanya im Biurim u-Peninim,* (Israel:

Rabbi Yekusiel Green, *Tanya im Maskil Le-Eitan, Sha'ar Ha-Yichud Ve-Ha-Emunah* (Kfar Chabad, 2002-3, Hebrew) 4 volumes. The section of Rabbi Green's commentary on chapters 1-6 has been translated into English in *Commentary on the Tanya: The Gate of Unity and Faith* (Kfar Chabad, 2006), 2 volumes.

Rabbi Adin Steinsalz *Biur Tanya,* (Jerusalem: Sifrei Milsa, 1997); one volume of this series is devoted to *Sha'ar Ha-Yichud Ve-Ha-Emunah.* English summaries of the commentary are published in Yehuda Hanegbi (ed.) *The Sustaining Utterance: Discourses on Chasidic Thought* (New Jersey: Jason Aronson, 1989).

Rabbi Avraham Alashvili, *Sha'ar Ha-Yichud Ve-Ha-Emunah ve-Igeres ha-Teshuvah in Perush Katzar* (Brooklyn: Kehos, 2015), is an expanded version of the author's *Tanya Mevuar* (Nachlas Har Chabad: Nachlas Sefer, 1998), and is the best short treatment of *Sha'ar Ha-Yichud Ve-Ha-Emunah.*

Rabbi Moshe Yehudah Kroll et. al, *Sefer Likutei Amarim Tanya* (Bnei Brak: Pe'er Mikdashim, 2014).

In addition to the above, *Gateway to Unity and Faith* has merited the following treatments devoted exclusively to this section of the *Tanya.*

Rabbi Aharon Horowitz of Starosselje (1766-1828), *Sha'arei Ha-Yichud Ve-ha-Emunah* (Shklov 1820; new edition, Jerusalem, 2016), is an extensive elaboration on the themes of Rabbi Shneur Zalman's *Sha'ar Ha-Yichud ve-ha-Emunah.* Rabbi Aharon was one of the great exponents of Chabad Chasidism in its second generation. Following the passing of his master, Rabbi Aharon established his own Chasidic court that, in some ways, competed with the court of Rabbi Shneur Zalman's son, Rabbi Dov Ber, and as a result Rabbi Aharon's works have not enjoyed too much popularity in later generations of Chabad.[61]

Machon Ma'or She-be-Torah, 2013-4), but the adaptation of Kirshenbaum and Feldman in this case is by far the superior work.

61. For a discussion of Rabbi Aharon's work and its relationship to the Tanya, see Rabbi Shmuel Ehrenfeld, *They Shall Revere You With the Sun* (Jerusalem: Machon Yam Ha-Chochmah, 2011), pp. 727-812). Rabbi Aharon's works have been the topic of interest in the academic community. See Naftali Loewenthal, *Communicating the Infinite: The Emergence of the Habad School* (Chicago University Press, 1990), chapter 4; Louis Jacobs, *Seeker of Unity: The Life and Works of Aaron of Starosselje* (London: Valentine

Rabbi Zalman Gopin (Rabbi Shimon Gopin ed.), *Shiurim Be-Chasidus, Sha'ar Ha-Yichud ve-ha-Emunah* (Brooklyn: Kehos, 2008). Rabbi Gopin's commentary builds on the work of Rabbi Yoel Kahn and is the most in-depth treatment available.

Rabbi Yisrael Nachum Wilhelm, *Yesodos ve-Shorashim be-Sha'ar Ha-Yichud ve-ha-Emunah* (Jerusalem: 2017) is not a running commentary but a series of essays on certain themes of the book.

Rabbi Michael Chanoch Golomb, *Yesodos be-Sha'ar Ha-Yichud ve-ha-Emunah* (Brooklyn: Central Yeshivas Yeshivas Tomchei Temimim, 2008), 2 pamphlets offering an in depth analysis of isolated passages from chapters 1-7.

Yechiel Harari, *Le-Hakir es Ha-Borei* (Israel: Hitbonenut, 2011, Hebrew), adapts the first seven chapters into summaries in modern Hebrew, aimed at a lay audience.

Rabbi Moshe Aharon Teichman, *Toras Ha-Besht Be-rei Chazal* (Israel: Kfar Chabad 2001), summarizes the themes of the book in detail for an educated orthodox audience (in pages 23-204).

Shmuel Yudaikin (ed.), *Sha'ar Ha-Yichud in Perush Amud Aish* (Bnei Brak: Da'as Kedoshim, 2000), collects discourses from the Fifth Lubavitcher Rebbe, Rabbi Shalom Dov Ber Schneerson, which are related to the themes of *Sha'ar Ha-Yichud ve-ha-Emunah,* but, in most cases, do not comment directly on it. A similar work, from the same editor, drawing from the works of the seventh Lubavitcher Rebbe, Rabbi Menachem Mendel Schneerson, is *Biurim be-Sefer Ha-Tanya,* volume 2 (Bnei Brak: 2003). These works should not be considered commentaries on the *Tanya;* they employ the text of the *Tanya* as a springboard to further readings drawn from the Chabad corpus.[62]

Mitchell, 2006); Rachel Elior, *The Theory of Divinity of Chasidus Chabad, Second Generation* (Jerusalem: Magnes 1982, Hebrew).

62 *Sha'ar Ha-Yichud Ve-Ha-Emunah* has also drawn the attention of non-orthodox/ academic authors. Notable examples include: Rachel Elior, *The Paradoxical Ascent to G-d: The Kabbalistic Theosophy of Habad Hasidism* (State University of New York Press, 1993), pp. 49-100; Dov Schwartz, *Habad's Thought from Beginning to End* (Israel: Bar Ilan Univeristy Press 2010) [Hebrew], pp. 23-114; Jacob Gotlieb, *Rationalism in Hasidic Attire: Habad's Harmonistic Approach to Maimonides* (Israel: Bar Ilan University Press 2009) [Hebrew], pp. 47-70; Arthur Green, *Seek My Face: A Jewish Mystical Theology* (Woodstock: Jewish Lights, 2006), pp. 3-67; Jay Michaelson, *Everything is G-d: The Radical Path of Nondual Judaism* (Shambhala, 2009); Sanford Drob, *Kaballah and Postmodernism: A Dialogue* (New York: Peter Lang, 2009) chapter 8.

ACKNOWLEDGMENTS

First and foremost I extend my gratitude to David and Lara Slager whose outstanding generosity has made this book possible, as well as most of my other works throughout the last decade. The Slager family have set an example to the Jewish community, both in their personal lives and with their outstanding philanthropic efforts towards an impressive array of causes across the globe. I wish David, Lara, and their precious children Hannah and Sara Malka, all the abundant blessings that they deserve.

I extend my heartfelt wishes to Rabbi Meyer Gutnick, co-founder and director of Kol Menachem publishing, who had the courage to invest in an unknown author, and since then has been an unfailing source of material support and moral encouragement for my work. Motivated by a great love for the Rebbe, and recognizing the urgency of spreading his Torah teachings, Rabbi Gutnick has chosen to invest his own natural talent at "getting things done" into a very worthy cause. In the merit of this, and all his many other impressive philanthropic efforts, may G-d bless him, together with his dear wife Shaindy, and all their wonderful children and grandchildren, with *chasidishe nachas* and only revealed and open goodness.

I am grateful to my father-in-law, Rabbi Yeremi Angyalfi for scrutinizing the entire text and offering many helpful corrections and comments; to Rabbi Shneur Zalman Gafnee and Rabbi Chaim Rapoport for critically reading parts of the manuscript. I extend my thanks to Rabbi Shmuel Rabin for carefully checking the Hebrew texts. For assistance with proofreading I thank Chanan Maister.

To my parents, Trevor and Denise Miller, for their love, for investing in my education and for supporting me in becoming a rabbi, even if they would have preferred I had become a doctor.

And finally, to my greatest support, my wife Chani, and to my wonderful children: Leah, Mendel, Mushka, Levi, Esther Miriam, Ariella and Menucha, my greatest pride and joy.

Chaim Miller
19th *Kislev* 5777

AUTHOR'S TITLE PAGE

4TH SIVAN REGULAR | 6TH SIVAN LEAP

This brief introductory section of Part Two of *Tanya* was written by the author to formally name this work and to state its purpose.

לִיקוּטֵי אֲמָרִים — The book *"An Anthology of Teachings"* (*Likutei Amarim*).

Both Parts One and Two of the *Tanya* are collectively named "An Anthology of Teachings." The *Tanya* is not an "anthology" in the sense of a "cut-and-paste" selection from other works; it's more of a *synthesis* of various teachings that the author had received, both written and oral, which he then enlarged upon and adapted for practical implementation in daily life.

The collected sermons of Rabbi Dov Ber of Mezritch (d. 1772), Rabbi Shneur Zalman's teacher, were published in 1781 with the same title, *Likutei Amarim,* and it is surely no coincidence that the *Tanya* (first published in 1796), was given the same name. While Rabbi Shneur Zalman undoubtedly put much of his own creative input into the pages of the *Tanya,* he chose to emphasize the direct continuity of his work with Rabbi Dov Ber's ideas by giving it the same name as his master's work.

Despite the author's choice of title, this book came to be generally known by the public as *"Tanya,"* the Hebrew word with which the book begins. (This name had been in common use before the *Tanya* was printed, when it had circulated in manuscript form). Already in the second printing of the work in 1799, the title *Tanya* formally appears, and has since become a permanent fixture.

חֵלֶק שֵׁנִי — Part Two.

As we noted in Part One, the *Tanya* was originally published as a single volume in two parts. (Our translation/commentary to Part One, *Sefer Shel Beinonim*, "The Book for Inbetweeners," is printed in a separate volume in this series.) Part Two, *Gateway to Oneness and Faith* (*Sha'ar Ha-Yichud ve-ha-Emunah*) focuses on the esoteric philosophy which forms the foundation of Chasidic thought.

(Though we cannot be certain, it appears that Rabbi Shneur Zalman had originally composed *Gateway to Oneness and Faith* as Part One of the book, but later made the decision to place the more practical *Book of the Inbetweeners* at the beginning of his published work.)

הנקרא בשם חינוך קטן

מלוקט מפי ספרים ומפי סופרים קדושי עליון נ"ע

The second printing of the *Tanya*, in 1799, included a third section, entitled *Letter on Repentance* (*Iggeres Ha-Teshuvah*), which had already been in broad circulation in manuscript form since the summer of 1792. A later printing, published posthumously by the author's sons in 1814, included a fourth part, *Sacred Letter* (*Igeres Ha-Kodesh*), containing various scholarly letters written by the author; and a fifth part, *Final Tract* (*Kuntres Acharon*), containing material which the author had composed at the same time the original *Tanya* was being written.

הַנִּקְרָא בְּשֵׁם חִינוּךְ קָטָן — Part Two of the *Tanya* is **called by the name, "Education of a Child"** (*Chinuch Katan*).

While this is the formal name of the second part of the *Tanya*, assigned by the author, the work has come to be known as *Gateway to Oneness and Faith*. But *Education of a Child* has remained as the title of the Author's Introduction.

The name *Education of a Child* reflects the theme of this work, which is aimed at providing a basic "education" in the Chasidic understanding of G-d and His relationship with the world, to provide a foundation for all worship. Since the reader will understand and "own" these ideas for himself, they will remain foundational, like a child's education.

מְלוּקָט מִפִּי סְפָרִים — This work is **anthologized from** various published **texts,** וּמִפִּי סוֹפְרִים קְדוֹשֵׁי עֶלְיוֹן נִשְׁמָתָם עֵדֶן — **and from** the unpublished wisdom of various **teachers of exceptional holiness, whose souls are in heaven.**

The author is intentionally vague about his sources, but that is not surprising when we consider that the original printing of the *Tanya* did not even bear the author's name!

The "published texts" which the *Tanya* quotes most extensively (besides the basic canon of Scripture, *Talmud* and *Midrash*), are: the *Zohar* and Rabbi Chaim Vital's *Etz Chaim* and *Pri Etz Chaim*. Maimonides' works are drawn upon, as is Rabbi Moshe Cordovero's *Pardes*. An internal Chabad tradition points to Rabbi Isaiah Horowitz's *Shnei Luchos Ha-Bris* (17th century) and the writings of Rabbi Yehudah Loew (Maharal) of Prague (d. 1609) as sources for the *Tanya*.

"Teachers of exceptional holiness, whose souls are in heaven" certainly refers to Rabbi Dov Ber of Mezritch (d. 1772), Rabbi Shneur Zalman's teacher, and Rabbi Dov Ber's teacher Rabbi Yisrael *Ba'al Shem Tov* (1698-1760) from whom the Chasidic movement originated. We should also include Rabbi Dov Ber's

מיוסד על פרשה ראשונה של קריאת שמע:

son, Avraham "the angel" (1739-1776), who was a personal teacher of Rabbi Shneur Zalman, and Rabbi Menachem Mendel of Vitebsk (d. 1788) who was a colleague and in many ways a teacher of Rabbi Shneur Zalman.

מְיוּסָד עַל פָּרָשָׁה רִאשׁוֹנָה שֶׁל קְרִיאַת שְׁמַע — Part Two of the *Tanya* is **based on the First Paragraph of the *Shema*,** as explained by the *Zohar*.

Part Two of the *Tanya* is an extended discussion of a comment in the *Zohar* that the opening of the *Shema* hints to two levels in the "unification" of G-d. (However, this will only be addressed directly later on, in Chapter Seven).

חנוך

לנער על פי דרכו גם כי יזקין לא
יסור ממנה הנה מדכתיב על פי דרכו
משמע שאינה דרך האמת לאמיתו
וא"כ מאי מעליותא שגם כי יזקין
לא יסור ממנה. אך הנה מודעת
זאת כי שרשי עבודת ה' ויסודותיה

AUTHOR'S INTRODUCTION
SECTION ONE: TWO TYPES OF LOVE

The First Book of *Tanya, Sefer Shel Beinonim,* guided us how to achieve an *emotional connection to G-d,* by generating feelings of love and reverence. This Second Book, *Sha'ar Ha-Yichud ve-ha-Emunah*, aims to enrich our *intellectual understanding* of G-d's existence and His relationship with the world.

In this introductory discourse, the author will explain how intellectual understanding and emotional connection are related, and how one acts as the foundation for the other.

חֲנוֹךְ לַנַּעַר עַל פִּי דַרְכּוֹ גַּם כִּי יַזְקִין לֹא יָסוּר מִמֶּנָּה — *"Educate a lad in his own way, when he grows old he will still not swerve from it"* (*Proverbs* 22:6).

Educating a young person in his "own way" implies that it is not a mature path, but one suitable for a child.

הִנֵּה מִדְּכְתִיב עַל פִּי דַרְכּוֹ מַשְׁמַע — **Now since the verse states,** *"Educate a lad in his own way,"* **it implies,** שֶׁאֵינָהּ דֶּרֶךְ הָאֱמֶת לַאֲמִיתוֹ — **that this is not the mature "way" of absolute truth,** but an imperfect path, tailored to the limited capabilities of a "lad."

וְאִם כֵּן — **And if this is the case,** מַאי מַעֲלִיּוּתָא שֶׁגַּם כִּי יַזְקִין לֹא יָסוּר מִמֶּנָּה — **what is the virtue that** *"when he grows old he will still not swerve from it"*?

Why would we hope that the child, on reaching adulthood, will still cling to the *immature* approach of his youth?

אַךְ הִנֵּה מוּדַעַת זֹאת — **However,** *"this thing is known"* (*Isaiah* 12:5), כִּי שָׁרְשֵׁי עֲבוֹדַת ה' וְיְסוֹדוֹתֶיהָ — **that the two roots and foundations of worshiping G-d,** הֵן דְּחִילוּ וּרְחִימוּ — **are reverence and love,** הַיִּרְאָה שֹׁרֶשׁ וִיסוֹד לְסוּר מֵרָע — **rev-**

הן דחילו ורחימו היראה שרש ויסוד
לסור מרע והאהבה לועשה טוב וקיום
כל מ"ע דאורייתא' ודרבנן כמו שיתב'
במקומן (ומצות החינוך היא ג"כ
במ"ע כמ"ש בא"ח סימן שמ"ג):
והנה באהבה כתיב בס"פ עקב אשר
אנכי מצוה אתכם לעשותה לאהבה
את ה' וגו' וצריך להבין איך שייך

erence is the root/foundation which motivates a person not to transgress any prohibitions, to **"turn away from evil"** (Psalms 34:14), וְהָאַהֲבָה לַעֲשֶׂה טוֹב — and love motivates the observance of positive commands, to **"do good"** (ibid.), וְקִיּוּם כָּל מִצְוֹת עֲשֵׂה דְּאוֹרַיְיתָא וּדְרַבָּנָן — namely, **the observance of all positive commands, both Biblical and Rabbinic,** כְּמוֹ שֶׁיִּתְבָּאֵר בִּמְקוֹמָן — **as will be explained** later, **in the appropriate place** (Part One, Chapter 4, 41).

The author uses the future tense here ("will be explained"), even though the explanation has appeared previously in Part One. This may simply be a printing error, but it could also be understood in light of an internal Chabad tradition that the author initially intended to make this volume Part One of the Tanya and later changed his mind (Notes on Tanya).

And — (וּמִצְוַת הַחִינוּךְ הִיא גַם כֵּן בְּמִצְוֹת עֲשֵׂה כְּמוֹ שֶׁכָּתוּב בְּאוֹרַח חַיִּים סִימָן שמ"ג) **the commandment to educate** a child in the observance of these commands, **applies also to positive commands, as stated in** Tur and Shulchan Aruch, Or-ach Chaim **chapter 343.**

While the verse ("educate a lad") speaks of a child under the age of Bar or Bas Mitzvah, who is not obligated to observe the commandments, there is nevertheless a requirement for the parents to educate a child in observance. This, the Tanya notes, includes a requirement to educate the child to observe positive commands.

If this is the case, then we must obviously educate the child to love G-d, which is the root and foundation of this observance. The child, though, will not have the same maturity of love as an adult, and his or her education will be a basic training in worship. (This point will prove significant later on in the author's introduction.)

וְהִנֵּה בְּאַהֲבָה כְּתִיב בְּסוֹף פַּרְשַׁת עֵקֶב — **Now concerning** the command to love G-d, **the verse states at the end of the** Torah **Portion of Ekev,** אֲשֶׁר אָנֹכִי מְצַוֶּה אֶתְכֶם לַעֲשׂוֹתָהּ לְאַהֲבָה אֶת ה' וְגוֹ' — **"which I command you to do it, to love G-d your G-d etc,"** (Deuteronomy 11:22), וְצָרִיךְ לְהָבִין — **and some clarification**

לשון עשייה גבי אהבה שבלב אך
העניין הוא דיש שני מיני אהבת ה'
האחת היא כלות הנפש בטבעה אל
בוראה כאשר תתגבר נפש השכלית
על החומר ותשפילהו ותכניעהו תחתיה
אזי תתלהב ותתלהט בשלהבת העולה
מאליה ותגל ותשמח בה' עושה
ותתענג על ה' תענוג נפלא והזוכים

is needed, אֵיךְ שַׁיָּיךְ לְשׁוֹן עֲשִׂיָּיה — why does the verse use **a verb of action,** ("*I command you to do it*"), גַּבֵּי אַהֲבָה שֶׁבַּלֵּב — **in reference to an emotion of the heart** ("*to love G-d*")?

It seems strange that the Torah describes loving G-d as something that we would "do" rather than "feel." How would you "do" love?

The *Tanya* will answer this question by drawing on a distinction we learned in Part One, that there are two types of love of G-d: one unattainable, except to a select few; the other, accessible to us all. The higher level of "great love" is the privilege of *tzadikim* (exceptionally pious individuals). The lower level is something we can all reach by disciplined meditation.

As we shall see, it is this second love to which our verse in *Deuteronomy* refers. Since it is a level accessible to us all, it is essentially "doable." And that is why the Torah uses a term of action, "*I command you to do it*," meaning to say: "I command you to do what is necessary to achieve it."

אַךְ הָעִנְיָין הוּא — **However, the explanation** of the verse in *Deuteronomy* is as follows.

הָאַחַת הִיא כְּלוֹת — **There are two types of love of G-d,** דְּיֵשׁ שְׁנֵי מִינֵי אַהֲבַת ה' הַנֶּפֶשׁ בְּטִבְעָהּ אֶל בּוֹרְאָהּ — **one is the "languishing of the soul"** (*kelos ha-nefesh*) **for its Creator, which is in the nature** of the soul itself (and not something acquired through meditation).

The *Tanya* explains this first type of love in more detail.

כַּאֲשֶׁר תִּתְגַּבֵּר נֶפֶשׁ הַשִּׂכְלִית עַל הַחוֹמֶר — **The first type of love is a product of the Intellectual Soul overcoming** the perception and allure of **the physical** senses, וְתַשְׁפִּילֵהוּ וְתַכְנִיעֵהוּ תַּחְתֶּיהָ — **deflating and subduing** the allure of the senses **under** its control, אֲזַי תִּתְלַהֵב וְתִתְלַהֵט — **as a result, that soul will be** "**ignited**" with **fiery** passion, בְּשַׁלְהֶבֶת הָעוֹלָה מֵאֵלֶיהָ — "*a flame that rises by itself*" (*Talmud, Shabbos* 21a), וְתָגֵל וְתִשְׂמַח בַּה' עוֹשָׂהּ — and the soul will "*rejoice and be gladdened in G-d*" (see *Joel* 2:23) **its Creator,** וְתִתְעַנֵּג עַל ה' תַּעֲנוּג נִפְלָא — and will "*delight in G-d*" (*Isaiah* 58:14), **with phenomenal pleasure.**

לְמַעֲלַת אהבה רבה זו הם הנקראים
צדיקים כדכתיב שמחו צדיקים בה'
אך לא כל אדם זוכה לזה כי לזה
צריך זיכוך החומר במאד מאד וגם
תורה ומעשים טובים הרבה לזכות
לנשמה עליונה שלמעלה ממדרגת רוח
ונפש כמ"ש בר"ח שער האהבה.
והשנית היא אהבה שכל אדם יוכל

This type of love is *not* the result of meditating on G-d's greatness. Rather, once the physical allure of the senses is "deflated and subdued," then instinctively the soul by its very nature will languish for G-d.

וְהַזּוֹכִים לְמַעֲלַת אַהֲבָה רַבָּה זוֹ הֵם הַנִּקְרָאִים צַדִּיקִים — **Those who merit to reach this level of "great love" are called** *tzadikim,* כְּדִכְתִיב שָׂמְחוּ צַדִּיקִים בַּה' — **as the verse implies that** only *"tzadikim are joyous with G-d"* (*Psalms* 97:12; see Part One, p. 178).

אַךְ לֹא כָּל אָדָם זוֹכֶה לָזֶה — **But not every person merits this** love of the *tzadik* (ibid. p. 172), כִּי לָזֶה צָרִיךְ זִיכּוּךְ הַחוֹמֶר בִּמְאֹד מְאֹד — **because it requires: a.) an extreme refinement of the physical** senses, which block this love experience, וְגַם תּוֹרָה וּמַעֲשִׂים טוֹבִים הַרְבֵּה — **and also: b.) a large amount of Torah and good deeds,** to draw lofty Divine energy into consciousness, לִזְכּוֹת לִנְשָׁמָה עֶלְיוֹנָה — **to merit to reach the higher** consciousness of *neshamah,* מִמַּדְרֵגַת רוּחַ וְנֶפֶשׁ — **which is above the** lower **levels of** *ruach* **and** *nefesh* consciousness, כְּמוֹ שֶׁכָּתוּב בְּרֵאשִׁית חָכְמָה שַׁעַר הָאַהֲבָה — **as stated** by Rabbi Eliyahu de Vidas, in *Reishis Chochmah, Gate of Love,* chapter 3, that the higher love must come from the consciousness of *neshamah.*

While our souls all *possess* the levels of *nefesh, ruach* and *neshamah* (see Part One, p. 49), the three levels do not always inform our consciousness directly. The *tzadik's* consciousness has transcended the levels of *ruach* and *nefesh,* which are closely associated with the body, and is aligned with the level of *neshamah* which can experience G-d directly, without the mediation of the senses. He or she does this through: a.) Overcoming the allure of the senses, to have an essentially disembodied connection with the Divine; b.) acquiring *"a large amount of Torah and good deeds"* to draw that consciousness back into his or her body (R' Hillel of Paritch).

Clearly, this is something not attainable by most of us. We therefore must work towards the second type of love.

וְהַשֵּׁנִית — **And the second** type of love of G-d, הִיא אַהֲבָה שֶׁכָּל אָדָם יוּכַל לְהַגִּיעַ אֵלֶיהָ — **is a love attainable by everyone.**

לְהַגִּיעַ אֵלֶיהָ כְּשֶׁיִתְבּוֹנֵן הֵיטֵב בְּעוּמְקָא
דְּלִבָּא בַּדְּבָרִים הַמְעוֹרְרִים אֶת הָאַהֲבָה
לַה' בְּלֵב כָּל יִשְׂרָאֵל. הֵן דֶּרֶךְ כְּלָל
כִּי הוּא חַיֵּינוּ מַמָּשׁ וְכַאֲשֶׁר הָאָדָם
אוֹהֵב אֶת נַפְשׁוֹ וְחַיָּיו. כֵּן יֶאֱהַב אֶת
ה' כַּאֲשֶׁר יִתְבּוֹנֵן וְיָשִׂים אֶל לִבּוֹ כִּי
ה' הוּא נַפְשׁוֹ הָאֲמִיתִּית וְחַיָּיו מַמָּשׁ
כמ"ש בַּזֹּהַר ע"פ נַפְשִׁי אִוִּיתִיךָ וְגו'.

While our emotions are not under our control, the second type of love is attainable because it is the *inevitable consequence* of thinking certain thoughts (which we *can* control).

כְּשֶׁיִּתְבּוֹנֵן הֵיטֵב בְּעוּמְקָא דְּלִבָּא — The second type of love will inevitably come **when you will meditate well, in the depths of your heart,** בַּדְּבָרִים הַמְעוֹרְרִים אֶת **— in** — upon ideas which arouse the love for G-d, הָאַהֲבָה לַה' — **in** the heart of all Israel.

The *Tanya* reminds us of two love meditations we have learned in Part One (*Sefer Shel Beinonim*), one "general" (in chapter 44), and another "detailed" (in chapters 46-49).

הֵן דֶּרֶךְ כְּלָל — You could use either the general meditation we learned above in Part One, Chapter 44, כִּי הוּא חַיֵּינוּ מַמָּשׁ — **how G-d is literally "our life"** (p. 578), וְכַאֲשֶׁר הָאָדָם אוֹהֵב אֶת נַפְשׁוֹ וְחַיָּיו, — **and when you will** contemplate how **you love your soul and your life,** כֵּן יֶאֱהַב אֶת ה' — **then you will come to love G-d,** כַּאֲשֶׁר יִתְבּוֹנֵן וְיָשִׂים אֶל לִבּוֹ, ה' — **by contemplating and taking to heart,** הוּא נַפְשׁוֹ הָאֲמִיתִּית וְחַיָּיו מַמָּשׁ — **that G-d really is your soul and your actual life.**

In Chapter 44 the *Tanya* teaches this meditation as follows: "*Since you, G-d, are my soul and my true life therefore, 'I have desired you,'* (Isaiah 26:9); *meaning that I desire and crave for you like a person desires his own life and soul. And just as a person becomes aware of how much he loves his life when he is weak and exhausted and he desires and craves that his energy should return (and similarly, when he goes to bed, he desires and yearns that his soul will be returned to him when he wakes up from his sleep), in the same way, I desire to draw inside me the Blessed Infinite Light, the true source of life*" (ibid. p. 567).

כְּמוֹ שֶׁכָּתוּב בַּזֹּהַר עַל פָּסוּק נַפְשִׁי אִוִּיתִיךָ וְגו' — As noted in Chapter 44, the above meditation is based on **the *Zohar's* commentary** (3, 68a) **to the verse, "*My soul, I have desired you* at night"** (Isaiah 26:9).

וְהֵן דֶּרֶךְ פְּרָט שֶׁכְּשֶׁבִּין וְיַשְׂכִּיל
בִּגְדוּלָתוֹ שֶׁל מִמְּ"ה הַקְּבָּ"ה דֶּרֶךְ פְּרָטִית
כַּאֲשֶׁר יוּכַל שְׂאֵת בְּשִׂכְלוֹ וּמַה שֶׁלְּמַעְלָה
מִשִּׂכְלוֹ וְאַחַ"כ יִתְבּוֹנֵן בְּאַהֲבַת ה'
הַגְּדוֹלָה וְנִפְלָאָה אֵלֵינוּ לֵירֵד לְמִצְרַיִם
עֶרְוַת הָאָרֶץ לְהוֹצִיא נִשְׁמוֹתֵינוּ מִכּוּר
הַבַּרְזֶל שֶׁהוּא הַסִּ"א רַ"ל לְקָרְבֵנוּ אֵלָיו
וּלְדַבְקֵנוּ בִּשְׁמוֹ מַמָּשׁ וְהוּא וּשְׁמוֹ אֶחָד
דְּהַיְינוּ שֶׁרוֹמְמָנוּ מִתַּכְלִית הַשִּׁפְלוּת
וְהַטּוּמְאָה לְתַכְלִית הַקְּדוּשָׁה וּגְדוּלָתוֹ
יִתְ' שֶׁאֵין לָהּ קֵץ וְתַכְלִית אֲזֵי כְמִים

76A

The *Zohar* states: *"You should love the Blessed Holy One with a true love of the soul, which is a complete love, a love of the nefesh and ruach, just as they (the nefesh and ruach) cling to the body and the body loves them, so must a person love the Blessed Holy One and cling to Him"* (*Zohar* 3, 68a; see ibid. p. 566).

The *Tanya* now reminds us of another "detailed" meditation, from Chapters 46-49.

וְהֵן דֶּרֶךְ פְּרָט — **Or** you could use **the detailed** meditation from Chapters 46-49, שֶׁכְּשֶׁבִּין וְיַשְׂכִּיל בִּגְדוּלָתוֹ שֶׁל מֶלֶךְ מַלְכֵי הַמְּלָכִים הַקָּדוֹשׁ בָּרוּךְ הוּא דֶּרֶךְ פְּרָטִית — **meditating upon and pondering in detail the greatness of the Blessed Holy One, the King,** and **King of kings,** כַּאֲשֶׁר יוּכַל שְׂאֵת בְּשִׂכְלוֹ — **as much as your mind can handle,** וּמַה שֶׁלְּמַעְלָה מִשִּׂכְלוֹ — **(and** also **transcending your intellect,** by realizing its limitations), וְאַחַר כָּךְ יִתְבּוֹנֵן בְּאַהֲבַת ה' הַגְּדוֹלָה וְנִפְלָאָה אֵלֵינוּ — **and then contemplating on the great and wondrous love G-d has shown for us** historically, לֵירֵד לְמִצְרַיִם עֶרְוַת הָאָרֶץ — **how despite His greatness He** lowered Himself and **came down to Egypt,** *"the land's depravity"* (*Genesis* 42:9), לְהוֹצִיא נִשְׁמוֹתֵינוּ מִכּוּר הַבַּרְזֶל שֶׁהוּא הַסִּטְרָא אָחֲרָא — **to extract our souls** from the *"iron-smelting furnace"* (*Deuteronomy* 4:20), the *sitra achra,* רַחֲמָנָא לְצְלָן — **may G-d protect us!** לְקָרְבֵנוּ אֵלָיו — **to bring us close to Him,** through the giving of the Torah, וּלְדַבְקֵנוּ בִּשְׁמוֹ מַמָּשׁ — **allowing us to attach ourselves literally to** the Torah, every word being **"His name"** (see *Ramban*, Introduction to *Commentary on the Torah*), וְהוּא וּשְׁמוֹ אֶחָד — **and** thereby **attach ourselves to Him, since He is one with His name,** דְּהַיְינוּ שֶׁרוֹמְמָנוּ מִתַּכְלִית הַשִּׁפְלוּת וְהַטּוּמְאָה — **which means that He has lifted us out from the most absolute depravity and impurity,** לְתַכְלִית הַקְּדוּשָׁה וּגְדוּלָתוֹ יִתְבָּרֵךְ — **to His most absolute holiness and greatness,** שֶׁאֵין לָהּ קֵץ וְתַכְלִית — **which has no end or limit.**

הַפָּנִים אֶל פָּנִים תִּתְעוֹרֵר הָאַהֲבָה בְּלֵב
כָּל מַשְׂכִּיל וּמִתְבּוֹנֵן בְּעִנְיָן זֶה בְּעוּמְקָא
דְלִבָּא לֶאֱהוֹב אֶת ה' אַהֲבָה עַזָּה
וּלְדָבְקָה בּוֹ בְּלֵב וְנֶפֶשׁ כְּמוֹ שֶׁיִּתְבָּאֵר
בִּמְקוֹמָהּ בַּאֲרִיכוּת. וְהִנֵּה עִנְיָן אַהֲבָה
זוֹ רָצָה מֹרֵע"ה לִיטַע בְּלֵב כָּל יִשְׂרָאֵל
בְּפָרְשָׁה וְעַתָּה יִשְׂרָאֵל וְגוֹ' בְּפָסוּק
לָה' אֱלֹהֶיךָ הַשָּׁמַיִם וְגוֹ' רַק בַּאֲבוֹתֶיךָ
חָשַׁק וְגוֹ' וּמַלְתֶּם וְגוֹ' בְּשִׁבְעִים נֶפֶשׁ

אֲזַי כַּמַּיִם הַפָּנִים לַפָּנִים תִּתְעוֹרֵר הָאַהֲבָה בְּלֵב כָּל מַשְׂכִּיל — Then through carrying out this meditation, **the heart of any thinking person will be awakened with love** for G-d, *"As in water, face reflects face"* (Proverbs 27:19), וּמִתְבּוֹנֵן בְּעִנְיָן זֶה בְּעוּמְקָא דְלִבָּא — by dwelling on this "detailed meditation," **in the depths of your heart,** לֶאֱהוֹב אֶת ה' אַהֲבָה עַזָּה — **leading you to love G-d intensely,** וּלְדָבְקָה בּוֹ בְּלֵב וְנֶפֶשׁ — **and to connect with Him, with heart and soul,** כְּמוֹ שֶׁיִּתְבָּאֵר בִּמְקוֹמָהּ בַּאֲרִיכוּת — **as will be explained at length in the** appropriate **place** (again, this is a reference to Part One, chapters 46-49).

5TH SIVAN REGULAR

If the second type of love (achieved through meditation), is required from us all, we would expect this method to be specified in the Torah. The *Tanya* now demonstrates that this is indeed the case.

וְהִנֵּה עִנְיָן אַהֲבָה זוֹ רָצָה מֹשֶׁה רַבֵּינוּ עָלָיו הַשָּׁלוֹם לִיטַע בְּלֵב כָּל יִשְׂרָאֵל — **Now Moses intended to plant in the heart of all Israel this** second, meditative path to **love,** בְּפָרְשָׁה וְעַתָּה יִשְׂרָאֵל וְגוֹ' — **in the passage** beginning with the verse, *"And now, Israel, what does the G-d your G-d ask of you but to revere G-d... to love Him"* (Deuteronomy 10:12), and ending with 11:22.

The contents of *Deuteronomy* 10:12-11:22 closely resemble the above meditation, as the *Tanya* now demonstrates.

בַּפָּסוּק הֵן לָה' אֱלֹהֶיךָ הַשָּׁמַיִם וְגוֹ' רַק בַּאֲבוֹתֶיךָ חָשַׁק וְגוֹ' וּמַלְתֶּם וְגוֹ' — Moses taught us the above meditation **in the verses,** *"Look, the heavens and the heavens beyond the heavens, the earth and all that is in it* **belong to G-d your G-d. G-d only desired your fathers,** *to love them, and chose their seed after them, chose you from all the peoples as on this day.* **And you shall circumcise** *the foreskin of your heart, nor shall you show a stiff neck anymore"* (ibid. 14-16), בְּשִׁבְעִים נֶפֶשׁ וְגוֹ' — **"With seventy persons** *did your fathers go down to Egypt, and now*

וגו' ואהבת וגו'. ולכן סיים דבריו על
אהבה זו אשר אנכי מצוה אתכם
לעשותה שהיא אהבה עשויה בלב
ע"י הבינה והדעת בדברים המעוררים
את האהבה וע"ז צוה כבר תחלה והיו
הדברים האלה אשר אנכי מצוך היום
על לבבך כדי שע"י תבא לאהבה
את ה' כדאיתא בספרי ע"פ זה.

G-d your G-d has set you like the stars of the heavens for multitude" (ibid. 22), וְאָהַבְתָּ וְגוֹ' — *"And you shall love G-d your G-d"* (ibid. 11:1).

Therefore Moוְלָכֵן סִיֵּם דְּבָרָיו עַל אַהֲבָה זוֹ אֲשֶׁר אָנֹכִי מְצַוֶּה אֶתְכֶם לַעֲשׂוֹתָהּ
ses concluded his words about this love with a term of action, **"which I command you to do it,"** (ibid. 22), שֶׁהִיא אַהֲבָה עֲשׂוּיָה בַּלֵּב — because it is a love which is practically possible ("doable") to have in your heart, עַל יְדֵי הַבִּינָה וְהַדַּעַת בִּדְבָרִים הַמְעוֹרְרִים אֶת הָאַהֲבָה — by meditating with *binah* (cognition), and *da'as* (regonition), on ideas that awaken love, such as the "general" and "detailed" meditation above.

This answers our earlier question, why the Torah uses a term of action, *"I command you to do it,"* for the emotion of love. The Torah means to say: "I command you to do what is necessary to achieve it," namely, thinking the appropriate thoughts with your mind which will *inevitably* produce the love.

וְעַל זֶה צִוָּה כְּבָר תְּחִלָּה — In the above verses Moses clarified how to practically implement what had been commanded previously, וְהָיוּ הַדְּבָרִים הָאֵלֶּה אֲשֶׁר אָנֹכִי מְצַוְּךָ הַיּוֹם עַל לְבָבֶךָ — *"And these words that I command you today shall be upon your heart"* (ibid. 6:6), כְּדֵי שֶׁעַל יְדֵי זֶה תָּבֹא לְאַהֲבָה אֶת ה' — since through this you will come to love G-d.

In Deuteronomy 6:5, we are commanded *"You shall love G-d with all your heart, soul and might."* The *Tanya* suggests here that the next verse clarifies how that love is to be achieved, *"And these words that I command you today shall be upon your heart,"* i.e., you will come to love G-d through reflection and meditation about G-d, through "these words" (of verse 5), "upon your heart."

But *Deuteronomy* 6:6 does not explain this meditation in detail. Moses therefore devotes a later passage (10:12-11:22, from which the *Tanya* has just cited highlights), to provide us with more detailed material for our love meditation.

כְּדְאִיתָא בְּסִפְרֵי עַל פָּסוּק זֶה — As stated in *Sifri* on this verse.

והנה על אהבה זו השנית שייך לשון
מצוה וצווי דהיינו לשום לבו ודעתו
בדברים המעוררים את האהבה אבל
באהבה ראשונ' שהיא שלהבת העולה
מאליה לא שייך לשון צווי ומצוה כלל
ולא עוד אלא שהיא מתן שכרן של
צדיקים לטעום מעין עו"הב בע"הז
שעליה נאמר עבודת מתנה אתן את

The *Tanya's* assertion, that *Deuteronomy* 6:6 clarifies the *method of imple-mentation* of 6:5, is sourced in the *Sifri* (a Tannaitic Commentary on the Book of *Deuteronomy*):

"'And these words which I command you this day shall be upon your heart.' Rebbi says: Why did Moses say this? Because Scripture says, 'You shall love G-d with all your heart,' but I do not know how one is to love G-d. So Scripture goes on to say, 'And these words which I command you this day shall be upon your heart,' meaning: take these words to heart, for in this way will you recog-nize He who spoke and the world came into being, and you will cling to His ways" (*Sifri*, section 33).

וְהִנֵּה עַל אַהֲבָה זוֹ הַשֵּׁנִית שַׁיָּיךְ לְשׁוֹן מִצְוָה וְצִוּוּי — Since there is a practical path to achieve **this second type of love, it's possible** to mandate it for everyone, **as a command,** דְּהַיְינוּ לָשׂוּם לִבּוֹ וְדַעְתּוֹ בַּדְּבָרִים הַמְעוֹרְרִים אֶת הָאַהֲבָה — the com-mand **being,** not to try to conjure emotion, which is not always possible, but **to take to heart and contemplate *ideas* that awaken love.**

אֲבָל בְּאַהֲבָה רִאשׁוֹנָה — **But regarding the first type of love** experienced by *tzadikim,* שֶׁהִיא שַׁלְהֶבֶת הָעוֹלָה מֵאֵלֶיהָ — which is *"a flame that rises by itself"* from the soul, and is not the direct product of a technique which everyone can apply, לֹא שַׁיָּיךְ לְשׁוֹן צִוּוּי וּמִצְוָה כְּלָל — **you cannot possibly legislate it as a command.**

וְלֹא עוֹד אֶלָּא שֶׁהִיא מַתַּן שְׂכָרָן שֶׁל צַדִּיקִים — **And what is more,** this first love is never directly achieved, but it is a **reward given to *tzadikim*,** לִטְעוֹם מֵעֵין עוֹלָם **so that they** "delight in G-d" **by tasting a little of the next world, while** still **in this world.**

שֶׁעָלֶיהָ נֶאֱמַר עֲבוֹדַת מַתָּנָה אֶתֵּן אֶת כְּהוּנַּתְכֶם — **As the verse states, *"I have giv-en you the service of your priesthood as a gift, etc.,"*** (*Numbers* 18:7), where "priesthood" is a metaphor for the love of G-d, כְּמוֹ שֶׁיִּתְבָּאֵר בִּמְקוֹמָה — **as will be explained in the appropriate place** (see *Sefer Shel Beinonim* chapters 14, 43; *Tanya, Igeres Ha-Kodesh* 6, 18).

כהוונתכם כמו שיתב׳ במקומה אך הנה
ידוע ליודעים טעמא דקרא מאי דכתיב
כי שבע יפול צדיק וקם ובפרט שהאדם
נקרא מהלך ולא עומד וצריך לילך
ממדרגה למדרגה ולא לעמוד במדרגה
אחת לעולם ובין מדרגה למדרגה טרם
שיגיע למדרגה עליונה ממנה הוא

SECTION TWO: THE "FALL" OF A TZADIK

6TH SIVAN REGULAR

Having familiarized ourselves with the two types of love, we can return to the question posed at the opening of this "Author's Introduction." The phrase "Educate a lad in *his own way*," implies that this is not a mature "way," but an imperfect path tailored to the limited capabilities of a "lad." If this is the case, what is the virtue that *"when he grows old he will still not swerve from it"*?

אַךְ הִנֵּה יָדוּעַ לַיּוֹדְעִים טַעֲמָא דִקְרָא — **However, Kabbalists are familiar with the** inner **meaning of the scripture,** מַאי דִכְתִיב כִּי שֶׁבַע יִפּוֹל צַדִּיק וָקָם — the explanation of **the verse, *"For seven times a tzadik falls and gets up"*** (Proverbs 24:16).

While the *tzadik* may not be plagued by the same challenges as the rest of us, that does not mean to say that his or her worship is static and devoid of growth. In fact, as this verse makes clear, a *tzadik* has periods of "falling" and subsequent growth.

וּבִפְרָט שֶׁהָאָדָם נִקְרָא מְהַלֵּךְ וְלֹא עוֹמֵד — **Especially as** every **human is "moving" and not "stationary"** (see *Zechariah* 3:7).

Angels are "stationary" in their worship, never shifting to a completely new paradigm of worship. Humans, by contrast, are capable of such a shift, and that is their hallmark (see Rabbi Shneur Zalman, *Torah Ohr* p. 30a). Certainly, then, the *tzadik* will demonstrate this uniquely human quality of radical growth.

וְצָרִיךְ לֵילֵךְ מִמַּדְרֵגָה לְמַדְרֵגָה וְלֹא לַעֲמוֹד בְּמַדְרֵגָה אַחַת לְעוֹלָם — **Since he or she** is human, the *tzadik* **must always ascend from level to level, and not remain "standing"** at the same level.

It is in this context that we can understand what it means for a *tzadik* to "fall."

וּבֵין מַדְרֵגָה לְמַדְרֵגָה טֶרֶם שֶׁיַּגִּיעַ לְמַדְרֵגָה עֶלְיוֹנָה מִמֶּנָּה — **And as** the *tzadik* **passes from one level to the next,** in the intermediate zone **before reaching the next**

בבחי' נפילה ממדרג' הראשונ' אך כי
יפול לא יוטל כתיב ואינה נקראת
נפילה אלא לגבי מדריגתו הראשונה
ולא לגבי שאר כל אדם ח"ו שאעפ"כ
הוא למעלה מכל האדם בעבודתו כי
נשאר בה בחי' רשימו ממדריגתו
הראשונה אך עיקרה מאהבה שנתחנך
והורגל בה מנעוריו בטרם שהגיע

level upwards, הוּא בִּבְחִינַת נְפִילָה מִמַּדְרֵגָה הָרִאשׁוֹנָה — he or she **is in a "fallen"** **state from the previous level.**

To enter a new paradigm, you must first detach yourself completely from previous patterns of thought and behavior. It is in this intermediate state, having left the previous level and not yet having embraced the next one, that the *tzadik* is described as "fallen."

(For example, in order to learn the Jerusalem Talmud properly, Rabbi Zeira fasted so that he would first forget the Babylonian Talmud, as related in *Bava Metzia* 85a. Rabbi Zeira fasted in order to forget how to study in the Babylonian fashion, which would have confused his study of the more elevated Jerusalem Talmud—*Notes on Tanya*.)

אַךְ כִּי יִפּוֹל לֹא יוּטָל כְּתִיב — **But the verse states, "***Though he falls, he will not be flung down"* (Psalms 37:24), וְאֵינָהּ נִקְרֵאת נְפִילָה אֶלָּא לְגַבֵּי מַדְרֵגָתוֹ הָרִאשׁוֹנָה — for the *tzadik* **is only referred to as "fallen" compared to his or her prior level,** וְלֹא לְגַבֵּי שְׁאָר כָּל אָדָם — **and not compared to other people,** חַס וְשָׁלוֹם — **G-d forbid,** שֶׁאַף עַל פִּי כֵן הוּא לְמַעְלָה מִכָּל הָאָדָם בַּעֲבוֹדָתוֹ — **since even while** this *tzadik* is in a "fallen" state, **his or her worship is still above the level of every** normal **person.**

The *tzadik* has not *literally* fallen. Compared to an ordinary person, the *tzadik* is still functioning on an elevated plane. The term "fallen" is only *relative* to the *tzadik's* prior level.

כִּי נִשְׁאַר בָּהּ בְּחִינַת רְשִׁימוּ מִמַּדְרֵיגָתוֹ הָרִאשׁוֹנָה — The *tzadik* has not literally fallen **since a remnant of his** or her **previous level remains** even in this interim period.

How, then, is the *tzadik* motivated to worship in this fallen state (beyond drawing from the remnant of his/her former self)?

אַךְ עִיקָרָהּ מֵאַהֲבָה שֶׁנִּתְחַנֵּךְ וְהוּרְגַּל בָּהּ מִנְּעוּרָיו — **But,** while in a "fallen" state, the *tzadik's* worship is motivated **mainly** not from this remnant, but **from the** type **of love** of G-d **in which he** or she **was educated and accustomed since**

למדרגת צדיק וז"ש גם כי יזקין וגו'.
והנה ראשית הדברים המעוררים האהבה
והיראה ויסודן היא האמונה הטהורה
ונאמנה ביחודו ואחדותו יתברך וית':

childhood, בְּטֶרֶם שֶׁהִגִּיעַ לְמַדְרֵגַת צַדִּיק — **before he** or she **reached the level of tzadik,** i.e., the second type of love discussed above, which is acquired through contemplation.

וְזֶהוּ שֶׁכָּתוּב גַּם כִּי יַזְקִין וְגוֹ' — **And this** provides an answer to our earlier question, on the verse "Educate a lad in his own way, **when he grows old he will still not swerve from it":** Why should a person sustain the "way" of his childhood, even in adulthood?

Now we can appreciate that this verse refers to the instance of a tzadik who has "fallen" (from the first type of love) while ascending from one level to the next, and must temporarily draw on residual tools of worship, which have been with him since childhood (i.e., the second type of love).

From all the above we see the importance of the second type of love, achieved through personal reflection, and becoming "accustomed" to worship through repeated practice (the "education of a child"). Ultimately this is the connection with G-d which stays with a person throughout his or her life, on the deepest level. Even a tzadik, who vastly transcends the worship of ordinary people, must sometimes rely on this second type of love, which he "owns" more deeply than his advanced worship.

SECTION THREE: THE IMPORTANCE OF FAITH

Now we turn to the main theme of this volume, faith in G-d.

וְהִנֵּה רֵאשִׁית הַדְּבָרִים הַמְעוֹרְרִים הָאַהֲבָה וְהַיִּרְאָה וִיסוֹדָן — **Now the initial step before, and foundation of, awakening love and reverence of G-d,** הִיא הָאֱמוּנָה הַטְּהוֹרָה וְנֶאֱמָנָה בְּיִחוּדוֹ וְאַחְדּוּתוֹ — **is the pure and devoted faith in G-d's oneness and nonduality,** יִתְבָּרֵךְ וְיִתְעַלֶּה — **may He be blessed and exalted,** which we will discuss in the coming chapters.

The practical techniques for awakening love and reverence of G-d have already been detailed in the First Book of Tanya. These techniques rely on contemplating G-d's greatness. So as a "foundation" to this work, we need to develop a more nuanced understanding of what it means that we believe "G-d is one" and why we believe He is nondual (i.e., that all existence is part of Him). It is to this that the Second Book of Tanya, Sha'ar Ha-Yichud ve-ha-Emunah, is devoted.

שער היחוד והאמונה

להבין מעט מזער מ"ש בזהר דשמע ישראל כו' הוא יחודא עילאה
ובשכמל"ו הוא יחודא תתאה:

AUTHOR'S OPENING

7TH SIVAN REGULAR | 7TH SIVAN LEAP

שַׁעַר הַיִּחוּד וְהָאֱמוּנָה — The second book of Tanya is called, *Gateway to Oneness and Faith.*

לְהָבִין מְעַט מִזְעֵר מַה שֶּׁכָּתוּב בַּזֹהַר — The purpose of this book is to give you at
least **a minimal understanding of what the** *Zohar* **states** (1, 12b), דִּשְׁמַע יִשְׂרָאֵל
גו' — that **Shema Yisra'el** *Hashem Elokenu Hashem Echad, "Hear, O Israel,
G-d is our G-d; G-d is one" (Deuteronomy* 6:4), הוּא יְחוּדָא עִילָּאָה — is "upper
unification" **(yichuda ila'ah),** וּבָרוּךְ שֵׁם כְּבוֹד מַלְכוּתוֹ לְעוֹלָם וָעֶד — and *Baruch
Sheim Kevod Malchuso Le'olam Va'ed, "Blessed be the name of His glo-
rious kingdom forever and ever,"* הוּא יְחוּדָא תַּתָּאָה — is "lower unification"
(yichuda tata'ah).

The Torah requires us to recite the *Shema* twice daily, a series of scriptural
passages which open with a declaration of faith in the One G-d.

The basic intention of the *Shema*, as required by Jewish Law, is *"to declare
G-d as King in the heavens and the earth"* (Shulchan Aruch, Orach Chaim
61:6). But According to the Kabbalah, in the *Shema* we affirm, not only G-d's
unity in the world, but also a unity *within G-d.* In the first verse of the
Shema ("Hear, O Israel, G-d is our G-d; G-d is one") we affirm that G-d's powers, which may seem to be diverse (since sometimes He rewards, sometimes
He punishes *etc.*), are, in fact, one. This is what the *Zohar* calls "upper unification" *(yichuda ila'ah).*

After saying the six words of Deuteronomy 6:4 *("Hear, O Israel, G-d is our
G-d; G-d is one"),* before continuing with Deuteronomy 6:5, we say, *Baruch
Sheim Kevod Malchuso Le'olam Va'ed, "Blessed be the name of His glorious
kingdom forever and ever"* (see *Talmud, Pesachim* 56a). This six-word formu-
la, says the Zohar, represents the six "directions" (energies) of the created
worlds that received energy from G-d's attributes. We should have this intention when saying this phrase, and it is referred to as "lower unification" *(yichuda tata'ah;* see Rabbi Moshe Cordovero, *Ohr Yakar* to *Zohar* ibid.).

The *Tanya*, however, will offer a deeper reading of these Zoharic terms. But first we need to immerse ourselves in the Ba'al Shem Tov's view of the universe which radically re-defined the monotheistic idea.

פרק א **וידעת** היום והשבות אל לבבך כי ה' הוא
האלהים בשמים ממעל ועל הארץ

CHAPTER 1

G-D'S CONTINUAL CREATION

SECTION ONE: EMBODIMENT OF DIVINE ENERGY IN CREATION

The simple statement that "G-d is One" is, in fact, surprisingly complex. Classically it has been interpreted to mean that G-d is the one and only real deity; all other gods are false (see *Mechilta, Exodus, Ba-Chodesh* 5).

The Kabbalists, however, were focused on a different concern when discussing the oneness of G-d, namely, the unity *within* G-d. While G-d interacts with the universe through His different "attributes" or "powers," we must be careful not to give these powers a separate identity from G-d. They are, in fact, merged with Him in a totally seamless unity, something that is beyond our full comprehension.

Many Kabbalistic texts have been devoted to this theme, and it will be the concern of the present work, Part Two of the *Tanya*, especially from Chapter 8 onwards.

Here in the first part of our book, the *Tanya* will elaborate upon another dimension of the "G-d is One" idea. It is a theme which became a cornerstone of the Chasidic revolution of the Ba'al Shem Tov, though it can be traced to earlier Jewish sources. Namely, that *G-d is the only true existence.*

That is not to say that the world does not exist at all. Rather, the world's existence is contingent on G-d, and therefore it has no *independent* existence.

Chasidic thought discerns this truth in the following verse.

וְיָדַעְתָּ הַיּוֹם וַהֲשֵׁבֹתָ אֶל לְבָבֶךָ כִּי ה' הוּא הָאֱלֹהִים בַּשָּׁמַיִם מִמַּעַל וְעַל הָאָרֶץ מִתָּחַת אֵין עוֹד — *"And you shall know today and take to your heart that G-d is G-d in the heavens above and in the earth below, there is none else"* (*Deuteronomy* 4:39).

"There is none else" can be read: "there is no other (independent) existence *at all* besides G-d."

The *Tanya* will devote several chapters to explain this idea. But first, we need to address another detail in the verse.

מתחת אין עוד. וצריך להבין וכי תעלה על דעתך שיש
אלהים נשרה במים מתחת לארץ שצריך להזהיר כ"כ
והשבות אל לבבך. הנה כתיב לעולם ה' דברך נצב
בשמים ופי' הבעש"ט ז"ל כי דברך שאמרת יהי רקיע
בתוך המים וגו' תיבות ואותיות אלו הן נצבות ועומדות

וְצָרִיךְ לְהָבִין — **We need to clarify** the following problem with this verse:

וְכִי תַעֲלֶה עַל דַּעְתְּךָ שֶׁיֵּשׁ אֱלֹהִים נִשְׁרָה בַּמַּיִם מִתַּחַת לָאָרֶץ — **Would you really think that there is a god inhabiting waters below the earth,** שֶׁצָּרִיךְ לְהַזְהִיר כָּל כָּךְ — **such that the verse has to warn us in such strong terms** that this is not the case, וַהֲשֵׁבוֹתָ אֶל לְבָבֶךָ — stating, *"and take it to your heart"?*

The verse instructs us to take its message "to heart," suggesting that some serious contemplation is required. But why *wouldn't* we think that "G-d is G-d... in the earth below"? Is the notion that there is "a god inhabiting waters below the earth" sufficiently credible that we need to "take to heart" that it is not true?

We will leave the answer to this question until much later (Chapter 6). First, we need to familiarize ourselves with the core mystical theology which will help us to understand why there is no other (independent) existence besides G-d.

הִנֵּה — **Now** to answer this question we need to delve into the following mystical secret, כְּתִיב לְעוֹלָם ה' דְּבָרְךָ נִצָּב בַּשָּׁמָיִם — the verse states, *"Forever, O G-d, Your word stands in the heavens"* (Psalms 119:89), וּפֵירֵשׁ הַבַּעַל שֵׁם טוֹב זִכְרוֹנוֹ לִבְרָכָה — **and the Ba'al Shem Tov, of blessed memory, explained** this verse as follows (see *Keser Shem Tov* section 194).

While the following teaching is actually sourced in *Midrash Tehillim* (ibid.), the *Tanya* attributes it to the *Ba'al Shem Tov* since he popularized it and taught it as a practical basis of worship (*Notes on Tanya*).

כִּי דְּבָרְךָ שֶׁאָמַרְתָּ — The *Ba'al Shem Tov* explained: **"Your word,"** G-d, **that You said,** in the six days of creation, יְהִי רָקִיעַ בְּתוֹךְ הַמַּיִם וְגוֹ' — such as *"Let*

A CHASIDIC THOUGHT

The so-called "act" of creation is really a process. *It is the story of the One entering the many.* It is the story of the formless infinite gradually garbing itself in a host of different forms.

"Creation" means that G-d did something *to Himself:* His energy emerges, gushes forth and *becomes* the universe.

לעולם בתוך רקיע השמים ומלובשות בתוך כל הרקיעים
לעולם להחיותם כדכתיב ודבר אלהינו יקום לעולם
ודבריו חיים וקיימים לעד כו' כי אילו היו האותיות
מסתלקות כרגע ח"ו וחוזרות למקורן היו כל השמים
אין ואפס ממש והיו כלא היו כלל וכמו קודם מאמר

there be a firmament in the midst of the waters, etc.," (*Genesis* 1:6), תֵּיבוֹת
הָאֵלּוּ הֵן נִצָּבוֹת וְעוֹמְדוֹת לְעוֹלָם בְּתוֹךְ רְקִיעַ הַשָּׁמַיִם — these Hebrew **words,**
and their constituent **letters,** *"forever stand in the heavens,"* וּמְלוּבָּשׁוֹת בְּתוֹךְ
כָּל הָרְקִיעִים לְעוֹלָם לְהַחֲיוֹתָם — since the energy of those letters **is embodied in
all the heavens "forever," to energize them.**

כְּדִכְתִיב וּדְבַר אֱלֹהֵינוּ יָקוּם לְעוֹלָם — **As the verse states,** *"the word of our G-d
shall stand for ever"* (*Isaiah* 40:8), וּדְבָרָיו חַיִּים וְקַיָּמִים לָעַד כוּ', **and we say,**
"Your word lives and sustains forever" (*Liturgy, Morning Prayer*).

Normally we look at language as a *convention,* to describe something which
is real and actual. For example, a chair exists regardless of what we call it. The
word "chair" is merely a label that we all agree upon so that this piece of furni-
ture can be identified.

PRACTICAL LESSONS

While they are record-
ed just once in the
Torah, G-d's ten cre-
ative statements are
"uttered" continuous-
ly to endow the uni-
verse with existence.

If G-d's creative
statements would
stop, even for a
moment, the universe
would cease to exist.

So look at the world
as a vibrant, pul-
sating "garment"
of the Divine.

But here the *Tanya* invites us to re-envision the relationship between language and reality. The universe,
we are told, only exists by virtue of (Divine/Hebrew)
language, which means: *language is reality* and *existence is convention.*

The words with which G-d creates the universe are
not incidental or a mere label of convenience. They
are the energy of the universe, the very power which
endows us with existence. *The letters are more "real"
than the universe itself.* The universe only "happens"
to exist because G-d has uttered a particular string of
words and letters.

כִּי אִילּוּ הָיוּ הָאוֹתִיוֹת מִסְתַּלְּקוֹת לְרֶגַע חַס וְשָׁלוֹם וְחוֹזְרוֹת
לִמְקוֹרָן — **For if the letters would disappear for a mo-
ment, G-d forbid, and return to their source** within
G-d, הָיוּ כָּל הַשָּׁמַיִם אַיִן וָאֶפֶס מַמָּשׁ — **all the heavens
would become absolutely** *"null and void"* (see *Isaiah*
40:17), וְהָיוּ כְּלֹא הָיוּ כְּלָל — **and it would be as if they
never had existed at all,** וּכְמוֹ קוֹדֶם מַאֲמַר יְהִי רָקִיעַ כוּ'
מַמָּשׁ — **just exactly as it was before** G-d said, *"Let
there be a firmament."*

יהי רקיע כו' ממש וכן בכל הברואים שבכל העולמות
עליונים ותחתונים ואפי' ארץ הלזו הגשמית ובחי' דומם
ממש אילו היו מסתלקות ממנה כרגע ח"ו האותיות
מעשרה מאמרות שבהן נבראת הארץ בששת ימי

A letter is a linguistic "vehicle" through which an idea may be expressed. G-d's letters are similarly "vehicles" or "packets" that deliver Divine creative energy to the world which are crucial to its existence.

The key emphasis here is that the creation of something-from-nothing is an *ongoing process.* G-d must constantly will all of existence into being, otherwise the universe would revert to primordial nothingness. "G-d's word" must continually be "spoken" to ensure the ongoing existence of every creation.

וְכֵן בְּכָל הַבְּרוּאִים שֶׁבְּכָל הָעוֹלָמוֹת עֶלְיוֹנִים וְתַחְתּוֹנִים — The same is true of all the creations in all the worlds, upper and lower, וַאֲפִילוּ אֶרֶץ הַלֵּזוּ הַגַּשְׁמִית — and even this physical earth, וּבְחִינַת דּוֹמֵם מַמָּשׁ — even completely inert matter, אִילוּ הָיוּ מִסְתַּלְקוֹת מִמֶּנָּה לְרֶגַע חַס וְשָׁלוֹם הָאוֹתִיּוֹת מֵעֲשָׂרָה מַאֲמָרוֹת שֶׁבָּהֶן נִבְרֵאת — if the letters (from the *"ten statements which the earth was created"* (Mishnah, Avos 5:1) in the six days of genesis), would disappear from the heavens, earth or even from inert matter, for a moment, G-d forbid, הָיְתָה חוֹזֶרֶת לְאַיִן וָאֶפֶס מַמָּשׁ — the heavens and earth would return to be absolutely *"null and void,"* כְּמוֹ לִפְנֵי שֵׁשֶׁת יְמֵי בְּרֵאשִׁית מַמָּשׁ — exactly as they were before the six days of genesis.

Chabad discourses often illustrate this idea with the analogy of a stone thrown into the air. In order to continue its ascent and counteract the gravitational pull downwards, the stone requires a continual supply of kinetic energy, provided by the initial thrust of the hand. As soon as this energy is exhausted,

A CHASIDIC THOUGHT

"Before anything was emanated, there was only the Infinite One (*Ein Sof*), which was all that existed. And even after He brought into being everything which exists, there is nothing but Him, and you cannot find anything that exists apart from Him, G-d forbid. For nothing exists devoid of G-d's power, for if there were, He would be limited and subject to duality, G-d forbid. Rather, G-d is everything that exists, but everything that exists is not G-d... Nothing is devoid of His G-dliness: everything is within it.... There is nothing but it."

Rabbi Moshe Cordovero (16th Cent.), *Elimah Rabasi*, p. 24d–25a.

בראשית היתה חוזרת לאין ואפס ממש כמו לפני ששת
ימי בראשית ממש וז"ש האר"י ז"ל שגם בדומם ממש
כמו אבנים ועפר ומים יש בחי' נפש וחיות רוחנית
דהיינו בחי' התלבשות אותיות הדבור מעשרה מאמרו'

the stone begins to fall. The upward *motion* of the rock is analogous to the *existence* of the world: If G-d's creative input were to cease, the world's existence would revert to its more "natural" state of nothingness.

The need for a constant sustaining force points to a crippling fragility which plagues the existence of all matter. The rock, in our analogy, never changes in substance or character; it has not become a new "species" of "flying rock"; rather, it is a rock that *happens* to be flying due to an *acquired* quality of kinetic motion. Ongoing creation teaches us that even when the world does enjoy existence, that existence is *an acquired property and not an inherent one.* In the same way that, even as it soars upwards, the stone's natural tendency is to fall downwards, the universe tends towards self-annihilation and "re-absorption" back into its Divine source. The apparently static phenomenon of the world's independent existence is, in fact, dynamically sustained by a constant creative drive. (For the above see: Rabbi Yoel Kahn, *Shiurim Be-Toras Chabad* (Kfar Chabad: 2006), pp. 152-5).

PRACTICAL LESSONS

G-d's creative energy, in the form of letters, is "downgraded" through switching and exchanging letters, so as to be compatible with the universe. Each created thing has its own unique "code" of letters.

The more switching/ exchanging takes place, the more the energy in the letters is diminished.

Through this process the Divine presence that fills the world has millions of different "faces."

The *Tanya* traces a source for this teaching of the *Ba'al Shem Tov* in the writings of *Arizal*.

וְזֶהוּ שֶׁאָמַר הָאֲר"י זִכְרוֹנוֹ לִבְרָכָה שֶׁגַם בְּדוֹמֵם מַמָּשׁ כְּמוֹ אֲבָנִים וְעָפָר וּמַיִם — **That is why Rabbi Isaac Luria, of blessed memory (***Arizal***) taught that even within completely inert matter, such as stones, earth and water,** יֵשׁ בְּחִינַת נֶפֶשׁ וְחַיּוּת רוּחָנִית — **there is a "soul," a spiritual energy** (*Etz Chaim* 39:3; 50:2).

Even stones and dirt are "alive" in the sense that G-d's life-energy must constantly be pumped into them to maintain their existence.

דְּהַיְינוּ בְּחִינַת הִתְלַבְּשׁוּת אוֹתִיּוֹת הַדִבּוּר מֵעֲשָׂרָה מַאֲמָרוֹת — **And this is** nothing other than the energy from **the letters of G-d's speech "in the "ten statements"** of genesis, **embodied in** the stones, earth and water, הַמְחַיּוֹת וּמְהַוּוֹת אֶת הַדּוֹמֵם — this energy from the letters **brings these inert things into being, and sustains**

המחיות ומהוות את הדומם להיות יש מאין ואפס
שלפני ששת ימי בראשית ואף שלא הוזכר שם אבן
בעשרה מאמרות שבתורה אעפ"כ נמשך חיות לאבן
ע"י צירופים וחילופי אותיו' המתגלגלות ברל"א שערים

their existence, לִהְיוֹת יֵשׁ מֵאַיִן וָאֶפֶס שֶׁלְפְנֵי שֵׁשֶׁת יְמֵי בְרֵאשִׁית — to be "some-thing" out of the *"null and void"* that was before the six days of genesis.

The withdrawal of G-d's creating and sustaining force to a thing would not only bring the thing itself to an end, it would eradicate *the very idea* of that thing. All its manifestations, past, present, and future, would cease to be, just like *"before the six days of genesis."*

SECTION TWO: CHANNELS OF FLOW

8TH SIVAN REGULAR

In Chapter Two, we will continue to explore the idea of continual creation and its implications. For the rest of this chapter we will address another, more technical issue concerning the creation of the universe though Divine letters.

Obviously, the "ten statements with which the earth was created" do not specify every species of plant, animal and every type of inert matter. How then do the letters of these "ten statements" energize *everything* in the universe?

וְאַף שֶׁלֹּא הוּזְכַּר שֵׁם אֶבֶן בַּעֲשָׂרָה מַאֲמָרוֹת שֶׁבַּתּוֹרָה — **And while the term "stone" is not mentioned in the ten statements** of genesis **in the Torah,** so how can we argue that it is the letters of the word "stone" that energizes all stones and brings them into being?

אַף עַל פִּי כֵן נִמְשָׁךְ חַיּוּת לָאֶבֶן — **Nevertheless, the stone still receives its energy through** letters from the ten statements, עַל יְדֵי צֵירוּפִים וְחִילוּפֵי אוֹתִיּוֹת — but in order to form the word "stone," **letters** must be **rearranged and switched.**

PRACTICAL LESSONS

The final "code" of Divine letters which powers an object is, in fact, its name in Hebrew.

Contemplate the energy and shape of the letters of your Hebrew name. They manifest a unique expression of G-d's energy within you.

Ultimately, the energy of any object can be traced back to the letters of the "ten statements." But in most instances, those letters will have to be "rearranged and switched" so as to be compatible with each individual object.

הַמִּתְגַּלְגְּלוֹת בְּרל"א שְׁעָרִים פָּנִים וְאָחוֹר כְּמוֹ שֶׁכָּתוּב בְּסֵפֶר יְצִירָה — The method of this rearrangement follows the **rotation of "the wheel of 231 gates, in forward and reverse,"** stated in *Sefer Yetzirah* (2:2-4).

פנים ואחור כמ"ש בס' יצירה עד שמשתלשל מעשרה
מאמרות ונמשך מהן צירוף שם אבן והוא חיותו של
האבן וכן בכל הנבראים שבעולם השמות שנקראים
בהם בלשון הקדש הן הן אותיות הדבור המשתלשלו'
ממדרגה למדרגה מעשרה מאמרות שבתורה ע"י
חילופים ותמורות האותיות ברל"א שערים עד שמגיעות
ומתלבשות באותו נברא להחיותו לפי שאין פרטי

77A

The "wheel of 231 gates" is a heavenly exchange system where the energy of one letter can be switched for the energy of any other. The wheel is drawn by placing all 22 letters on the circumference of a circle, and connecting each letter to every other letter with a line, which results in 231 pathways.

"Twenty-two elemental letters. He engraved them, carved them, weighed them, permuted them, and transposed them, forming with them everything formed and everything destined to be formed. Twenty-two elemental letters. He set them in a wheel with 231 gates, turning forward and backward…. How did He permute them? Alef with them all, all of them with alef; beis with them all, all of them with beis; and so with all the letters, turning round and round, within 231 gates" (Sefer Yetzirah 2:2-4).

PRACTICAL LESSONS

The majesty and oneness of G-d are manifest in the most basic and simple types of being, including dirt and stones.

The simplest things, when appreciated with reverence, can take on an entirely new meaning.

עַד שֶׁמִּשְׁתַּלְשֵׁל מֵעֲשָׂרָה מַאֲמָרוֹת וְנִמְשָׁךְ מֵהֶן צֵירוּף שֵׁם אֶבֶן — The **rearrangement** of letters **of the ten statements** continues through the "wheel" **until the eventual result is the word** *even* **(stone),** וְהוּא חַיּוּתוֹ שֶׁל הָאֶבֶן — **which is the life-force of the stone.**

וְכֵן בְּכָל הַנִּבְרָאִים שֶׁבָּעוֹלָם — **And the same is true for all the created objects in the world,** הַשֵּׁמוֹת שֶׁנִּקְרָאִים בָּהֶם בִּלְשׁוֹן הַקֹּדֶשׁ — **the names which they are called in** Biblical Hebrew, **the sacred tongue,** הֵן הֵן אוֹתִיּוֹת הַדִּבּוּר הַמִּשְׁתַּלְשְׁלוֹת מִמַּדְרֵגָה לְמַדְרֵגָה מֵעֲשָׂרָה מַאֲמָרוֹת שֶׁבַּתּוֹרָה — **are nothing other than the letters spoken in the ten statements** of Genesis **in the Torah, after passing down from level to level,** עַל יְדֵי חִילּוּפִים וּתְמוּרוֹת הָאוֹתִיּוֹת בְּרל"א שְׁעָרִים — **through switching and exchanging the letters through the 231 gates,** עַד שֶׁמַּגִּיעוֹת וּמִתְלַבְּשׁוֹת בְּאוֹתוֹ נִבְרָא לְהַחֲיוֹתוֹ — **to the point** at which those letters **can reach and become embodied in that creation, to energize it,** because they spell its name.

הנבראים יכולים לקבל חיותם מעשרה מאמרות עצמן
שבתורה שהחיות הנמשך מהן עצמן גדול מאד מבחי'
הנבראים פרטיים ואין כח בהם לקבל החיות אלא ע"י
שיורד החיות ומשתלשל ממדרגה למדרגה פחותה
ממנה ע"י חילופים ותמורות האותיות וגימטריאות

The *Tanya* refers to two different methods of rearranging letters, "switching" (*chiluf*) and "exchanging" (*temurah*). While these two methods sound similar, they do in fact differ "as much as the heavens transcend the earth" (*Ramak, Pardes* 30:5).

"Switching" is a process of taking the *same letters* and changing their order, like an anagram. When letters are "exchanged" they are swapped for *different letters* (through the "wheel") which are then arranged into the desired word (ibid.).

Exchanging the letters is a very different process because it *diminishes energy* significantly, much more so than with switching. But this is actually a helpful thing, as the *Tanya* will now explain.

לְפִי שֶׁאֵין פְּרָטֵי הַנִּבְרָאִים יְכוֹלִים לְקַבֵּל חַיּוּתָם מֵעֲשָׂרָה מַאֲמָרוֹת עַצְמָן שֶׁבַּתּוֹרָה — This process is necessary **because individual created objects can't receive their energy directly from** the energy of **the ten statements** of genesis **in the Torah,** שֶׁהַחַיּוּת הַנִּמְשָׁךְ מֵהֶן עַצְמָן גָּדוֹל מְאֹד מִבְּחִינַת הַנִּבְרָאִים פְּרָטִיִּים — **because the energy flowing from** the ten statements **themselves is much too great for individual creations** to receive, וְאֵין כֹּחַ בָּהֶם לְקַבֵּל הַחַיּוּת אֶלָּא עַל יְדֵי שֶׁיּוֹרֵד הַחַיּוּת וּמִשְׁתַּלְשֵׁל מִמַּדְרֵגָה לְמַדְרֵגָה פְּחוּתָה מִמֶּנָּה — **and they are only able to receive this energy once the energy has been downgraded multiple levels,** עַל יְדֵי חִילוּפִים וּתְמוּרוֹת הָאוֹתִיּוֹת — **through switching and exchanging letters.**

Why do we need switching and exchanging at all? Why did G-d not simply list every entity that He wished to create in the "ten statements" of genesis?

The *Tanya* answers: The "ten statements" contain a raw, primordial energy that, generally speaking, "is too great for individual creations." Switching and exchanging is the necessary process by which this raw energy is "downgraded multiple levels" so that it can be compatible with ordinary creations.

So far we have learned that energy may be dimmed through either a.) switch-

שֶׁהֵן חֶשְׁבּוֹן הָאוֹתִיּוֹת עַד שֶׁיּוּכַל לְהִתְצַמְצֵם וּלְהִתְלַבֵּשׁ
וּלְהִתְהַוּוֹת מִמֶּנּוּ נִבְרָא פְּרָטִי וְזֶה שְׁמוֹ אֲשֶׁר יִקְרְאוּ לוֹ
בְּלה״ק הוּא כְּלִי לַחַיּוּת הַמְצוּמְצָם בְּאוֹתִיּוֹת שֵׁם זֶה
שֶׁנִּשְׁתַּלְשֵׁל מֵעֲשָׂרָה מַאֲמָרוֹת שֶׁבַּתּוֹרָה שֶׁיֵּשׁ בָּהֶם כֹּחַ
וְחַיּוּת לִבְרוֹא יֵשׁ מֵאַיִן וּלְהַחֲיוֹתוֹ לְעוֹלָם דְּאוֹרַיְיתָא
וְקוּדְשָׁא בְּרִיךְ הוּא כּוּלָּא חַד:

ing, or b.) exchanging of letters. We will now learn of a third method, which results in an even greater dimming of light.

וְגִימַטְרִיָאוֹת שֶׁהֵן חֶשְׁבּוֹן הָאוֹתִיּוֹת — **And c.) through *gematrios* (sing. *gematria*),** the exchange of **letters** based on their **numerical values.**

Through *gematria,* letters are exchanged into numbers and then back into letters again. These additional transmutations result in a greater diminishing of the light than through "exchanging."

The three processes of a.) switching, b.) exchanging and c.) *gematria* are needed to dim the raw, primordial light of the "ten statements,"

עַד שֶׁיּוּכַל לְהִתְצַמְצֵם וּלְהִתְלַבֵּשׁ וּלְהִתְהַוּוֹת מִמֶּנּוּ נִבְרָא פְּרָטִי — **to the point where** the energy has been sufficiently diminished so that it can become embodied in that particular creation, to bring it into existence.

The final product, of manipulating all these letters, is a Hebrew word:

וְזֶה שְׁמוֹ אֲשֶׁר יִקְרְאוּ לוֹ בִּלְשׁוֹן הַקֹּדֶשׁ — **And this is the name by which** this particular creation **is called in the sacred tongue,** Biblical Hebrew.

An object's name in Biblical Hebrew is not a mere convention applied for the purposes of identification; it is the very life-force of that object. The name can be traced back to the raw energy of the "ten statements," after which the letters were processed and diminished by switching, exchanging and *gematrios.*

הוּא כְּלִי לַחַיּוּת הַמְצוּמְצָם בְּאוֹתִיּוֹת שֵׁם זֶה — **That name is the "vessel"** which delivers **the diminished energy found in the letters of this name,** שֶׁנִּשְׁתַּלְשֵׁל מֵעֲשָׂרָה מַאֲמָרוֹת שֶׁבַּתּוֹרָה — **which are a derivative of the ten statements of the Torah,** שֶׁיֵּשׁ בָּהֶם כֹּחַ וְחַיּוּת לִבְרוֹא יֵשׁ מֵאַיִן וּלְהַחֲיוֹתוֹ לְעוֹלָם — **that have the power and energy to create something-from-nothing and to energize it forever,** דְּאוֹרַיְיתָא וְקוּדְשָׁא בְּרִיךְ הוּא כּוּלָּא חַד — **since** *"the Torah and G-d are totally one"* (see *Zohar* 1, 24a; 2, 60a).

The Torah is not merely authored by G-d, its letters represent an *encapsulation of G-d's energy.* Just as G-d has the power to create, His letters in the Torah possess that power too, since "the Torah and G-d are totally one."

(We will elaborate on this point later on, in Chapter 12.)

פרק ב והנה   מכאן תשובת המינים וגילוי שורש
טעותם הכופרים בהשגחה פרטית

CHAPTER 2

MORE ON CONTINUOUS CREATION

SECTION ONE: A RATIONAL BASIS FOR CONTINUOUS CREATION

9TH SIVAN REGULAR | 8TH SIVAN LEAP

Chapter Two continues the theme of Chapter One, elaborating on the necessity for G-d's continuous energetic presence in the world (in the form of "letters of the Torah") to sustain the world's existence.

וְהִנֵּה מִכָּאן תְּשׁוּבַת הַמִּינִים — **From the above** discussion in Chapter One, **we have an** intelligent **response to heretics (*minim*).**

Who are these "heretics" and why are they addressed here in the *Tanya*?

Judaism requires us to *"know how to respond to the heretic"* (*Mishnah, Avos* 2:14), so as to defend the principles of our faith. But the *Tanya* is not a polemical work, and it is unlikely that the author was expecting many "heretics" to be reading this text, or to be influenced by it.

Rather, the author was of the opinion that *faith in the received wisdom of Judaism must be supported by rational argument.* Having accepted the received wisdom of Chapter One (that G-d creates the world continually through the letters of the "statements of genesis"), it would now be helpful to know why this must be the case, rationally speaking. Our exercise in "responding to heretics" is important even if we never engage with any actual heretics, as it is beneficial *to us* to understand the necessity of continual creation.

וְגִילוּי שׁוֹרֶשׁ טָעוּתָם — **And a clarification of the root of the error of** these heretics.

The *Tanya* teaches us here a Chasidic approach to arguments about faith. Debating issues directly is often ineffective since it involves a strong element of oneupmanship, where each side is trying to outdo the other, rather than a frank discussion. The outcome often depends on the skill of the debaters, rather than the validity of their arguments. So the best approach is to clarify *"the root* of the error," the conceptual principle which is the source of misunderstanding (see *Ha-Lekach ve-ha-Libuv*).

הַכּוֹפְרִים בְּהַשְׁגָּחָה פְּרָטִית — The error of **those** heretics who agree that G-d cre-

וּבְאוֹתוֹ וּמוֹפְתֵי הַתּוֹרָה שְׁטוֹעֵי' בְּדִמְיוֹנָם הַכּוֹזֵב שֶׁמְדַמִּין
מַעֲשֵׂה ה' עוֹשֶׂה שָׁמַי' וָאָרֶץ לְמַעֲשֵׂה אֱנוֹשׁ וְתַחְבּוּלוֹתָיו כִּי

ated the world something-from-nothing but **who deny** the possibility of **Divine providence.**

In his *Principles of Faith*, Rambam writes, *"Principle Ten is that G-d knows man's actions and does not remove His eye from them, rejecting the view that 'G-d has abandoned the earth'"* (*Commentary to the Mishnah, Sanhedrin, beg. chapter chelek*).

A denial of this principle renders a person a *min,* a heretic (ibid.; *Mishneh Torah, Laws of Teshuvah* 3:7).

These "heretics" accept that only one G-d exists and that He created the world something-from-nothing, but they fail to understand how He could retain His utter oneness and at the same time, be *intimately involved* with the world. If G-d is truly one, they argue, how could He be closely connected with a world of multiplicity? If He were to know and directly control so many details, wouldn't those details impose some detail in Him? Rather, the heretics conclude, He must be an initial and *distant* cause of everything that exists (*Notes on Tanya*).

וּבְאוֹתוֹת וּמוֹפְתֵי הַתּוֹרָה — **And** for the same reason these heretics deny the possibility of Divine intervention, such as the **miracles and wonders** stated **in the Torah.**

The heretics argue: If G-d is truly one He must be distant from our world of multiplicity, therefore He cannot directly intervene in the world's affairs, to bring about a miracle (ibid.).

The *Tanya* now addresses the "root error" of this ideology.

שֶׁמְדַמִּין **They mistakenly imagine in their minds,** שֹׁטוֹעִים בְּדִמְיוֹנָם הַכּוֹזֵב — **a similarity between G-d's act of** *"making heavens and earth"* (*Psalms* 115:15), מַעֲשֵׂה ה' עוֹשֶׂה שָׁמַיִם וָאָרֶץ — and *"the work of* לְמַעֲשֵׂה אֱנוֹשׁ וְתַחְבּוּלוֹתָיו *man and his schemes"* (cf. *Liturgy, Day of Atonement*).

The core error of the heretics is *thinking in human terms about G-d*. They impose certain features of human creative work on the Divine, and come to mistaken conclusions.

The *Tanya* now clarifies more precisely the error which results from such thinking.

PRACTICAL LESSONS

Humans never really create something-from-nothing. So you can't understand Divine creation by comparing it to human creation.

כאשר יצא לצורף כלי שוב אין הכלי צריך לידי הצורף
כי אף שידיו מסולקות הימנו והולך לו בשוק הכלי קיים
בתבניתו וצלמו ממש כאשר יצא מידי הצורף כך
מדמין הסכלים האלו מעשה שמים וארץ אך טח מראות
עיניהם ההבדל הגדול שבין מעשה אנוש ותחבולותיו
שהוא יש מיש רק שמשנה הצורה והתמונה מתמונת

כִּי כַּאֲשֶׁר יָצָא לַצּוֹרֵף כְּלִי — **Because** in the case of human creative work, **when a metalworker finishes a utensil,** שׁוּב אֵין הַכְּלִי צָרִיךְ לִידֵי הַצּוֹרֵף — **that utensil** exists independently, **and no longer requires the metalworker's hands.**

כִּי אַף שֶׁיָּדָיו מְסוּלָקוֹת הֵימֶנּוּ — **For even when** the metalworker's **hands will cease to have any involvement with the vessel,** וְהוֹלֵךְ לוֹ בַּשּׁוּק — **and he will go off** elsewhere **in the marketplace,** הַכְּלִי קַיָּים בְּתַבְנִיתוֹ וְצַלְמוֹ מַמָּשׁ כַּאֲשֶׁר יָצָא מִידֵי הַצּוֹרֵף — **that utensil remains exactly the same, in its shape and form, as when it left the metalworker's hands.**

כָּךְ מְדַמִּין הַסְּכָלִים הָאֵלוּ מַעֲשֵׂה שָׁמַיִם וָאָרֶץ — **That is how those fools,** the heretics, **imagine that** G-d **made the heavens and the earth!**

The heretics fail to understand that the existence of matter is *not* autonomous, and must be sustained by G-d. Human "creation" only carves form *within existing matter*; it does not create the matter itself.

אַךְ טַח מֵרְאוֹת עֵינֵיהֶם — **But** *"their eyes are plastered over"* (*Isaiah* 44:18), הַהֶבְדֵּל הַגָּדוֹל שֶׁבֵּין מַעֲשֵׂה אֱנוֹשׁ וְתַחְבּוּלוֹתָיו — and they fail to see **the major distinction between** *"the work of man and his schemes,"* שֶׁהוּא יֵשׁ מִיֵּשׁ — which is not *real* creation, but forming **something-from-something,** רַק שֶׁמְּשַׁנֶּה — **just a morphing of form and appearance,** מִתְּמוּנַת חֲתִיכַת הַצּוּרָה וְהַתְּמוּנָה — from what initially **is shaped as a chunk of silver to** adopt **the appearance of a utensil,** כֶּסֶף לִתְמוּנַת כְּלִי — **and they** לְמַעֲשֵׂה שָׁמַיִם וָאָרֶץ שֶׁהוּא יֵשׁ מֵאַיִן

A CHASIDIC THOUGHT

"Everything is in G-d's hand. *There is nothing outside Him.* This is what it really means to believe in G-d's existence. It's common to believe that there is a G-d, but people do not always affirm that He is all. And that's a problem, as it implies you could leave the domain of G-d. Therefore, the belief in G-d's existence must be that *He is everything* and *nothing is outside Him*."

Rabbi Judah Loew (Maharal) of Prague, *Gevuros Hashem* (London, 1964, p. 181).

חתיכת כסף לתמונת כלי למעשה שמים וארץ שהוא
יש מאין והוא פלא גדול יותר מקריעת ים סוף עד"מ
שהוליך ה' את הים ברוח קדים עזה כל הלילה ויבקעו
המים ונצבו כמו נד וכחומה ואילו הפסיק ה' את הרוח
כרגע היו המים חוזרים וניגרים במורד כדרכם וטבעם

confuse this **with G-d's _"making heavens and earth,"_ which is** genuinely **some-thing-from-nothing.**

If G-d's energy would depart for a moment, the world would cease to exist. The heretics do not appreciate this fact because they look at creation in human terms, and imagine that it could exist on its own without G-d. But the reason why human "creations" exist without the continual involvement of their creator is because they are not really creations at all, but merely a _shift in form_ within preexisting matter.

SECTION TWO: AN ILLUSTRATION FROM THE SEA SPLITTING

To further illustrate the need for G-d's continual creative involvement with the world, the _Tanya_ offers us an analysis of the splitting of the Reed Sea.

(Obviously, this proof was not intended for the heretics who deny "miracles and wonders stated in the Torah." Rather it is to help the _Tanya's_ believing readers understand the concept more clearly—_Notes on Tanya_).

וְהוּא פֶּלֶא גָּדוֹל יוֹתֵר מִקְרִיעַת יַם סוּף עַל דֶּרֶךְ מָשָׁל — Creation of some-thing-from-nothing is **a greater wonder than** a miracle **such as the splitting of the Reed Sea,** שֶׁהוֹלִיךְ ה' אֶת הַיָּם בְּרוּחַ קָדִים עַזָּה כָּל הַלַּיְלָה וַיִּבָּקְעוּ הַמַּיִם — when _**"G-d led the sea with a mighty east wind all night... and the waters were split apart"**_ (_Exodus_ 14:21), וְנִצְבוּ כְמוֹ נֵד וּכְחוֹמָה — and the waters, _**"stood up like a mound"**_ (ibid. 15:8), **and like _"a wall"_** (ibid. 14:22).

The _Tanya_ here follows the view of _Rashbam_ that the splitting of the sea was actually caused by the wind which blew all night (and not by supernatural intervention).

וְאִילוּ הִפְסִיק ה' אֶת הָרוּחַ כְּרֶגַע — **And** the verse stresses that "G-d led the sea with a mighty east wind _all night,"_ to indicate that **if G-d had stopped the wind for a moment,** הָיוּ הַמַּיִם חוֹזְרִים וְנִגְּרִים בְּמוֹרָד — the sea **would have returned** _"like **water rushing down a slope"**_ (_Micah_ 1:4), כְּדַרְכָּם וְטִבְעָם — **which is** water's **way and nature,** וְלֹא קָמוּ כְּחוֹמָה בְּלִי סָפֵק — **and** the waters **would undoubtedly not have stood like a wall.**

To maintain a situation which is unnatural, a constant input is required. If G-d had not blown a wind "all night," there would not be sufficient force to main-

ולא קמו כחומה בלי ספק אף שהטבע הזה במים גם כן
נברא ומחודש יש מאין שהרי חומת אבנים נצבת
מעצמה בלי רוח רק שטבע המים אינו כן וכ"ש וק"ו

tain the water "like a wall," against its natural tendency to be "rushing down a slope."

The *Tanya's* proof is not from the *existence* of the waters in the sea, but their natural *tendency* (their "way and nature") to flow downwards. Since that tendency is constant, its reversal also requires a wind which does not stop.

And if the reversal of a mere tendency requires G-d's sustained involvement, all the more so must that be true of its very existence!

PRACTICAL LESSONS

The universe is like a wall of water being held up by a strong wind of G-d's creative energy. If the wind were to stop flowing for a moment, the wall would collapse.

Existence is not given and secure; it is flimsy and transient.

אַף שֶׁהַטֶּבַע הַזֶּה בַּמַּיִם גַּם כֵּן נִבְרָא וּמְחוּדָשׁ יֵשׁ מֵאַיִן — **Even though this tendency of water** to *"rush down a slope"* **is also created and innovated by G-d, something-from-nothing.**

Above we argued that the "natural" state of water was to flow down (and therefore its reversal, to make water stand, required constant input from G-d.) Here the *Tanya* notes that this is really an oversimplification, since nothing in this world is naturally "as it is" without G-d's constant input. Even water's tendency to flow downwards is created, and like all created things, it must also be constantly renewed by G-d.

שֶׁהֲרֵי חוֹמַת אֲבָנִים נִצֶּבֶת מֵעַצְמָהּ בְּלִי רוּחַ — **As we see that a wall of bricks will stand on its own, without any wind** to hold it up, רַק שֶׁטֶּבַע הַמַּיִם אֵינוֹ כֵן — **whereas the nature of water is not like that,** so the tendencies of each thing in the world (its properties) are clearly something assigned by G-d *in addition* to the thing's actual existence.

9TH SIVAN LEAP

To sum up: every physical entity has both a.) existence and b.) properties/tendencies. If even the tendencies require G-d's continuous input for them to be sustained,

וְכָל שֶׁכֵּן וְקַל וָחֹמֶר בִּבְרִיאַת יֵשׁ מֵאַיִן — **then how much more so is it definitely the case with creation** of an entity's existence **something-from-nothing,** that G-d's continuous input is required.

Creation of something-from-nothing is clearly more impressive than splitting the Reed Sea since:

בבריאת יש מאין שהיא למעלה מהטבע והפלא ופלא
יותר מקריעת ים סוף עאכ"ו שבהסתלקו' כח הבורא מן
הנברא ח"ו ישוב הנברא לאין ואפס ממש אלא צריך
להיות כח הפועל בנפעל תמיד להחיותו ולקיימו והן
בחי' אותיות הדבור מעשרה מאמרות שבהם נבראו
וע"ז נאמר ואתה מחיה את כולם אל תקרי מחיה אלא

שֶׁהִיא לְמַעְלָה מֵהַטֶּבַע — Creation of something-from-nothing **is supernatural.**

While it was a miracle for the wind to blow all night, splitting the sea exactly when it was needed by the Israelites to save their lives, it was nevertheless not a violation of the laws of Physics (according to the *Tanya's* reading here, following *Rashbam*). The waters split because that was the *natural effect* of wind blowing all night, without interruption.

If G-d's constant input was required for the lesser (natural) wonder of the splitting of the sea, all the more so is His constant input required for the greater (supernatural) wonder of creating the world!

וְהַפְלֵא וָפֶלֶא יוֹתֵר מִקְּרִיעַת יַם סוּף — Creation of something-from-nothing is **doubly more astonishing than the splitting of the Reed Sea.**

It is "doubly" more astonishing since: a.) Creation is something-from-nothing, and not merely something-from-something; b.) Creation alters not only the properties of an entity, but its very existence.

עַל אַחַת כַּמָּה וְכַמָּה שֶׁבְּהִסְתַּלְּקוּת כֹּחַ הַבּוֹרֵא מִן הַנִּבְרָא חַס וְשָׁלוֹם — **All the more so, then, if the Creator's power would leave the creation, G-d forbid,** יָשׁוּב הַנִּבְרָא — the creation **would return to be absolutely** *"null and void"* לְאַיִן וָאֶפֶס מַמָּשׁ (see *Isaiah* 40:17).

SECTION THREE: MORE ON DIVINE LETTERS

In chapter 1, the *Tanya* taught us that the powers which G-d constantly infuses into the universe, to keep it in existence, are *the Divine letters of the creation story* (the "ten statements" of genesis). We now continue with this theme.

אֶלָּא צָרִיךְ לִהְיוֹת כֹּחַ הַפּוֹעֵל בַּנִּפְעָל תָּמִיד לְהַחֲיוֹתוֹ וּלְקַיְּימוֹ — **Rather,** as we have now demonstrated, **the causal power (G-d) must constantly be present within the effect** (creation), **to energize and sustain it,** otherwise the effect would revert to nothingness, וְהֵן הֵן בְּחִינוֹת אוֹתִיּוֹת הַדִּבּוּר מֵעֲשָׂרָה מַאֲמָרוֹת שֶׁבָּהֶם נִבְרָאוּ — **and this** causal power **is nothing other than the spoken letters of the "ten statements"** of genesis **through which** the universe **was created.**

מהוה דהיינו יש מאין ואתה הן בחי' האותיות מאל"ף
ועד תי"ו וה"א היא ה' מוצאות הפה מקור האותיות
ואף שאין לו דמות הגוף הרי מקרא מלא דבר הכתוב

וְעַל זֶה נֶאֱמַר וְאַתָּה מְחַיֶּה אֶת כּוּלָם — **That is why** our Sages commented **on the verse,** *"And You (ve-atah) give life to them all"* (Nechemia 9:6), אַל תִּקְרֵי מְחַיֶּה — **"Do not read** *mechayeh,* **'give life,'** *but mehaveh,* **'bring into being'"** (cited in *Pardes* 6:8 in the name of the Sages), דְּהַיְינוּ יֵשׁ מֵאַיִן — **namely,** creation **something-from-nothing.**

The force which sustains our existence, giving it life (*mechayeh*), actually brings it into existence (*mehaveh*) too.

However the *Tanya's* particular interest here is in the first word of this quote, *ve-atah,* "And You" (spelled *vav-alef-tav-hei*).

וְאַתָּה הֵן בְּחִינוֹת הָאוֹתִיוֹת מֵאָלֶ"ף וְעַד תָּי"ו — **The word** *ve-atah,* which contains the Hebrew alphabet's first letter, *alef,* and its last letter, *tav,* alludes to all **the letters from** *alef* **to** *tav.*

The letters *alef* and *tav* in the word *ve-atah* span the whole of the Hebrew alphabet, hinting to all the letters. These letters are the energetic "packets" by which G-d sustains the world.

"And you give life to the world" is to be read: "And the twenty-two letters (*ve-atah*) bring the world into being (*mehaveh*)."

וְהֵ"א הִיא ה' מוֹצָאוֹת הַפֶּה — **And the** *hei* at the end of the word *ve-atah,* alludes to **the five organs of speech,** the throat, palate, tongue, teeth and lips (*Sefer Yetzirah* 2:3), מְקוֹר הָאוֹתִיוֹת — **which are,** metaphorically, **the source of the** spoken **letters** in G-d.

So, to be precise, "And you give life to the world" is to be read: "And the twenty-two letters *spoken by G-d's five organs of speech* bring the world into being."

Obviously, such physical references to G-d are not meant literally, as the *Tanya* immediately clarifies.

וְאַף שֶׁאֵין לוֹ דְּמוּת הַגּוּף — **And while** G-d *"has no body, nor image of a body"* (*Piyut Yigdal; Rambam's* Third Principle of Faith), הֲרֵי מִקְרָא מָלֵא דְּבֶר הַכָּתוּב — **nevertheless, Scripture will often speak of** G-d's speech in human terms, such as וַיְדַבֵּר ה' וַיֹּאמֶר ה' — **"G-d spoke," or "G-d said."**

וידבר ה' ויאמר ה' והיא בחי' התגלות הכ"ב אותיות
עליונות לנביאי' ומתלבשות בשכלם והשגתם במראה
הנבואה וגם במחשבתם ודיבורם כמ"ש רוח ה' דבר בי
ומלתו על לשוני וכמ"ש האר"י ז"ל [בשער הנבואה]
וכעין זה היא התלבשות האותיות בברואים כדכתיב
בדבר ה' שמים נעשו וברוח פיו כל צבאם רק שהיא
ע"י השתלשלות רבות ועצומות עד שיורדות לעשיה

References to G-d "speaking" are indeed metaphorical, but they are never-theless a physical example which accurately mirrors a spiritual process.

וְהִיא בְּחִינַת הַתְגַלוֹת הַכ"ב אוֹתִיוֹת עֶלְיוֹנוֹת לַנְבִיאִים — **And this** analogy, of G-d's speech, **refers to the disclosure of the twenty-two supernal letters to the prophets,** וּמִתְלַבְּשׁוֹת בְּשִׂכְלָם וְהַשָׂגָתָם בְּמַרְאֵה הַנְבוּאָה — **which are "dressed" in their minds and thoughts,** manifesting **in their prophetic visions,** וְגַם בְּמַחֲשַׁבְתָּם — **as well as in their thoughts and their speech,** כְּמוֹ שֶׁכָּתוּב רוּחַ ה', וְדִיבּוּרָם — **as the verse states, "The spirit of G-d spoke with me, and His word was on my tongue"** (2 Samuel 23:2), וּכְמוֹ שֶׁאָמַר הָאַר"י זִכְרוֹנוֹ לִבְרָכָה — **and as Arizal taught,** [בְּשַׁעַר הַנְבוּאָה] — **in** Sha'ar Ha-Nevuah (chapter 2).

The association of prophecy with a "text" of Divine speech is not incidental. The same letters which G-d used to create the world are received by the proph-ets as a disclosure of Divine energy in their minds, and subsequently, their speech.

וּכְעֵין זֶה הִיא הִתְלַבְּשׁוּת הָאוֹתִיוֹת בַּבְּרוּאִים — **The way in which the** supernal **letters are embodied in the creations resembles this,** כְּדִכְתִיב בִּדְבַר ה' שָׁמַיִם נַעֲשׂוּ וּבְרוּחַ פִּיו כָּל צְבָאָם — **as the verse states, "By the word of G-d the heavens were made, and by the breath of His mouth, all their hosts"** (Psalms 33:6).

PRACTICAL LESSONS

Prophecy represents an intermediate level of Divine "letters," lower than the Torah, but higher than the "letters" as they are found power-ing this world.

The prophet sees the very letters ("packets" of Divine energy) which G-d uses to create the world, and they are absorbed by his mind in a similar way in which the world must absorb that energy to remain in existence.

רַק שֶׁהִיא עַל יְדֵי הִשְׁתַּלְשְׁלוּת רַבּוֹת וַעֲצוּמוֹת — **Only,** in contrast to the prophets, where the supernal letters are manifested *directly*, creation **is through many powerful downgrades,** עַד שֶׁיוֹרְדוֹת לַעֲשִׂיָה גוּפָנִית — **until** this **physical World of**

גופנית משא"כ השגת הנביאי' היא באצילו' המתלבבשת בעולם הבריאה:

Asiyah (Action) is reached, מַה שֶּׁאֵין כֵּן הַשָּׂגַת הַנְּבִיאִים — unlike prophecy, הִיא בַּאֲצִילוּת הַמִּתְלַבֶּשֶׁת בְּעוֹלַם הַבְּרִיאָה — which is a disclosure from the highest World of *Atzilus* that is embodied in the World of *Beriah* (Creation).

The elevated consciousness of the prophet is much closer than the world to the source of the Divine letters. The letters need pass through only *one world* to enter the mind of the prophet (*Atzilus* to *Beriah*), whereas to reach the physical world their energy must be "downgraded" through *four worlds* (*Atzilus* to *Asiyah*). Nevertheless, the underlying principle is the same: G-d's energy is encapsulated in the "vessels" of the letters of the Torah, and these, in turn, are absorbed and "embodied" below to provide both prophecy and creative power.

78A פֶּרֶק ג וְהִנֵּה אַחֲרֵי הַדְּבָרִי׳ וְהָאֱמֶת הָאֵלֶּה כָּל מַשְׂכִּיל
עַל דָּבָר יָבִין לְאָשׁוּרוֹ אֵיךְ שֶׁכָּל נִבְרָא
וְיֵשׁ הוּא בָּאֱמֶת נֶחְשָׁב לְאַיִן וָאֶפֶס מַמָּשׁ לְגַבֵּי כֹּחַ הַפּוֹעֵל
וְרוּחַ פִּיו שֶׁבַּנִּפְעַל הַמְהַוֶּה אוֹתוֹ תָּמִיד וּמוֹצִיאוֹ מֵאַיִן מַמָּשׁ

CHAPTER 3

QUESTIONS OF IDENTITY

SECTION ONE: THE FLIMSINESS OF EXISTENCE

10TH SIVAN REGULAR | 10TH SIVAN LEAP

In Chapter One we were introduced to the *Ba'al Shem Tov's* teaching that creation is a *constant process.* If G-d would cease for a moment to energize the world with creative power, the world would cease to exist.

Chapter Two continued to explore this theme with a rational approach, demonstrating how G-d's energetic presence in the world is a logical necessity.

Here in Chapter Three we will approach the idea of continual creation from a different angle. The previous discussions have been theoretical: *If* G-d would cease to create the world constantly, it would cease to exist. But, thankfully, He has not done so, and we are still here. So how is the idea of continual creation meaningful to us now that G-d has chosen to sustain our existence constantly?

וְהִנֵּה אַחֲרֵי הַדְּבָרִים וְהָאֱמֶת הָאֵלֶּה — Now *"after* hearing *these true words"* (2 *Chronicles* 32:1), כָּל מַשְׂכִּיל עַל דָּבָר — everyone *"who looks into the matter"* (*Proverbs* 16:20), יָבִין לְאָשׁוּרוֹ אֵיךְ שֶׁכָּל נִבְרָא וְיֵשׁ הוּא בָּאֱמֶת נֶחְשָׁב לְאַיִן וָאֶפֶס מַמָּשׁ — will thoroughly understand how every created entity is genuinely and literally considered *"null and void"* (see *Isaiah* 40:17), לְגַבֵּי כֹּחַ הַפּוֹעֵל וְרוּחַ פִּיו שֶׁבַּנִּפְעַל — in relation to the causal power (G-d), *"the breath of His mouth,"* (*Psalms* 33:6), within the effect (creation), הַמְהַוֶּה אוֹתוֹ תָּמִיד — the causal power which continually brings all created entities into being, וּמוֹצִיאוֹ מֵאַיִן מַמָּשׁ לְיֵשׁ — taking them out from absolute nothingness, to become "something."

While it is true that the world does exist, the fact that a constant creative input is required from G-d affects the identity of the world. Since we cannot exist for a moment without Divine energy, our existence is flimsy and insubstantial.

In fact, as the *Tanya* puts it, our existence is "null and void." That does not mean to say that we do not exist at all, but *"in relation to the causal power (G-d)... which brings all created entities into being,"* we are *"null and void."*

ליש ומה שכל נברא ונפעל נראה לנו ליש וממשו' זהו
מחמת שאין אנו משיגים ורואים בעיני בשר את כח ה'
ורוח פיו שבנברא אבל אילו ניתנה רשות לעין לראות
ולהשיג את החיות ורוחניות שבכל נברא השופע בו
ממוצא פי ה' ורוח פיו לא היה גשמיות הנברא וחומרו

We are utterly dependent on the "causal power," so our existence has no independence at all from that power and is really just an expression of it.

But if we are "null and void," why does it not seem that way? Why does it appear very much the case that we do enjoy an independent existence?

וּמַה שֶׁכָּל נִבְרָא וְנִפְעָל נִרְאֶה לָנוּ לְיֵשׁ וּמַמָּשׁוּת — **And as for the fact that every created thing appears to us as real and substantial,** and not "null and void," זֶהוּ מֵחֲמַת שֶׁאֵין אָנוּ מַשִׂיגִים וְרוֹאִים בְּעֵינֵי בָשָׂר אֶת כֹּחַ ה' וְרוּחַ פִּיו שֶׁבַּנִבְרָא — **that is** only **because we fail to grasp, and tangibly see, the power of G-d, the *"breath of His mouth,"*** in every **created thing.**

Our senses offer us a veiled perspective of reality. They cannot detect the "causal power" of G-d in the universe, so they perceive an effect without a cause. They see the result of what G-d has produced, without noticing G-d's hand in every detail. Therefore our senses mistake something which is "null and void" for being "real and substantial."

אֲבָל אִילוּ נִיתְּנָה רְשׁוּת לָעַיִן לִרְאוֹת וּלְהַשִׂיג אֶת הַחַיוּת וְרוּחָנִיוּת שֶׁבְּכָל נִבְרָא — **But** *"if the eye were granted permission to see"* (*Talmud, Berachos* 6b), **and grasp the spiritual energy in every created thing,** הַשׁוֹפֵעַ בּוֹ מִמוֹצָא פִּי ה' וְרוּחַ פִּיו — **that flows into it from** *"the utterance of G-d's mouth"* (*Deuteronomy* 8:3) **and** *"the breath of His mouth,"* לֹא הָיָה גַּשְׁמִיוּת הַנִבְרָא וְחוּמְרוֹ וּמַמָּשׁוֹ נִרְאֶה כְּלָל לְעֵינֵינוּ — **our eyes would no longer perceive the physical, coarse, substantial** dimension **of the created entity.**

Obviously, the physical eye can't see something spiritual, so why does the *Tanya* entertain the possibility here?

The *Tanya's* view is that *your reality is determined by your consciousness.* You can accept what your senses tell you, that the physical world is substantial and enjoys independent existence; or you can choose for your reality to be determined by the conclusions of your mind.

If, over a period of time, you contemplate the idea that G-d creates the world constantly and that the universe enjoys no independent existence, after a

PRACTICAL LESSONS

Dependency erodes identity. Since our existence is dependent on G-d, we are "null and void." We have no true being of our own. We simply reflect G-d.

וממשו נראה כלל לעינינו כי הוא בטל במציאות ממש
לגבי החיות והרוחניות שבו מאחר שמבלעדי הרוחניו'
היה אין ואפס ממש כמו קודם ששת ימי בראשי' ממש
והרוחניות השופע עליו ממוצא פי ה' ורוח פיו הוא לבדו
המוציאו תמיד מאפס ואין ליש ומהוה אותו א"כ אפס

while, that becomes your truth, your reference point with which you interpret sensory information. You will still see a physical world, but you will have trained yourself to not be deceived by its illusion.

כִּי הוּא בָּטֵל בִּמְצִיאוּת מַמָּשׁ לְגַבֵּי הַחַיּוּת וְהָרוּחָנִיּוּת שֶׁבּוֹ — If you could see G-d's creative power, you would see how the world's separate identity **is completely voided by the spiritual energy in it,** מֵאַחַר שֶׁמִּבַּלְעֲדֵי הָרוּחָנִיּוּת הָיָה אַיִן וָאֶפֶס מַמָּשׁ — **because without that spiritual** energy, the created thing would be **absolutely** *"null and void"* (see *Isaiah* 40:17), כְּמוֹ קוֹדֶם שֵׁשֶׁת יְמֵי בְּרֵאשִׁית מַמָּשׁ — **exactly as it was before the six days of creation.**

וְהָרוּחָנִיּוּת הַשּׁוֹפֵעַ עָלָיו — In reality, **the spiritual** energy **which flows to** each created entity, מִמּוֹצָא פִּי ה' וְרוּחַ פִּיו — from *"the utterance of G-d's mouth"* and *"the breath of His mouth,"* הוּא לְבַדּוֹ הַמּוֹצִיאוֹ תָּמִיד מֵאֶפֶס וָאַיִן לְיֵשׁ וּמְהַוֶּה אוֹתוֹ — **is the exclusive** power **that transforms it constantly from** *"null and void"* into **"something," bringing it into being.**

אִם כֵּן אֶפֶס בִּלְעָדוֹ בֶּאֱמֶת — And **this being the case, there is no true** existence **other than** G-d.

When the *Tanya* states that *"there is no true existence other than G-d,"* and that the universe is *"null and void,"* it doesn't mean that we don't exist at all, and that the world is an illusion. We do exist, but in a state of utter dependence on G-d. Like a fetus inside a mother, which has no identity of its own because it has not separated from its source, we are *inside G-d's creative power* and still identified with Him. (And much more so, since a mother merely sustains, but does not create, her fetus constantly.)

Scholars have described this view as *panentheism* (literally "all in G-d"). It is not that you don't exist; you just don't exist like you think you do. "You" are really something that happens within G-d, like a ripple on a "sea" of the Divine.

A CHASIDIC THOUGHT

Embracing the truth that nothing exists outside G-d is the foundational principle of an awakened mystical life.

בלעדו באמת והמשל לזה הוא אור השמש המאיר
לארץ ולדרים שהוא זיו ואור המתפשט מגוף השמש
ונראה לעין כל מאיר על הארץ ובחלל העולם והנה זה
פשוט שאור וזיו הזה ישנו ג"כ בגוף וחומר כדור השמש
עצמו שבשמים שאם מתפשט ומאיר למרחוק כ"כ
כ"ש שיוכל להאיר במקומו ממש רק ששם במקומו
ממש נחשב הזיו הזה לאין ואפס ממש כי בטל
ממש במציאות לגבי גוף כדור השמש שהוא

SECTION TWO: A PHYSICAL ILLUSTRATION OF PANENTHEISM

11TH SIVAN REGULAR | 11TH SIVAN LEAP

Since the notion of our existence being "null and void" is counterintuitive, and a radical departure from ordinary consciousness, the *Tanya* will devote the rest of this chapter to making the idea more relatable with a physical illustration. (It would also be helpful to re-read Part One of the *Tanya*, chapters 20-21, where a different illustration was offered.)

וְהַמָּשָׁל לָזֶה — **A** physical **illustration of this,** הוּא אוֹר הַשֶּׁמֶשׁ הַמֵּאִיר לָאָרֶץ וְלַדָּרִים — **is from the** sunlight which **"shines on the earth and its inhabitants"** (*Liturgy, Blessing Yotzer Ohr*), שֶׁהוּא זִיו וְאוֹר הַמִּתְפַּשֵׁט מִגּוּף הַשֶּׁמֶשׁ — **light rays which have emerged from the globe of the sun,** וְנִרְאֶה לְעֵין כֹּל מֵאִיר עַל הָאָרֶץ וּבַחֲלַל הָעוֹלָם — **and they are visible to everyone, shining on the earth and in the atmosphere.**

וְהִנֵּה זֶה פָּשׁוּט שֶׁאוֹר וְזִיו הַזֶּה יֶשְׁנוֹ גַּם כֵּן בְּגוּף וְחוֹמֶר כַּדּוּר הַשֶּׁמֶשׁ עַצְמוֹ שֶׁבַּשָּׁמַיִם — **Now obviously, these light rays are also found inside the physical globe of the sun itself,** the globe that we see **in the sky,** שֶׁאִם מִתְפַּשֵׁט וּמֵאִיר לְמֵרָחוֹק — **for if** the light rays **can spread out and shine at such a distance** to reach the earth, **they can certainly shine in their own locality,** כָּל כָּךְ כָּל שֶׁכֵּן שֶׁיּוּכַל לְהָאִיר בִּמְקוֹמוֹ מַמָּשׁ — **only** רַק שֶׁשָּׁם בִּמְקוֹמוֹ מַמָּשׁ נֶחְשַׁב הַזִּיו הַזֶּה לְאַיִן וָאֶפֶס מַמָּשׁ **there, in their own locality** inside the globe of the sun, **one ray is considered completely "null and void."**

Obviously, you would have a hard time spotting one ray of light inside the sun. But the *Tanya's* argument here is not simply a matter of *quantity* (that there is so much light in the sun that one ray is not discernible), but an issue of *logic*. The sun and its rays are in a cause-and-effect relationship and therefore:

כִּי בָּטֵל מַמָּשׁ בִּמְצִיאוּת לְגַבֵּי גוּף כַּדּוּר הַשֶּׁמֶשׁ שֶׁהוּא מְקוֹר הָאוֹר וְהַזִּיו הַזֶּה — One ray of light is "null and void" in the sun's globe **since its identity is voided by the sun's globe, which is the source of that light ray.**

מְקוֹר הָאוֹר וְהַזִּיו הַזֶּה שֶׁהַזִּיו וְהָאוֹר הַזֶּה אֵינוֹ רַק
הָאָרָה מְאִירָה מִגּוּף וְעֶצֶם כַּדּוּר הַשֶּׁמֶשׁ רַק בַּחֲלַל
הָעוֹלָם תַּחַת כָּל הַשָּׁמַיִם וְעַל הָאָרֶץ שֶׁאֵין כָּאן גּוּף
כַּדּוּר הַשֶּׁמֶשׁ בִּמְצִיאוּת נִרְאָה כָּאן הָאוֹר וְהַזִּיו הַזֶּה
לְיֵשׁ מַמָּשׁ לְעֵין כֹּל וְנוֹפֵל עָלָיו כָּאן שֵׁם יֵשׁ בֶּאֱמֶת

78B

מַה שֶּׁכֵּן כְּשֶׁהוּא בִּמְקוֹרוֹ בְּגוּף הַשֶּׁמֶשׁ אֵין נוֹפֵל עָלָיו שֵׁם
יֵשׁ כְּלָל רַק שֵׁם אַיִן וָאֶפֶס כִּי בֶּאֱמֶת הוּא שָׁם לְאַיִן וָאֶפֶס
מַמָּשׁ שֶׁאֵין מֵאִיר שָׁם רַק מְקוֹרוֹ לְבַדּוֹ שֶׁהוּא גּוּף
הַשֶּׁמֶשׁ הַמֵּאִיר וְאֶפֶס בִּלְעָדוֹ וְכַדְּבָרִים הָאֵלֶּה מַמָּשׁ

The light ray has no identity *within its source*. Or, in logical terms, an effect has no identity while it is still within its cause.

שֶׁהַזִּיו וְהָאוֹר הַזֶּה אֵינוֹ רַק הָאָרָה מְאִירָה מִגּוּף וְעֶצֶם כַּדּוּר הַשֶּׁמֶשׁ — **Because the light ray** is merely an *effect* of the sun, being **nothing other than light shining from the actual globe of the sun,** which is its cause.

רַק בַּחֲלַל הָעוֹלָם תַּחַת כָּל הַשָּׁמַיִם וְעַל הָאָרֶץ — **Only, in the earth's atmosphere,** *"under the skies"* (*Deuteronomy* 4:19), **and on the earth** itself, שֶׁאֵין כָּאן גּוּף כַּדּוּר הַשֶּׁמֶשׁ בִּמְצִיאוּת — **where the sun's globe** (the cause) **is not present,** נִרְאָה כָּאן הָאוֹר וְהַזִּיו הַזֶּה לְיֵשׁ מַמָּשׁ לְעֵין כֹּל — **the ray of light** (the effect) *does* **appear to us all as a separate entity,** וְנוֹפֵל עָלָיו כָּאן שֵׁם יֵשׁ בֶּאֱמֶת — **and it can appropriately be called a real "entity."**

When the ray of light leaves the sun's globe, it acquires its own identity as an "effect."

מַה שֶּׁאֵין כֵּן כְּשֶׁהוּא בִּמְקוֹרוֹ בְּגוּף הַשֶּׁמֶשׁ — **But this is not the case when it is in its source, in the sun's globe,** אֵין נוֹפֵל עָלָיו שֵׁם יֵשׁ כְּלָל — **where it could not be termed an "entity" at all,** רַק שֵׁם אַיִן וָאֶפֶס — **it is just termed** *"null and void,"* כִּי בֶּאֱמֶת הוּא שָׁם לְאַיִן וָאֶפֶס מַמָּשׁ — **because it really is** *"null and void"* **there,** שֶׁאֵין מֵאִיר — שָׁם רַק מְקוֹרוֹ לְבַדּוֹ שֶׁהוּא גּוּף הַשֶּׁמֶשׁ — **since all that is recognizable there is its source, the sun's globe,** הַמֵּאִיר וְאֶפֶס בִּלְעָדוֹ — **that is the only thing apparent, nothing else.**

PRACTICAL LESSONS

If you were able to see the Divine energy that sustains the world constantly, you would see that everything is G-d.

12TH SIVAN LEAP

The *Tanya* applies this illustration to our case.

וְכַדְּבָרִים הָאֵלֶּה מַמָּשׁ בִּדְמוּתָם כְּצַלְמָם — *"Similar to these ways"* (*Genesis* 39:19), **precisely, both in** *"image and likeness"* (ibid. 5:3), mirroring the above analogy

בדמותם כצלמם הם כל הברואים לגבי שפע האלהי
מרוח פיו השופע עליהם ומהוה אותם והוא מקורם והם
עצמם אינם רק כמו אור וזיו מתפשט מן השפע ורוח
ה' השופע ומתלבש בתוכם ומוציאם מאין ליש ולכן
הם בטלים במציאות לגבי מקורם כמו אור השמש
שבטל במציאות ונחשב לאין ואפס ממש ואינו נקרא
בשם יש כלל כשהוא במקורו רק תחת השמים שאין
שם מקורו כך כל הברואי' אין נופל עליהם שם יש כלל
אלא לעיני בשר שלנו שאין אנו רואים ומשיגים כלל

הֵם כָּל הַבְּרוּאִים לְגַבֵּי שֶׁפַע of light rays losing their identity within the sun's globe,
הָאֱלֹהִי מֵרוּחַ פִּיו — are all creations voided of their separate identity by the flow
of Divine energy from the *"breath of His mouth,"* הַשׁוֹפֵעַ עֲלֵיהֶם וּמְהַוֶּה אוֹתָם
וְהוּא מְקוֹרָם — which flows to the creations, brings them into being and is their
source, וְהֵם עַצְמָם אֵינָם רַק כְּמוֹ אוֹר וְזִיו מִתְפַּשֵׁט מִן הַשֶׁפַע וְרוּחַ ה' — and the creations themselves have no more identity than a light ray which emanates from
the Divine source of flow, the "breath of G-d" הַשׁוֹפֵעַ וּמִתְלַבֵּשׁ בְּתוֹכָם — which
flows into and becomes embodied within them, וּמוֹצִיאָם מֵאַיִן לְיֵשׁ — transforming them from nothing-to-something.

וְלָכֵן הֵם בְּטֵלִים בִּמְצִיאוּת לְגַבֵּי מְקוֹרָם — Therefore,
their identity is voided by their source, כְּמוֹ אוֹר
הַשֶׁמֶשׁ שֶׁבָּטֵל בִּמְצִיאוּת — like the sunlight within
the globe of the sun, which has no separate identity, וְנֶחְשָׁב לְאַיִן וָאֶפֶס מַמָשׁ — and is considered literally *"null and void,"* וְאֵינוֹ נִקְרָא בְּשֵׁם יֵשׁ כְּלָל כְּשֶׁהוּא
בִּמְקוֹרוֹ — and, while it is within its source, cannot be
termed an "entity" at all, רַק תַּחַת הַשָׁמַיִם — and only
in the earth's atmosphere, *"below the skies,"* שָׁאֵין
שָׁם מְקוֹרוֹ — where its source is not present, can it
be called an independent "entity."

PRACTICAL LESSONS

What you see in front
of you now is the
Divine. G-d is the sub-
stance of all things.
There is no thing
that is not pulsating
with Divine energy.

Our perception of the world is like the ray that has
left the sun; we discern the existence of separate
things. But, in reality, the world's existence resembles
the light ray inside the sun, which has no identity of its own and is absorbed in
its source/cause.

כָּךְ כָּל הַבְּרוּאִים אֵין נוֹפֵל עֲלֵיהֶם שָׁם יֵשׁ כְּלָל — Similarly, all the creations cannot be termed separate "entities" at all אֶלָּא לְעֵינֵי בָשָׂר שֶׁלָנוּ שֶׁאֵין אָנוּ רוֹאִים
וּמַשִׂיגִים כְּלָל אֶת הַמָקוֹר — other than to our physical eyes, that do not per-

אֶת הַמָּקוֹר שֶׁהוּא רוּחַ ה' הַמְהַוֶּה אוֹתָם. וְלָכֵן נִרְאֶה
לְעֵינֵינוּ גַּשְׁמִיּוּת הַנִּבְרָאִים וְחוֹמְרָם וּמַמָּשָׁם שֶׁהֵם יֵשׁ
גָּמוּר כְּמוֹ שֶׁנִּרְאֶ' אוֹר הַשֶּׁמֶשׁ יֵשׁ גָּמוּר כְּשֶׁאֵינוֹ בִּמְקוֹרוֹ
רַק שֶׁבָּזֶה אֵין הַמָּשָׁל דּוֹמֶה לַנִּמְשָׁל לְגַמְרֵי לְכְאוֹרָה
שֶׁבַּמָּשָׁל אֵין הַמָּקוֹר בִּמְצִיאוּת כְּלָל בַּחֲלַל הָעוֹלָם וְעַל
הָאָרֶץ שֶׁנִּרְאֶה שָׁם אוֹרוֹ לְיֵשׁ גָּמוּר מַשְׁאֵ"כ כָּל הַבְּרוּאֵ'
הֵם בִּמְקוֹרָם תָּמִיד רַק שֶׁאֵין הַמָּקוֹר נִרְאֶה לְעֵינֵי בָשָׂר
וְלָמָּה אֵינָם בְּטֵלִים בִּמְצִיאוּת לִמְקוֹרָם אַךְ לְהָבִין זֶה
צָרִיךְ לְהַקְדִּים:

ceive or grasp the spiritual **source** of these creations **at all,** שֶׁהוּא רוּחַ ה' הַמְהַוֶּה אוֹתָם — **which is the "breath of G-d" which brings them into being,** וְלָכֵן נִרְאֶה לְעֵינֵינוּ גַּשְׁמִיּוּת הַנִּבְרָאִים וְחוֹמְרָם וּמַמָּשָׁם — **and that is why we see the cre- ations as physical, material and substantive,** שֶׁהֵם יֵשׁ גָּמוּר — **appearing as a real** independent **entity,** כְּמוֹ שֶׁנִּרְאֶה אוֹר הַשֶּׁמֶשׁ יֵשׁ גָּמוּר כְּשֶׁאֵינוֹ בִּמְקוֹרוֹ — **just as sunlight appears to be a real entity when it is outside its source.**

Our physical illustration is, however, imperfect, as the *Tanya* now observes.

רַק שֶׁבָּזֶה אֵין הַמָּשָׁל דּוֹמֶה לַנִּמְשָׁל לְגַמְרֵי לְכְאוֹרָה — **There is, however, one re- spect in which our analogy does not appear to be a perfect reflection of what it attempts to represent,** שֶׁבַּמָּשָׁל אֵין הַמָּקוֹר בִּמְצִיאוּת כְּלָל בַּחֲלַל הָעוֹלָם וְעַל הָאָרֶץ — **because in our analogy, the source,** the sun, **is not actually present in the earth's atmosphere, or on the earth,** שֶׁנִּרְאֶה שָׁם אוֹרוֹ לְיֵשׁ גָּמוּר — **and it is only** because the light is distant from its source, **that the light appears there,** on earth, **as a separate entity.**

כָּל הַבְּרוּאִים הֵם בִּמְקוֹרָם תָּמִיד — **This is not true, however,** in reality, מַה שֶּׁאֵין כֵּן — **where all the creations** *are* **continually within their source, G-d,** רַק שֶׁאֵין הַמָּקוֹר נִרְאֶה לְעֵינֵי בָשָׂר — **and it is only that the source is not** *visible* **to the eye.**

Our analogy depicts a shift from an effect absorbed in its cause (a light ray in- side the sun), to the effect's emergence from the cause, to become a separate entity (a light ray on earth). But nothing ever leaves the presence of G-d! Our eyes may perceive that to be the case, but it does not reflect actual reality. In the *Tanya's* analogy, we are all rays inside the sun's globe; we are an "effect" but not one which has departed from its Cause.

וְלָמָּה אֵינָם בְּטֵלִים בִּמְצִיאוּת לִמְקוֹרָם — **Why, then, are** all creations **not voided of their identity by their source** which *is* present?

אַךְ לְהָבִין זֶה צָרִיךְ לְהַקְדִּים — **To answer this question, we first need to clarify another matter,** in the following chapter.

The *Tanya* ends this chapter with a hanging question. This is unusual, as Chasidic texts prefer not to shed doubt on matters of faith, leaving them unanswered.

In this case, however, it is not G-d's existence that is being questioned, but our own existence. If we are all "within G-d," like rays of sun in the sun, how do we possibly have any existence at all?

Over such an ego-deflating question, the *Tanya* is happy for us to ponder for a while.

פרק ד כי הנה כתיב כי שמש ומגן ה' אלהים
פי' מגן הוא נרתק לשמש להגן שיוכלו

CHAPTER 4

THE DIVINE ATTRIBUTES
SECTION ONE: THE NAMES OF G-D

12TH SIVAN REGULAR | 13TH SIVAN LEAP

This chapter begins to answer a question posed at the end of chapter 3: *"Why, then, are all creations not voided of their identity by their source which is present"*? If we are all "within" G-d, so to speak, the power which creates us, how do we possess the consciousness of independent existence? Why does our existence simply not dissolve, like a light ray within the sun, and become indistinguishable from G-d?

כִּי הִנֵּה כְּתִיב כִּי שֶׁמֶשׁ וּמָגֵן ה' אֱלֹהִים — **Now the verse states,** *"For a sun and shield is G-d, Almighty (Havayah Elokim)"* (*Psalms* 84:12).

While there is only one G-d, He is nevertheless referred to in Judaism by many different names, reflecting different *types of activity* that He performs. When He appears to act kindly, we use a name reflecting G-d's benevolence. When He appears to act harshly, a different name is in order.

Does G-d really act kindly and then harshly, or is He, in fact, consistent and we are simply unable to fathom that?

The Kabbalists teach that G-d *in His essence* does not change, but He did *emanate* different Divine energies, or "attributes," that are responsible for different types of activity. When G-d acts *through a particular Divine energy,* we call Him by a name reflecting that energy.

Psalms 84:12 mentions two Divine names: 1.) The Tetragrammaton, G-d's four-lettered name (spelled *yud-hei* followed by *vav-hei*), commonly referred to as *Havayah.* 2.) *Elokim,* which literally means "judge."

The verse compares these two names, *Havayah* and *Elokim,* to a "sun" and "shield." First the *Tanya* will clarify the meaning of the sun's "shield."

פֵּירוּשׁ מָגֵן הוּא נַרְתֵּק לַשֶּׁמֶשׁ — **A "shield" here refers to the sun's protective layer,** לְהָגֵן שֶׁיּוּכְלוּ הַבְּרִיּוֹת לְסָבְלוֹ — **which protects** us **creatures, so that we can withstand its** heat and radiation.

הבריות לסבלו כמארז"ל לעתיד לבא הקב"ה מוציא
חמה מנרתקה רשעים נידונין בה כו' וכמו שהנרתק
מגין בעד השמש כך שם אלהים מגין לשם הוי"ה ב"ה
דשם הוי"ה פירושו שמהוה את הכל מאין ליש   79A

The *Midrash* describes the outer layer of the sun as having protective qualities: *"In the future, G-d will remove the sun from its protective layer and will
use it to burn the wicked, as the verse states, 'For the day is coming, burning
like an oven... and that coming day will burn them up' (Malachi 3:19)" (Genesis
Rabah 6:6).*

כְּמַאֲמַר רַבּוֹתֵינוּ זִכְרוֹנָם לִבְרָכָה — **As our sages of blessed memory taught,**
לֶעָתִיד לָבֹא הַקָּדוֹשׁ בָּרוּךְ הוּא מוֹצִיא חַמָּה מִנַּרְתֵּקָהּ רְשָׁעִים נִידוֹנִין בָּהּ כו' — **that in
the future era, the Blessed Holy One will remove the sun from its protective
layer, and the wicked will be judged by it,** *etc.*

*"In the world to come, there is no purgatory (Gehinom). Rather, the Blessed
Holy One will bring the sun out of its protective layer and He will heat the wicked, but heal the righteous through it. The wicked will be brought to judgment
by it" (Talmud, Nedarim 8b; see Zohar 3, 17a).*

The *Tanya* now applies the concept of "sun" and "shield" to clarify the meaning of the two names, *Havayah* and *Elokim.*

וּכְמוֹ שֶׁהַנַּרְתֵּק מֵגֵן בְּעַד הַשֶּׁמֶשׁ כָּךְ שֵׁם אֱלֹהִים מֵגִין לְשֵׁם הֲוָיָ"ה בָּרוּךְ הוּא — **Just as
the protective layer shields the sun,** the Divine energy represented by the
name *Elokim* **shields** the Divine energy represented by the **blessed name
Havayah** (see *Zohar 2, 229b*).

Havayah represents G-d's power of *disclosure* and revelation, like a sun
which emits light. *Elokim* is the "protective layer" of the sun, G-d's power to
withhold revelation so that it does not hurt or overwhelm us.

SECTION TWO: BENEVOLENCE AND DISCLOSURE ENERGY

First we will turn to the name *Havayah* and explain how its function is suggested by its name.

דְּשֵׁם הֲוָיָ"ה — **For** the last three letters of **the name Havayah** (*hei-vav-hei,*
spelling *HoVeH,* literally, "brings into being"), פֵּירוּשׁוֹ שֶׁמְּהַוֶּה אֶת הַכֹּל מֵאַיִן לְיֵשׁ
— **imply that** G-d (*Havayah*) **brings everything into being** (*meHaVeH*), some-
thing-from-nothing (*Zohar 3, 257b; Pardes 1:9*).

G-d's bringing the world into being is an act of benevolence and disclosure.
He gains nothing from creating the world; it expresses His pure kindness. And
the creation process expresses Divine powers, so it is an act of disclosure.

וְהָיוּ"ד מְשַׁמֶּשֶׁת עַל הַפְּעוּלָה שֶׁהִיא בִּלְשׁוֹן הֹוֶה וְתָמִיד
כְּדְפֵרֵשׁ"י עַ"פ כָּכָה יַעֲשֶׂה אִיּוֹב כָּל הַיָּמִים וְהַיְינוּ הַחַיּוּת
הַנִּשְׁפָּע בְּכָל רֶגַע מַמָּשׁ בְּכָל הַבְּרוּאִים מְמּוֹצָא פִּי ה'
וְרוּחוֹ וּמְהַוֶּה אוֹתָם מֵאַיִן לְיֵשׁ בְּכָל רֶגַע כִּי לֹא דַי לָהֶם
בְּמַה שֶׁנִּבְרְאוּ בְּשֵׁשֶׁת יְמֵי בְרֵאשִׁית לִהְיוֹת קַיָּימִים בָּזֶה

This explains the last three letters of the name *Havayah*.

וְהָיוּ"ד — **And the** first letter of *Havayah,* **yud,** מְשַׁמֶּשֶׁת עַל הַפְּעוּלָה — **modifies** the last three letters, **the verb** "brings into being," שֶׁהִיא בִּלְשׁוֹן הֹוֶה וְתָמִיד — **so that it is in the present tense, and continuous.**

Havayah, then, is an energy of benevolence and disclosure through which G-d constantly brings all existence into being.

The *Tanya* cites a proof of the grammatical significance of a *yud* preceding a verb.

כְּדְפֵרֵשׁ רַשִׁ"י עַל פָּסוּק כָּכָה יַעֲשֶׂה אִיּוֹב כָּל הַיָּמִים — **As** *Rashi* **comments on the verse, "Thus would Job do (ya'aseh) at all times"** (*Job* 1:5), *"He would always do in this manner"* (*Rashi* ibid.).

PRACTICAL LESSONS

Elokim represents a Divine power which shields us from the reality that we have no independent existence.

As *Rashi* clarifies, the *yud* at the beginning of the verb *ya'aseh* renders it present and continuous.

וְהַיְינוּ הַחַיּוּת הַנִּשְׁפָּע בְּכָל רֶגַע מַמָּשׁ בְּכָל הַבְּרוּאִים — G-d's constant "bringing into being" of the creations, suggested by the name *Havayah,* **refers to the energy which flows literally every moment into all the creations,** מְמּוֹצָא פִּי ה' וְרוּחוֹ — **from** *"the utterance of G-d's mouth"* (*Deuteronomy* 8:3) and *"His breath"* (*Psalms* 33:6), וּמְהַוֶּה אוֹתָם מֵאַיִן לְיֵשׁ בְּכָל רֶגַע — **which brings them into being every moment, something-from-nothing.**

כִּי לֹא דַי לָהֶם בְּמַה שֶׁנִּבְרְאוּ בְּשֵׁשֶׁת יְמֵי בְרֵאשִׁית לִהְיוֹת קַיָּימִים בָּזֶה — **For the** initial **creative act of the six days of genesis is not sufficient for their existence to be sustained,** כְּמוֹ שֶׁנִּתְבָּאֵר לְעֵיל — **as explained above** in chapters 1-2.

The phenomenon which we have described at length, in the first chapters, of G-d continually bringing the world into being is a function of G-d acting as *Havayah.*

As we have learned, G-d's willingness to create the world is an expression of His benevolence. The *Tanya* now elaborates on this theme, clarifying how creation and benevolence are connected.

כמ"ש לעיל. והנה בסידור שבחיו של הקב"ה כתיב
הגדול הגבור כו' ופי' הגדול היא מדת חסד והתפשטות
החיות בכל העולמות וברואים לאין קץ ותכלית להיות
ברואים מאין ליש וקיימים בחסד חנם ונקראת גדולה כי
באה מגדולתו של הקב"ה בכבודו ובעצמו כי גדול ה'

וְהִנֵּה בְּסִדּוּר שְׁבָחָיו שֶׁל הַקָּדוֹשׁ בָּרוּךְ הוּא — **Now, in the list of attributes** with which Moses praised G-d (*Deut.* 10:17), echoed in our daily liturgy, in the *Amidah* prayer,' — כְּתִיב הַגָּדוֹל הַגִּבּוֹר כו' — **the verse states,** *"Master of masters, **the great and mighty...** G-d,"* — וּפֵירוּשׁ הַגָּדוֹל הִיא מִדַּת חֶסֶד — **The term "great" (gadol)** **refers to the Divine attribute of chesed, "kindness"** (*Tikunei Zohar,* sec. 22).

G-d's energy of disclosure and benevolence is referred to in the Kabbalah as His power of *chesed* (literally "kindness"). In earlier Kabbalistic works it was common to refer to *chesed* as *gedulah,* the attribute of "greatness" mentioned in *Deuteronomy* 10:17 (see, for example, *Zohar* 3, 248b).

Chesed and *gedulah* are synonymous. *Gedulah* implies "growth" and "expansion." Therefore *chesed* "is called *GeDuLah,* since all the other Divine energies grow (*misGaDLim*) from it" (Rabbi Moshe Cordovero, *Pardes* 23:3).

Chesed (*gedulah*) is "benevolent," not only in powering the creation of the universe, but also in emanating all the other Divine energies.

וְהִתְפַּשְּׁטוּת הַחַיּוּת בְּכָל הָעוֹלָמוֹת וּבְרוּאִים לְאֵין קֵץ וְתַכְלִית — *Chesed* powers **the endless and limitless flow of energy to all the worlds and creations,** לִהְיוֹת בְּרוּאִים מֵאַיִן לְיֵשׁ וְקַיָּימִים — **in order that they should be created** continually **something-from-nothing, and remain in existence,** בְּחֶסֶד חִנָּם — **due to the unconditional chesed** of G-d.

Based upon this thought, *Tanya* offers us another insight into why *chesed* is also called *gedulah.*

וְנִקְרֵאת גְּדוּלָה — This *chesed* energy, constantly powering creation, **is referred to as gedulah,** **"greatness,"** כִּי בָאָה מִגְּדוּלָתוֹ שֶׁל הַקָּדוֹשׁ בָּרוּךְ הוּא בִּכְבוֹדוֹ וּבְעַצְמוֹ — **since it expresses the greatness of G-d Himself,** כִּי גָדוֹל ה' וְלִגְדוּלָתוֹ אֵין חֵקֶר — **for *"Great is G-d... His greatness cannot be fathomed"*** (Psalms 145:3).

Only G-d can create the world, something-from-nothing. That is why the Divine attribute which powers creation is called *gedulah* ("greatness"), because it expresses the unique greatness of G-d.

וְלִגְדוּלָתוֹ אֵין חֵקֶר וְלָכֵן מַשְׁפִּיעַ ג"כ חַיּוּת וְהִתְהַוּוּת מֵאַיִן
לְיֵשׁ לְעוֹלָמוֹת וּבְרוּאִים אֵין קֵץ שֶׁטֶּבַע הַטּוֹב לְהֵטִיב
וְהִנֵּה כְּמוֹ שֶׁמִּדָּה זוֹ הִיא שִׁבְחוֹ שֶׁל הַקָּבָּ"ה לְבַדּוֹ שֶׁאֵין
בִּיכוֹלֶת שׁוּם נִבְרָא לִבְרוֹא יֵשׁ מֵאַיִן וּלְהַחֲיוֹתוֹ וְגַם מִדָּה

And the very same attribute is also called *chesed* ("kindness"), since,

וְלָכֵן מַשְׁפִּיעַ גַּם כֵּן חַיּוּת וְהִתְהַוּוּת מֵאַיִן לְיֵשׁ לְעוֹלָמוֹת וּבְרוּאִים אֵין קֵץ — it is this attribute **that provides limitless energy for the endless worlds and creations, to bring them into being.**

The themes of "greatness" and "benevolence" are intertwined. Since G-d is "great" *therefore* He is benevolent.

שֶׁטֶּבַע הַטּוֹב לְהֵטִיב — **Since** *"if you're good, you're generous"* (Rabbi Naftali Hertz Bacharach, *Eimek Ha-Melech*, 1:1).

If you had unlimited funds, you would become a generous person. You wouldn't feel that by giving something away you would be lacking yourself. Since G-d is infinite, He is also generous; one leads to the other.

SECTION THREE: G-D AND HIS ATTRIBUTES

13TH SIVAN REGULAR | 14TH SIVAN LEAP

We have now touched upon G-d's attribute of *chesed/gedulah,* which is represented by the name *Havayah* (the "sun" in our verse in *Psalms*). Before continuing to discuss the name *Elokim,* G-d's power of restraint and diminishment (the "shield" in our verse), the *Tanya* gives us an important clarification about the nature of Divine attributes.

וְהִנֵּה כְּמוֹ שֶׁמִּדָּה זוֹ הִיא שִׁבְחוֹ שֶׁל הַקָּדוֹשׁ בָּרוּךְ הוּא לְבַדּוֹ — **Now just as this attribute** of *chesed/gedulah* **is something by which G-d** exclusively **is praised,** the same is true of G-d's attribute of restraint and diminishment.

Only G-d can create a world, but restraint and diminishment appears to be something we can all do. The *Tanya* will argue that this is not the case. All the Divine attributes are wondrous and unfathomable. Just as we cannot understand the miracle of creation, we cannot possibly fathom the unique qualities of G-d's powers of diminishment.

But before we turn to the miracle of diminishment, the *Tanya* dwells for a moment on the miracle of creation.

שֶׁאֵין בִּיכוֹלֶת שׁוּם נִבְרָא לִבְרוֹא יֵשׁ מֵאַיִן וּלְהַחֲיוֹתוֹ — **For no created entity can make something-from-nothing and** then **energize it,** וְגַם מִדָּה זוֹ הִיא לְמַעְלָה

זו היא למעלה מהשכלת כל הברואים והשגתם שאין
כח בשכל שום נברא להשכיל ולהשיג מדה זו ויכלתה
לברוא יש מאין ולהחיותו כי הבריאה יש מאין הוא דבר
שלמעלה משכל הנבראים כי היא ממדת גדולתו של
הקב״ה והקב״ה ומדותיו אחדות פשוט כדאיתא בז״הק
דאיהו וגרמוהי חד וכשם שאין ביכולת שום שכל
נברא להשיג בוראו כך אינו יכול להשיג מדותיו וכמו

מֵהַשְׂכָּלַת כָּל הַבְּרוּאִים וְהַשָּׂגָתָם — this attribute being also beyond the grasp and understanding of all creations, שֶׁאֵין כֹּחַ בְּשֵׂכֶל שׁוּם נִבְרָא לְהַשְׂכִּיל וּלְהָשִׂיג מִדָּה זוּ וְיִכָלְתָּה לִבְרוֹא יֵש מֵאַיִן וּלְהַחֲיוֹתוֹ — since no creation is capable of understanding or grasping this attribute and its ability, to create something-from-nothing and then energize it, כִּי הַבְּרִיאָה יֵש מֵאַיִן הוּא דָּבָר שֶׁלְמַעְלָה מִשֵּׂכֶל הַנִּבְרָאִים — for creation of something-from-nothing is not intelligible by us creations, כִּי הִיא מִמִּדַּת גְּדוּלָתוֹ שֶׁל הַקָּדוֹשׁ בָּרוּךְ הוּא — since it is powered by G-d's attribute of gedulah, "greatness."

But what, exactly, is an "attribute"? How is it part of the one G-d, and at the same time assigned to a specific task?

וְהַקָּדוֹשׁ בָּרוּךְ הוּא וּמִדּוֹתָיו אַחֲדוּת פָּשׁוּט — G-d is totally one with His attributes, כְּדְאִיתָא בַּזֹּהַר הַקָּדוֹשׁ דְּאִיהוּ וְגַרְמוֹהִי חַד — as the holy Zohar states, "He and the attributes that He causes are one" (Tikunei Zohar 3b).

While the attributes did not always exist, and they were emanated at a certain point in time by G-d, they are nevertheless part of Him. The emanation process occurred within G-d. (We will discuss this at length in Chapters 8-11.)

וּכְשֵׁם שֶׁאֵין בִּיכוֹלֶת שׁוּם שֵׂכֶל נִבְרָא לְהָשִׂיג בּוֹרְאוֹ — And therefore, in the same way that no created intellect can grasp its Creator, כָּךְ אֵינוֹ יָכוֹל לְהָשִׂיג מְדוֹתָיו — likewise, the created intellect cannot grasp the attributes of the Creator, which are totally one with Him.

The attributes themselves are Divine. They are not "G-d" but "G-dliness"; not the "emanator," but "emanations." Like light emerging from a source, they share the properties of the source and are Divine themselves.

SECTION FOUR: G-D'S POWER OF RESTRAINT

Now we turn to discuss the Divine name Elokim, which refers to G-d's power of restraint and diminishment (the "shield" in our verse), which throughout the Kabbalah is referred to as gevurah.

שאין ביכולת שום שכל נברא להשיג מדת גדולתו
שהיא היכולת לברוא יש מאין ולהחיותו כדכתיב עולם
חסד יבנה כך ממש אין ביכלתו להשיג מדת גבורתו
של הקב"ה שהיא מדת הצמצום ומניעת התפשטות
החיות מגדולתו מלירד ולהתגלות על הנבראים

79B

וּכְמוֹ שֶׁאֵין בִּיכוֹלֶת שׁוּם שֵׂכֶל נִבְרָא לְהַשִּׂיג מִדַּת גְּדוּלָתוֹ — Since the attributes themselves are Divine, therefore **in the same way that no created intellect can grasp** G-d's **attribute of "greatness"** (chesed), שֶׁהִיא הַיְכוֹלֶת לִבְרוֹא יֵשׁ מֵאַיִן וּלְהַחֲיוֹתוֹ — **which is the power to create something-from-nothing and energize it,** כְּדִכְתִיב עוֹלָם חֶסֶד יִבָּנֶה — **as the verse states, "the world is built by chesed"** (Psalms 89:3), כָּךְ מַמָּשׁ אֵין בִּיכָלְתּוֹ לְהַשִּׂיג מִדַּת גְּבוּרָתוֹ שֶׁל הַקָּדוֹשׁ בָּרוּךְ הוּא — **so too, it is impossible** for the created intellect **to grasp G-d's attribute of gevurah.**

As we learned above, *Deuteronomy* 10:17 refers to the two primary attributes of G-d as *"great (gadol) and mighty (gibor)."* GaDoL, we have seen, refers to GeDuLah, G-d's power of creation and disclosure; GiBoR refers to the opposite power of GeVuRah, which restrains, diminishes, judges and punishes.

שֶׁהִיא מִדַּת הַצִּמְצוּם — *Gevurah* being **the attribute of diminishment (tzimtzum),** וּמְנִיעַת הִתְפַּשְׁטוּת הַחַיּוּת מִגְּדוּלָתוֹ — **the withholding of energy from** G-d's attribute of **gedulah.**

As we have seen above from Rabbi Moshe Cordovero's *Pardes, gedulah* is the source of all the universe's energy. But an excess of revelation and energy is dangerous, just as too much good food leads to illness. Therefore, G-d emanated an opposing energy of diminishment and restraint, which is called *gevurah.*

מִלֵּירֵד וּלְהִתְגַּלּוֹת עַל הַנִּבְרָאִים — *Gevurah* **prevents** energy and revelation **from coming down and being disclosed to the creations,** לְהַחֲיוֹתָם וּלְקַיְּימָם בְּגִילּוּי — **so as to energize and sustain them overtly.**

The word "overtly" is highly significant here. If G-d completely restrained and diminished the emanation of His energy, there would be nothing left to power the world. The diminishment, then, was more of a *veiling* than an actual blocking of G-d's energy. The energy still reaches us, and that is why we exist; but we don't realize that it reaches us (it isn't *overt*), and so our sense of independence is not erased.

This is what sets apart G-d's power of diminishment from ours. When we turn down the volume, there is less noise. If we turn it down completely, there is nothing to be heard. But G-d is able to "turn down the volume" of His emana-

לְהַחֲיוֹתָם וּלְקַיְּימָם בְּגִילּוּי כ"א בְּהֶסְתֵּר פָּנִים שֶׁהַחַיּוּת מִסְתַּתֵּר בְּגוּף הַנִּבְרָא וּכְאִילּוּ גוּף הַנִּבְרָא הוּא דָּבָר בִּפְנֵי עַצְמוֹ וְאֵינוֹ הִתְפַּשְּׁטוּת הַחַיּוּת וְהָרוּחָנִיּוּת כְּהִתְפַּשְּׁטוּת הַזִּיו וְהָאוֹר מֵהַשֶּׁמֶשׁ אֶלָּא הוּא דָּבָר בִּפְנֵי עַצְמוֹ וְאַף שֶׁבֶּאֱמֶת אֵינוֹ דָּבָר בִּפְנֵי עַצְמוֹ אֶלָּא כְּמוֹ הִתְפַּשְּׁטוּת הָאוֹר מֵהַשֶּׁמֶשׁ מִכָּל מָקוֹם הֵן הֵן גְּבוּרוֹתָיו

tion in a way that we hear it *and* we don't. We "hear" it and absorb it enough to keep us in existence; but we also don't hear it, in the sense that we don't feel G-d creating us at every moment.

כִּי אִם בְּהֶסְתֵּר פָּנִים — **Rather, there is a** *"Hiding of G-d's face"* (see *Deuteronomy* 31:17-18), שֶׁהַחַיּוּת מִסְתַּתֵּר בְּגוּף הַנִּבְרָא — **meaning that** Divine **energy is present within** every **created entity, but hidden there,** וּכְאִילּוּ גוּף הַנִּבְרָא הוּא דָּבָר בִּפְנֵי עַצְמוֹ — **and it's as if the created entity remains independent** from the energy within it.

Again the stress is "it's *as if* the created entity remains independent," because, as stated above, the presence of G-d's energy is not "overt."

G-d's *gevurah* doesn't *prevent* us from receiving His energy; it *modifies* what we receive, so that we don't sense that it is coming from G-d. This is conveyed by the Biblical metaphor of *"Hiding G-d's face"*: we receive energy from G-d but we don't see His "face," we don't realize that it's coming directly from Him.

וְאֵינוֹ הִתְפַּשְּׁטוּת הַחַיּוּת וְהָרוּחָנִיּוּת כְּהִתְפַּשְּׁטוּת הַזִּיו וְהָאוֹר מֵהַשֶּׁמֶשׁ — **When there is** *"Hiding of G-d's face,"* **spiritual energy does not flow** from Him overtly, **like a light ray from the sun,** אֶלָּא הוּא דָּבָר בִּפְנֵי עַצְמוֹ — **but rather, separately.**

That doesn't mean the energy is *genuinely* separate from G-d, (which would be impossible, since nothing is outside G-d). Rather, it *appears to us* as separate, whereas in reality, it is not.

וְאַף שֶׁבֶּאֱמֶת אֵינוֹ דָּבָר בִּפְנֵי עַצְמוֹ — **Even though, in reality,** this spiritual energy **is not separate,** אֶלָּא כְּמוֹ הִתְפַּשְּׁטוּת הָאוֹר מֵהַשֶּׁמֶשׁ — **but** even this "hidden" spiritual energy shines to the creations **like light emerging from the sun.**

Gevurah, however, does not create an illusion. It creates *a perception* of independent reality, and that itself is real. In our consciousness, we do feel separate and independent, and from our perspective that is reality. G-d made it that way.

הֵן הֵן גְּבוּרוֹתָיו — **Nevertheless,** even though we don't perceive it, מִכָּל מָקוֹם שֶׁל הַקָּדוֹשׁ בָּרוּךְ הוּא — these diminishments *"are, in fact, expressions of G-d's might (gevurah)"* (*Yalkut Shimoni,* par. 1071; cf. *Yoma* 69b).

של הקדוש ברוך הוא אשר כל יכול לצמצם החיות
והרוחניות הנשפע מרוח פיו ולהסתירו שלא יבטל גוף
הנברא במציאות וזה אין בשכל שום נברא להשיג
מהות הצמצו' וההסתר ושיהיה אעפ"כ גוף הנברא נברא
מאין ליש כמו שאין יכולת בשכל שום נברא להשיג

The *Tanya* wants us to reconfigure the way we perceive reality. Instead of wondering, "I see a world, but does G-d exist?", we should be thinking, "obviously G-d exists, but *how am I here?*"

The answer to that question is that, through His power of *gevurah,* G-d has modified the way He energizes us so that we do not notice His presence. The apparent absence of G-d is, in fact, *a perception that He created.*

To convey this point, the *Tanya* borrows the Talmudic phrase, *"they are, in fact, expressions of G-d's might (gevurah)."* Even G-d's concealment, the apparent absence of G-d, is an expression of a wondrous Divine power, the ability to modify the energy that we receive so that we do not realize it comes from G-d.

PRACTICAL LESSONS

Creation was an act of G-d's self-revelation, the Divine emerging from hiding.

But, paradoxically, this revelation takes place *through* hiding, since the One is now veiled by the many.

אֲשֶׁר כֹּל יָכוֹל לְצַמְצֵם הַחַיוּת וְהָרוּחָנִיּוּת הַנִּשְׁפָּע מֵרוּחַ פִּיו — And G-d, **being omnipotent, is able to diminish the spiritual energy that flows from** *"the breath of His mouth,"* (*Psalms* 33:6), וּלְהַסְתִּירוֹ שֶׁלֹּא יְבַטֵּל גוּף הַנִּבְרָא בִּמְצִיאוּת — **hiding** that energy **so that it does not obliterate the individual identities of the creations** at the very same time it energizes them and brings them into existence!

— וְזֶה אֵין בְּשֵׂכֶל שׁוּם נִבְרָא לְהַשִּׂיג מַהוּת הַצַּמְצוּם וְהַהֶסְתֵּר **And no created intellect can understand the nature of this diminishment and hiding,** due to its contradictory dynamic, וְשֶׁיִּהְיֶה אַף עַל פִּי כֵן גוּף הַנִּבְרָא נִבְרָא מֵאַיִן לְיֵשׁ — **that,** while simultaneously hiding and concealing energy, **it nevertheless brings about the creation of an entity, something from nothing.**

כְּמוֹ שֶׁאֵין יְכוֹלֶת בְּשֵׂכֶל שׁוּם נִבְרָא לְהַשִּׂיג מַהוּת הַבְּרִיאָה מֵאַיִן לְיֵשׁ — Diminishment, *gevurah,* is an unfathomable wonder, **just as no created intellect can understand the nature of** *chesed* which powers **creation of something-from-nothing.**

Creation of something-from-nothing is an obvious miracle that clearly defies comprehension, since no mortal can do it. Diminishment, on the other hand, would seem to make more sense, since withholding is something we do all the time.

מהות הבריאה מאין ליש. [והנה בחי' הצמצום
והסתר החיות נקרא בשם כלים והחיות עצמו נקרא

The *Tanya*, however, has made clear that G-d's power of diminishment has a wondrous property which sets it apart from our own. G-d can *simultaneously give and withhold*. At the same time He appears to us as withholding, He is actually giving. Both are true: one from the consciousness of *worldly perception,* and the other from the perspective of *heavenly truth*. While it is ultimately incomprehensible, the *Tanya* invites us to raise our consciousness to the perspective of heavenly truth, that whenever our senses perceive the absence of G-d, we should take to heart that this perceived absence is, in fact, an expression of G-d's might (*gevurah*).

SECTION FIVE: THE KABBALAH OF "DIMINISHMENT"

14TH SIVAN REGULAR | 15TH SIVAN LEAP

From the above discussion you might imagine that G-d's powers of disclosure (*chesed/gedulah*) and diminishment (*gevurah*) are two totally separate forces which have nothing to do with each other, since they perform opposite tasks.

In reality, however, they are deeply integrated. Our verse in Psalms makes this point quite clearly, *"For a sun and shield is Havayah/Elokim." Elokim* (diminishment) is not independent from *Havayah* (disclosure); it is, in fact, the "shield" of the sun itself.

To make this point clearer, the *Tanya* now cites symbols of the Kabbalah which describe these two powers and their deep integration.

[וְהִנֵּה בְּחִינַת הַצִּמְצוּם וְהֶסְתֵּר הַחַיּוּת נִקְרָא בְּשֵׁם כֵּלִים — **Now** in Kabbalistic symbolism, **powers of "diminishment" and "hiding" are called** *keilim,* **"vessels,"** וְהַחַיּוּת עַצְמוֹ נִקְרָא בְּשֵׁם אוֹר — **and the** disclosure of **energy itself is called** *ohr,* **"light."**

The Kabbalists grappled extensively with the problem of how the Divine attributes could be on the one hand, totally unified with one G-d, and yet, on the other hand, produce different effects. As is the way of Kabbalah, they attempted to solve the problem not with logic, but with rich symbolism.

They described two components to each of the attributes: "lights" and "vessels." The lights, emerging directly from G-d, retain the energy of G-d's abstract, undefined oneness. The "vessels" modify and shape the light, imposing specific attributes on it.

The "lights" have an energy of disclosure; the "vessels," an energy of diminishment.

בשם אור שכמו שהכלי מכסה על מה שבתוכו כך
בחי׳ הצמצום מכסה ומסתיר האור והחיות השופע
והכלים הן הן האותיות ששרשן ה׳ אותיות מנצפ״ך
שהן ה׳ גבורות המחלקות ומפרידות ההבל והקול
בה׳ מוצאות הפה להתהוות כ״ב אותיות ושרש הה׳

The *Tanya* explains why the symbol of a "vessel" was chosen to describe a spiritual energy.

שֶׁכְּמוֹ שֶׁהַכְּלִי מְכַסֶּה עַל מַה שֶׁבְּתוֹכוֹ — **For just as a vessel hides its contents,** כָּךְ בְּחִינַת הַצִּמְצוּם מְכַסֶּה וּמַסְתִּיר הָאוֹר וְהַחַיּוּת הַשׁוֹפֵעַ — **so too, the powers of diminishment hide and conceal the light and energy which flows** through them.

As we have seen, the *Tanya* considers language to be of extreme importance and the words of Scripture are understood to be the embodiment of Divine energies.

וְהַכֵּלִים הֵן הֵן הָאוֹתִיּוֹת — **And the "vessels" are, in fact, letters** (see Rabbi Chaim Vital, *Otzaros Chaim, Sha'ar Ha-Nekukim* chapter 1).

Letters on their own are meaningless. It is only when they are strung together in a certain sequence that they can capture ideas. The letters and the ideas they represent can therefore be compared to "vessels" and "lights" respectively.

This symbolism helps us to appreciate further how the attributes are deeply integrated.

שֶׁשָּׁרְשָׁן ה׳ אוֹתִיּוֹת מנצפ״ך — **For the source of** the letters **are** the five organs of verbal articulation, represented by **the five letters** *mem, nun, tzadik, pey, chaf,* שֶׁהֵן ה׳ גְבוּרוֹת הַמְּחַלְּקוֹת וּמַפְרִידוֹת הַהֶבֶל — **which are five forces of** *gevurah,* וְהַקּוֹל בְּה׳ מוֹצָאוֹת הַפֶּה — **that divide and separate breath/voice through the five organs of speech,** לְהִתְהַוּוֹת כ״ב אוֹתִיּוֹת — **to produce twenty-two letters.**

In order to pronounce the twenty-two letters (which, in Hebrew, are all consonants), five organs of articulation are needed, larynx, palate, tongue, teeth, and

---

A CHASIDIC THOUGHT

"All forms in the universe emerge from letters. You will not find a form that does not have an image in the letters or in the combination of two, three, or more of them. This is a principle hinted to in the sequence of the alphabet, and the matters are ancient, deep waters that have no limit" (Rabbi Ya'akov Ben Sheishes, *Meishiv Devarim Nechochim,* p. 154).

גְּבוּרוֹת הוּא בוּצִינָא דְּקַרְדּוּנִיתָא שֶׁהִיא גְּבוּרָה עִילָאָה
דְּעַתִּיק יוֹמִין וְשֹׁרֶשׁ הַחֲסָדִים הוּא גַּ״כ חֶסֶד דְּעַתִּיק יוֹמִין
כַּיָּדוּעַ לִי״ח:

lips. These function by taking the pure sound of the breath, "dividing" and "separating" it into consonant sounds. The five organs therefore represent powers of *gevurah,* whose energy is one of diminishment and atomization. Among the letters themselves, these forces are represented by the final letters, which denote the end of one word, *dividing* it from the next.

(There are precisely *five* forces of *gevurah* since each of the emotional attributes *chesed, gevurah, tiferes, netzach* and *hod* contains some *gevurah* within it. This is because, since the attributes are deeply integrated, each one contains a little of the other's energy. The attributes of *yesod* and *malchus* are not counted here since they do not add any new content, but merely combine and harmonize the energies they receive from the other attributes.)

וְשֹׁרֶשׁ הַה׳ גְּבוּרוֹת הוּא בּוּצִינָא דְּקַרְדּוּנִיתָא — **And the source of the five forces of *gevurah* is** the level called by the Zohar ***butzina de-kardunisa,*** "**light out of darkness**" (*Zohar* 1, 15a), שֶׁהִיא גְּבוּרָה עִילָאָה דְּעַתִּיק יוֹמִין — **which is the lofty** *gevurah* **of *Atik Yomin*** ("Ancient of Days"—*Daniel* 7:9).

Atik Yomin is a level within the Divine which transcends all attributes; it is aloof (*ne'tak*) from revealed powers ("days"). Nevertheless, it is the source of them. The *gevurah* within *Atik Yomin,* referred to by the Zohar as *butzina de-kardunisa,* is the source of all Divine *gevurah* powers.

וְשֹׁרֶשׁ הַחֲסָדִים הוּא גַּם כֵּן חֶסֶד דְּעַתִּיק יוֹמִין — **And the source of the powers of** *chesed* **is also *Atik Yomin,*** כַּיָּדוּעַ לְיוֹדְעֵי חָכְמָה נִסְתָּרָה — **as scholars of the Kabbalah are aware.**

This explains how the vessels have the power to transform the light and impose a certain form on it. Since both the vessels and light (*gevurah* and *chesed*) are derived from the same source, therefore they have equal power, so to speak.

In any case, the above ideas underscore the theme of this chapter, that G-d's powers of disclosure and diminishment are not separate powers, but are deeply integrated within the One G-d.

פרק ה והנה על זה אמרו רז"ל בתחלה עלה
במחשבה לברוא את העולם
במד"הד ראה שאין העולם מתקיים שתף בו מדת

CHAPTER 5

MORE ON THE ATTRIBUTES

SECTION ONE: THE DIVINE ATTRIBUTES ARE REAL

15TH SIVAN REGULAR | 16TH SIVAN LEAP

This chapter continues the discussion in Section Four of the previous chapter, concerning the Divine attributes. In this chapter we will learn that the attributes are real, and not merely metaphorical; that they cannot be understood by humans, even through prophecy; but they can be grasped, to some extent, by the soul in the afterlife.

וְהִנֵּה עַל זֶה אָמְרוּ רַבּוֹתֵינוּ זִכְרוֹנָם לִבְרָכָה — **This is the meaning of what our Sages taught,** בִּתְחִלָּה עָלָה בְּמַחֲשָׁבָה לִבְרוֹא אֶת הָעוֹלָם בְּמִדַּת הַדִּין רָאָה שֶׁאֵין הָעוֹלָם מִתְקַיֵּים שִׁתֵּף בּוֹ מִדַּת רַחֲמִים — *"Originally, G-d thought to create the world with His attribute of judgment, but He saw that the world wouldn't last, so He added His attribute of compassion"* (*Genesis Rabah* 12:15).

If we were to look at G-d's attribute of judgment (*gevurah*) as a totally independent power from His attribute of *chesed*, this statement would make no sense. How could G-d possibly *"create the world with His attribute of judgment"* if all *gevurah* does is conceal, diminish and hide?

It must be the case, as we have argued in Chapter Four, that there is a deep integration between *chesed* and *gevurah*. *Chesed* provides the energy, *gevurah,* the containment; *chesed* is the light, *gevurah,* the vessel. So when, *"Originally, G-d thought to create the world with His attribute of judgment,"* it means that in the careful balance between *chesed* and *gevurah*, G-d originally intended there to be more *gevurah*, so that His creative power (*chesed*) would be completely hidden.

However, *"He saw that the world wouldn't last."* If our purpose is to bring awareness of G-d and to disclose His presence, then too much *gevurah* would make that task impossible.

"So He added His attribute of compassion." To what does this refer?

רחמים דהיינו התגלות אלהות על ידי צדיקים
ואותות ומופתים שבתורה. והנה על זה אמרו
בזהר דלעילא בסטרא דקדושה עילאה אית ימינא

דְּהַיְינוּ הִתְגַּלּוּת אֱלֹהוּת עַל יְדֵי צַדִּיקִים — The "added compassion" **refers to the** supernatural **Divine revelations brought about by** *tzadikim,* וְאוֹתוֹת וּמוֹפְתִים שֶׁבַּתּוֹרָה — **and the** miraculous **signs and wonders in the Torah.**

Normally, G-d's light is safely and effectively contained in His "vessels." This ensures that the universe runs stably, and that nature runs its course.

When G-d (temporarily) increases the amount of light, so that the vessel "overflows," a miracle happens. These occasional violations of the natural order shift the disclosure/concealment equilibrium towards more disclosure, making the universe viable.

The *Tanya* now cites a teaching from the Zohar which describes G-d's powers of *chesed* and *gevurah.*

וְהִנֵּה עַל זֶה אָמְרוּ בַּזֹּהַר — **And this is what the** *Zohar* **refers to when it states,** דִּלְעֵילָּא בְּסִטְרָא דִּקְדוּשָׁה עִילָּאָה אִית יְמִינָא וְאִית שְׂמָאלָא — **that** *"above, in the holy lofty domain,"* i.e., within the Divine realm of G-d's attributes, *"there is right and there is left"* (*Zohar* 1, 53a), דְּהַיְינוּ חֶסֶד וּגְבוּרָה — "right" and "left" **referring to** *chesed* **and** *gevurah* respectively.

You might be inclined to think that G-d's benevolence and judgment are human constructs based on our limited ability to understand the One G-d. If He is unlimited, doesn't He defy any classification into specific character traits?

Jewish philosophers, such as Maimonides, would say that this is definitely the case. *"The Torah speaks in human terms"* (*Sifre* 112), describing G-d as sometimes generous, sometimes punishing, but that, the philosophers argue, is our impression, and not the actual reality. Just as one single fire will melt some substances and harden others, the One G-d acts in one single way, but the effect is different, depending on the recipients.

PRACTICAL LESSONS

The little miracles you witness every day are hints of G-d's compassion; His gift to help you to cope in a world of strict law and justice.

The Kabbalists sharply rejected this world-view. They taught that while G-d's *essence* is one, infinite and devoid of any character (it is *Ein Sof,* "without end"), His *attributes* are not just a figment of the human mind, they are real. G-d emanated these attributes, and they exist in the Divine realm: *"Above, in the holy lofty domain... there is right and there is left."*

וְאִית שְׂמָאלָא דְהַיְינוּ חֶסֶד וּגְבוּרָה פִּי' דְּשַׁתֵּיהֶן הֵן
מִדוֹת אֱלֹהוּת לְמַעְלָה מִשֵּׂכֶל הַנִּבְרָאִים וְהַשָּׂגָתָם
דְּאִיהוּ וְגַרְמוֹהִי חַד בְּעוֹלָם הָאֲצִילוּת וְאַף הַשָּׂגַת
מֹשֶׁה רַבֵּינוּ עָלָיו הַשָּׁלוֹם בִּנְבוּאָתוֹ לֹא הָיְתָה בְּעוֹלָם
הָאֲצִילוּת אֶלָּא עַל יְדֵי הִתְלַבְּשׁוּתוֹ בְּעוֹלָם הַבְּרִיאָה

When G-d acts benevolently He uses His power of *chesed* ("right"), and when He judges, the attribute of *gevurah* ("left") is at work.

פֵּירוּשׁ דְּשַׁתֵּיהֶן הֵן מִדוֹת אֱלֹהוּת — What the *Zohar* means is that both *chesed* and *gevurah* are real, Divine attributes, לְמַעְלָה מִשֵּׂכֶל הַנִּבְרָאִים וְהַשָּׂגָתָם — which elude the grasp of mortal intellect, דְּאִיהוּ וְגַרְמוֹהִי חַד בְּעוֹלָם הָאֲצִילוּת — since, in the World of *Atzilus (Emanation)*, "He and the attributes that He causes are one" (*Tikunei Zohar* 3b).

It turns out that the world's identity and form is more real than we had previously imagined. While everything we argued in Chapters 1-3 remains true (the world's identity is voided by the Divine energy that creates it constantly), it is nevertheless also true (from our perspective) that the world's identity is real. From our view point, *"all creations are **not** voided of their identity by their source"* (end of chap. 3), because our separateness is maintained by the Divine attribute of *gevurah*. So even if you could see the Divine attributes, from that vantage point the world would still exist.

SECTION TWO: THE LIMITATIONS OF PROPHECY

As we have just learned, the Divine attributes "elude the grasp of mortal intellect." To underscore this point further, the *Tanya* will show that even the prophets did not merit to perceive the Divine attributes.

וְאַף הַשָּׂגַת מֹשֶׁה רַבֵּינוּ עָלָיו הַשָּׁלוֹם בִּנְבוּאָתוֹ — And even what Moses, of blessed memory, grasped through his prophecy, לֹא הָיְתָה בְּעוֹלָם הָאֲצִילוּת אֶלָּא עַל יְדֵי — was not a direct vision of the World of *Atzilus* הִתְלַבְּשׁוּתוֹ בְּעוֹלָם הַבְּרִיאָה — (Emanation), but seen through the filtering of the World of *Beriah* (Creation).

The realm of Divine attributes is called in the Kabbalah, the World of *Atzilus* (Emanation). Since these attributes are totally one with G-d, they cannot be perceived by man. Even the prophets, who did envision G-d more directly, had to perceive Him through a veil. That veiled perspective is called the World of *Beriah* (Creation).

"Creation" implies separateness; "Emanation," oneness. Trying to perceive oneness from a perspective of separateness is like trying to fit a square peg

וְאַף גַם זֹאת לֹא בִּשְׁתֵּי מִדּוֹת אֵלּוּ חוּ"ג אֶלָּא עַל יְדֵי
הִתְלַבְּשׁוּתָן בְּמִדּוֹת שֶׁלְּמַטָּה מֵהֶן בְּמַדְרֵגָה שֶׁהֵן מִדּוֹת
נֶצַח הוֹד יְסוֹד [כמ"ש בשער הנבואה] רַק שֶׁמָּתָן

into a round hole: they are totally incompatible. Even the prophecy of Moshe, which was the greatest in history, only managed to perceive G-d's oneness through the veil of separation.

The *Tanya's* point here is to impress upon us the Divine nature of the attributes themselves. Since G-d "emanated" *chesed* and *gevurah,* they may appear as "tools" or "creations" just like everything else in the universe. There is, however, a major distinction: the attributes are *Divine*; they are one with G-d; everything else which G-d made is separate from Him. Even the prophets could not bridge this gap.

וְאַף גַם זֹאת לֹא בִּשְׁתֵּי מִדּוֹת אֵלּוּ חֶסֶד וּגְבוּרָה — **And even** Moshe's veiled vision of the attributes in the World of *Beriah* **was not a vision of the two attributes,** *chesed* **and** *gevurah,* in the World of *Beriah,* אֶלָּא עַל יְדֵי הִתְלַבְּשׁוּתָן בַּמִּדּוֹת שֶׁלְּמַטָּה מֵהֶן בְּמַדְרֵגָה — **but** *chesed* **and** *gevurah* **as they are filtered by the attributes a level below them** in the World of *Beriah.*

Moses could not even perceive the filtered version of *chesed* and *gevurah* in the World of *Beriah.* In the World of *Beriah* itself, further filtering and diminishing had to take place before "the greatest of all prophets" could perceive the attributes.

שֶׁהֵן מִדּוֹת נֶצַח הוֹד יְסוֹד — **Namely** a filter at the level of **the attributes of** *netzach* **("endurance"),** *hod* **("splendor") and** *yesod* **("foundation")** of *Beriah,* [כְּמוֹ שֶׁכָּתוּב בְּשַׁעַר הַנְּבוּאָה] — **as stated in** *Sha'ar Ha-Nevu'ah,* chapter 1.

In any spiritual world, the "delivery system" which carries energies over into the next, lower world, is the triad of energies *netzach, hod* and *yesod. Netzach* is the "vehicle" for *chesed, hod* the "vehicle" for *gevurah,* and they are synthesized by *yesod* for delivery to the next world. It is these lower energies which were perceived by the prophets.

SECTION THREE: THE SOUL'S EXPERIENCE IN THE AFTERLIFE

While the prophets were not able to receive the energy of the Divine attributes *chesed* and *gevurah* directly, the souls of the righteous (*tzadikim*) in *Gan Eden* (Heaven) *do* manage to grasp some of this energy.

רַק שֶׁמַּתַּן שְׂכָרָם שֶׁל צַדִּיקִים בְּגַן עֵדֶן — **Only, the reward for** *tzadikim* **in** *Gan Eden,* הוּא הַשָּׂגַת הִתְפַּשְׁטוּת הַחַיּוּת וְאוֹר הַנִּמְשָׁךְ מִשְׁתֵּי מִדּוֹת אֵלּוּ — **is** to have

שכרם של צדיקים בגן עדן הוא השגת התפשטות
החיות ואור הנמשך משתי מדות אלו חו"ג והוא
מזון נשמות הצדיקים שעסקו בתורה לשמה בעו"הז

some **grasp of the energy which seeps out, and** some of **the light which flows, from these two attributes,** חֶסֶד וּגְבוּרָה — *chesed* and *gevurah*.

As the *Talmud* states, that *"the tzadikim sit with their crowns on their heads, enjoying the splendor of the Presence of G-d"* (*Berachos* 17a), which means that *"they know and grasp some of G-d's truth"* (*Rambam, Laws of Teshuvah* 8:2).

The *Tanya* here interprets this to mean that the souls of *tzadikim* actually experience some of the energy of *chesed* and *gevurah* of *Atzilus*, without it being filtered through the World of *Beriah* (as was the case with the prophets).

PRACTICAL LESSONS

G-d's many attributes are, in fact, totally one with His being. Don't be disturbed if you can't understand that, even Moses, the greatest of all prophets, couldn't fully grasp it either.

But, amazingly, in the afterlife, your soul will get a real taste of this truth.

וְהוּא מְזוֹן נִשְׁמוֹת הַצַּדִּיקִים — **And this** revelation is the "food" for the souls of *tzadikim* in the next world, שֶׁעָסְקוּ בַּתּוֹרָה לִשְׁמָהּ בָּעוֹלָם הַזֶּה — in reward for their authentic Torah study in this world.

As we learned in Part One of *Tanya*, Chapter Five: *"Torah is called 'bread' and 'food' of the soul, for just as physical bread nourishes your body only when it is actually absorbed inside you... the same is true with your soul's knowledge and mastery of Torah, when you study it well, focusing the mind, to the point where the Torah is absorbed by your intellect, merging with it to become one, then it provides nourishment for the soul, and life for it, from the Giver of life, the Blessed Infinite Light, which is 'dressed' in His wisdom, in His Torah, now absorbed inside it...."*

"The mitzvos performed during your life provide 'garments' for your soul in the afterlife, while the Torah which you studied authentically (lishmah) in this world will be 'food' for your soul in the afterlife.... The term lishmah in this case means: the intention to attach your soul to G-d through understanding the Torah, according to your mind's ability" (*The Practical Tanya*, volume 1, pp. 80-81).

If even Moses was not capable of perceiving the energy of the Divine attributes, without his existence being obliterated, how is it possible for the souls in *Gan Eden* to receive it?

כִּי מֵהִתְפַּשְׁטוּת שְׁתֵּי מִדּוֹת אֵלּוּ נִמְתַּח רָקִיעַ עַל
הַנְּשָׁמוֹת שֶׁבְּגַן עֵדֶן וְרָקִיעַ זֶה נִקְרָא רָזָא דְאוֹרַיְיתָא
וּבוֹ סוֹד כ"ב אוֹתִיּוֹת הַתּוֹרָה הַנְּתוּנָה מִשְׁתֵּי מִדּוֹת

To answer this question the *Tanya* cites a teaching from the *Zohar* and *Etz Chaim* (sources are cited below).

כִּי מֵהִתְפַּשְׁטוּת שְׁתֵּי מִדּוֹת אֵלּוּ — **Because it is from the seepage of** energy from **these two attributes,** *chesed* and *gevurah*, נִמְתַּח רָקִיעַ עַל הַנְּשָׁמוֹת שֶׁבְּגַן עֵדֶן — **that a "firmament" is stretched over the souls in** *Gan Eden.*

The presence of a "firmament" in *Gan Eden* enables the souls to receive this energy. This "firmament" is a product of the Torah study of these souls, and the Torah provides the "firmament's" protective power, enabling the souls to receive the energy of the Divine attributes.

As the Zohar clarifies, this firmament is made of "fire and water" (*gevurah* and *chesed*) and therefore provides the power to integrate these two attributes.

וְרָקִיעַ זֶה נִקְרָא רָזָא דְאוֹרַיְיתָא — **And this "firmament" is called** by the *Zohar,* *raza d'oraisa* **("secret of the Torah"),** וּבוֹ סוֹד כ"ב אוֹתִיּוֹת הַתּוֹרָה — **for it has the** mystical **power of the twenty-two letters,** the Hebrew alphabet used to write **the Torah.**

Once the Torah is given in this world, there must be a distinction between do's and don'ts, *chesed* and *gevurah*. But in its heavenly setting, the "secret" of the Torah integrates *chesed* and *gevurah* perfectly.

הַנְּתוּנָה מִשְׁתֵּי מִדּוֹת אֵלּוּ — **And the Torah was given** to us **through these two attributes,** *chesed* and *gevurah,* כְּדִכְתִיב מִימִינוֹ אֵשׁ דָּת לָמוֹ — **as the verse states,** *"from His right hand, fiery-law (aish-das) for them"* (*Deuteronomy* 33:2).

The Torah's power to integrate *chesed* and *gevurah* is indicated by Scripture. The Torah ("law") is both from G-d's "right hand" (*chesed*) and it is also "fiery" (*gevurah*).

וּמֵרָקִיעַ זֶה נוֹטֵף טַל לִמְזוֹן הַנְּשָׁמוֹת — **And it is from this "firmament" that dew drips to feed the souls.**

The protective power of Torah, which enables souls to withstand great revelation, is compared to "dew." As we learned in Part One, Chapter 36:

"The 'dew of Torah' is referred to by Scripture as 'strength' because it em-powers you to withstand intense revelation, as in the teaching of our Sages, of blessed memory, 'Whoever immerses himself in Torah (in this world), the dew of Torah will revive him (in the future)'" (*The Practical Tanya,* volume 1, p. 407).

דְּהַיְינוּ יְדִיעַת סוֹד כ"ב אוֹתִיּוֹת הַתּוֹרָה — **This protective power comes from the knowledge of the secret of the twenty-two letters of the** Hebrew alphabet, in

אֵלּוּ כדכתיב מימינו אֵשׁ דָּת לָמוֹ וּמֵרָקִיעַ זֶה נוֹטֵף
טַל לִמְזוֹן הַנְּשָׁמוֹת דְּהַיְינוּ יְדִיעַת סוֹד כ"ב אוֹתִיּוֹת
הַתּוֹרָה כִּי הָרָקִיעַ הַזֶּה הוּא סוֹד הַדַּעַת וְהַתּוֹרָה הִיא
מְזוֹן הַנְּשָׁמוֹת בְּג"ע וְהַמִּצְוֹת הֵן לְבוּשִׁים כמבואר
כל זה [בזהר ויקהל דף ר"ט ור"י ובע"ח שער מ"ד
פרק ג']:

the **Torah,** כִּי הָרָקִיעַ הַזֶּה הוּא סוֹד הַדַּעַת — since "firmament" is a secret code
for *da'as.*

As we have learned, *da'as* is a power which *"incorporates chesed and gevu-rah"* (ibid. chapter 3, p. 63). *Da'as,* therefore, is the secret by which the "firma-ment" is able to "incorporate" and synthesize the conflicting powers of *chesed* and *gevurah.*

וְהַתּוֹרָה הִיא מְזוֹן הַנְּשָׁמוֹת בְּגַן עֵדֶן — And the Torah is "food" for the souls in *Gan Eden,* וְהַמִּצְוֹת הֵן לְבוּשִׁים — whereas the *mitzvos* are "garments."

The *mitzvos* are certainly do's and don'ts, so how do they provide integrative power?

The *Tanya* answers that the energy of the *mitzvos* is not fully absorbed by the souls, but envelopes them like a "garment." Therefore it does not disturb the deep integration of *chesed* and *gevurah* which is achieved by the souls through the Torah that they have learned.

בַּזֹהַר וַיַּקְהֵל דַּף ר"ט וְר"י וּבְעֵץ] — And all this has been clarified, כְּמְבוֹאָר כָּל זֶה — in the *Zohar, Vayakhel,* 2, **209-210** and *Etz Chaim,* [חַיִּים שַׁעַר מ"ד פֶּרֶק ג' **Gate 44** (in the 1782 Koritz edition; in current editions, Gate 43), **chapter 3.**

פרק ו והנה שם אלהים הוא שם מדת הגבורה
והצמצום ולכן הוא גם כן
בגימטריא הטבע לפי שמסתיר האור שלמעלה
המהוה ומחיה העולם ונראה כאילו העולם עומד
ומתנהג בדרך הטבע ושם אלהים זה הוא מגן ונרתק

808

INTEGRATING THE ATTRIBUTES

SECTION ONE: HOW THE DIVINE ATTRIBUTES WORK TOGETHER

16TH SIVAN REGULAR | 17TH SIVAN LEAP

In the previous chapters, the *Tanya* has explained how creation is a product of two Divine attributes, *chesed* (disclosure; generosity) and the counter-force of *gevurah* (diminishment; control). Until this point we have understood that these two attributes have opposite functions, but in this chapter we will discover that, in reality, the dynamic is far more nuanced.

וְהִנֵּה שֵׁם אֱלֹהִים הוּא שֵׁם מִדַּת הַגְּבוּרָה וְהַצִּמְצוּם — **Now the** Divine **name** *Elokim* **represents G-d's attribute of** *gevurah* **and** power of **diminishment,** וְלָכֵן הוּא גַּם כֵּן בְּגִימַטְרִיָּא הַטֶּבַע — **which is why it has the** *gematria* **(numerical value) of** eighty-six, the same as the word *ha-teva* ("nature"), לְפִי שֶׁמַּסְתִּיר הָאוֹר שֶׁלְמַעְלָה הַמְהַוֶּה וּמְחַיֶּה הָעוֹלָם — **be-** **cause** G-d's attribute of *gevurah* **conceals the Divine light that brings the world into being and energizes it,** וְנִרְאֶה כְּאִילּוּ הָעוֹלָם עוֹמֵד וּמִתְנַהֵג בְּדֶרֶךְ הַטֶּבַע — **so** **it looks as if the world exists and operates naturally** and autonomously.

PRACTICAL LESSONS

The Divine name *Elokim* represents Diminishment, the veil of nature, hiding G-d's overwhelming power.

As we have learned, the Divine name *Elokim* represents G-d's power of diminishment. This, the *Tanya* notes here, is hinted to by the fact that the Hebrew word *Elokim* has the same numerical value as the word *ha-teva* ("nature"), because nature, the appearance that the world runs on its own without G-d, is only possible through the diminishment and hiding of G-d's presence.

לשם הוי"ה להעלים האור והחיות הנמשך משם
הוי"ה ומהוה מאין ליש שלא יתגלה לנבראים
ויבטלו במציאות והרי בחי' גבורה זו וצמצום הזה
הוא גם כן בחי' חסד שהעולם יבנה בו וזו היא
בחי' גבורה הכלולה בחסד והנה מהתכללות המדות

וְשֵׁם אֱלֹהִים זֶה הוּא מָגֵן וְנַרְתֵּק לְשֵׁם הֲוָיָ"ה — **This name,** *Elokim*, **is the "shield"** **and "protective layer" of the** energy represented by the **name** *Havayah*.

In Chapter Four, the *Tanya* explained the role of the Divine names *Elokim* and *Havayah* with the verse, *"For a sun and shield is G-d, Almighty (Havayah Elokim)" (Psalms* 84:12). *Havayah* represents G-d's power of revelation and disclosure, like the sun which emanates light. *Elokim* resembles the sun's "protective sheath," which diminishes the light so that it does not overwhelm us.

לְהַעֲלִים הָאוֹר וְהַחַיּוּת הַנִּמְשָׁךְ מִשֵּׁם הֲוָיָ"ה וּמְהַוֶּה מֵאַיִן לְיֵשׁ — *Elokim* **conceals the** Divine **light and energy of the name** *Havayah*. **which brings** us **into existence, something-from-nothing,** שֶׁלֹּא יִתְגַּלֶּה לַנִּבְרָאִים וְיִבָּטְלוּ בִּמְצִיאוּת — **and this con**cealment is necessary **so that** the energy of *Havayah* **doesn't become** too **revealed to us creations, which would cause** our sense of independent **existence to be erased.**

This is a brief summary of what we have learned above, from the beginning of chapter 4. Now the *Tanya* will introduce a new element to the discussion.

וַהֲרֵי בְּחִינַת גְּבוּרָה זוֹ וְצִמְצוּם הַזֶּה הוּא גַּם כֵּן בְּחִינַת חֶסֶד — **So this quality of** *ge-vurah* **and this diminishment** power **really is a type of kindness** (*chesed*), שֶׁהָעוֹלָם יִבָּנֶה בּוֹ — **since the world is built on it.**

Up to this point, we have understood *gevurah* (diminishment) to be the opposite of *chesed* (disclosure). For example, *gevurah* would be equivalent to the structure and discipline in your life, which enables you to hold down a job and do necessary tasks, so that you will later have the opportunity for pleasure and relaxation (*chesed*). The two forces work in dynamic tension.

A CHASIDIC THOUGHT G-d diminished His light, so to speak, like a father who "diminishes" his intellect and speaks childish things to engage with his toddler. The father behaves in all sorts of childish ways, *and the father even loves this childishness,* so that the child should enjoy being with him *(Magid of Mezritch, Ohr Torah,* beginning).

זו בזו נראה לעין דאיהו וגרמוהי חד שהן מדותיו
כי מאחר שהן ביחוד גמור עמו לכן הן מתייחדות

But here the *Tanya* observes that, in essence, *gevurah is itself a form of chesed* (kindness). *Gevurah* is "tough love," the restraint necessary to make G-d's loving act of creating you possible.

וְזוֹ הִיא בְּחִינַת גְּבוּרָה הַכְּלוּלָה בְּחֶסֶד — **And it is, in fact, the subdivision of *gevurah* within *chesed*.**

In the Kabbalah, each energy/attribute (*sefirah*) contains a little of all the other energies, even opposing ones. G-d did this to make the universe viable, otherwise the energies would end up destroying each other.

![PRACTICAL LESSONS]

Gevurah, then, contains an element of *chesed* within it; and, likewise, *chesed* contains an element of *gevurah*.

Chesed-within-*gevurah* ensures that the diminishment of G-d's light is constructive, for the sake of creation. And *gevurah*-within-*chesed* enables G-d's light to shine at the correct (disciplined) intensity, appropriate for each world and created entity (see *Notes on Tanya*).

17TH SIVAN REGULAR | 18TH SIVAN LEAP

The *Tanya* now brings a logical proof for the idea that all attributes contain a little of all the other attributes as "subdivisions."

וְהִנֵּה מֵהִתְכַּלְלוּת הַמִּדּוֹת זוֹ בָּזוֹ — **Now, from** this idea **that the attributes all contain subdivisions of the other** attributes, נִרְאֶה לָעַיִן דְּאִיהוּ וְגַרְמוֹהִי חַד — **it is self-evident that** *"He and the attributes that He causes are one"* (*Tikunei Zohar* 3b), שֶׁהֵן מְדוֹתָיו — *i.e.,* **they are** G-d's **attributes,** כִּי מֵאַחַר שֶׁהֵן בְּיִחוּד גָּמוּר עִמּוֹ — **because since they are seamlessly merged with** G-d, לָכֵן הֵן מִתְיַחֲדוֹת זוֹ בָּזוֹ — **therefore** the attributes are also **integrated with each other,** וּכְלוּלוֹת זוֹ מִזּוֹ — **and they contain** a little **of one another.**

If the attributes had been created separate from G-d, it would be conceivable that they would be totally opposed to each other, just as fire is completely extinguished by water. But since, in reality, the attributes are one with G-d, they defy binary opposition and are able to embrace contradiction, like their Creator.

זו בזו וכלולות זו מזו כמאמר אליהו ואנת הוא
דקשיר לון ומיחד לון וכו' ובר מינך לית יחודא
בעילאי כו' וז"ש והשבות אל לבבך כי ה' הוא
האלהים פירוש ששני שמות אלו הם אחד ממש
שגם שם אלהים המצמצם ומעלים האור הוא בחי'

This, the *Tanya* asserts, is a "self-evident" fact. It is impossible that G‑d's kindness (*chesed*) could be devoid of discipline, or that G‑d's might (*gevurah*) would be devoid of compassion.

The *Tanya* cites a source for this idea, from the *Tikunei Zohar*.

וְאַנְתְּ הוּא דְקָשִׁיר לוֹן וּמְיַחֵד לוֹן וְכוּ' — **As in the discourse of Elijah,** כְּמַאֲמַר אֵלִיָּהוּ — *"You are the one who binds and unites them..."* וּבַר מִינָּךְ לֵית יְחוּדָא בְּעִילָּאֵי כוּ' — *"without You, there is no unity above"* (*Tikunei Zohar* 17a).

Since G‑d is one with His attributes (He "binds and unites them"), therefore they co-exist harmoniously (*"without You, there is no unity above"*).

With the above in mind, we now return to explain the verse with which our book opened, *Deuteronomy* 4:39.

וְזֶהוּ שֶׁכָּתוּב וַהֲשֵׁבוֹתָ אֶל לְבָבֶךָ כִּי ה' הוּא הָאֱלֹהִים — **And this is the meaning of the verse** — *"And you shall know today and take to your heart that G‑d (Havayah) is G‑d (Elokim)"* (*Deuteronomy* 4:39), פֵּירוּשׁ שְׁנֵי שֵׁמוֹת אֵלוּ הֵם אֶחָד מַמָּשׁ —

A CHASIDIC THOUGHT

I only have an independent mind because G‑d's presence is concealed. If, at any moment, He were to reverse this, space and time would implode, since the distinctions which make finite existence possible would be erased.

My consciousness is, in a sense, a lie. My separate mind can only exist because G‑d has hidden His presence. If that veil is removed, I will be reabsorbed in His oneness.

On the other hand, this is a real book and I am reading it. The world really does exist; it is not an illusion. G‑d *actually did* "create the heavens and the earth."

My very consciousness—and therefore, every object and experience it perceives—is both true and a lie at the very same time. It is true because this world is real; but it is a lie because my reality can only exist if Divine concealment (a lie) is in place.

חֶסֶד כְּמוֹ שֵׁם הֲוָי"ה מִשּׁוּם שֶׁמִּדּוֹתָיו שֶׁל הַקָּדוֹשׁ
בָּרוּךְ הוּא מִתְיַחֲדוֹת עִמּוֹ בְּיִחוּד גָּמוּר וְהוּא
וּשְׁמוֹ אֶחָד שֶׁמִּדּוֹתָיו הֵן שְׁמוֹתָיו וְאִם כֵּן מִמֵּילָא
תֵּדַע שֶׁבַּשָּׁמַיִם מִמַּעַל וְעַל הָאָרֶץ מִתַּחַת אֵין עוֹד

Namely you must know **that these two names,** *Havayah* and *Elokim,* **are literal-ly one** integrated system, שֶׁגַּם שֵׁם אֱלֹהִים הַמְצַמְצֵם וּמַעֲלִים הָאוֹר הוּא בְּחִינַת חֶסֶד כְּמוֹ שֵׁם הֲוָי"ה — **that even the name** *Elokim (gevurah),* **which diminishes and hides** G-d's **light, is really kindness** *(chesed),* **like the name** *Havayah,* מִשּׁוּם שֶׁמִּדּוֹתָיו שֶׁל הַקָּדוֹשׁ בָּרוּךְ הוּא מִתְיַחֲדוֹת עִמּוֹ בְּיִחוּד גָּמוּר — **because** G-d's **attri-butes are seamlessly merged with Him.**

Deuteronomy 4:39 instructs us to "know" and "take to heart" that "*Havayah* is *Elokim.*" The meaning of this cryptic phrase is precisely what we have ex-plained above, that even *chesed* (*Havayah*), is not devoid of *gevurah* (*Elokim*), and *gevurah* is not devoid of *chesed,* since each contains an element of the other.

Or, to put it in other terms, "*Havayah* is *Elokim,*" since the goal of disclosure (*Havayah*) is to be sufficiently contained (through *Elokim*) for the world to be able to receive it. And "*Elokim* is *Havayah,*" since the goal of diminishment (*Elokim*) is to make the disclosure (of *Havayah*) possible.

The *Tanya* cites one final proof, from the *Zohar.*

וְהוּא וּשְׁמוֹ אֶחָד — **And this is the meaning of the phrase,** *"He and His name are one"* (*Zohar* 2, 86a), שֶׁמִּדּוֹתָיו הֵן שְׁמוֹתָיו — **since His "attributes" are His "names."**

While G-d's names (attributes) differ, each having different meanings, they are deeply integrated towards a unified action and goal.

SECTION TWO: THE WORLD'S (NON)EXISTENCE, REVISITED

Before chapter 6 we looked at the Divine attributes as different, sometimes opposing powers. Now we understand that they are deeply integrated and each share an element of the other. What difference does that make in our understanding of the creation process?

As we shall see, this nuanced understanding of the attributes will be quite significant.

וְאִם כֵּן מִמֵּילָא תֵּדַע שֶׁבַּשָּׁמַיִם מִמַּעַל וְעַל הָאָרֶץ מִתַּחַת אֵין עוֹד — When you *"take to your heart that G-d (Havayah) is G-d (Elokim)"* and realize that the attributes each contain all the others, **you will inevitably come to know** the truth stated

פי' שגם הארץ החומרית שנראית יש גמור לעין
כל היא אין ואפס ממש לגבי הקדוש ברוך הוא
כי שם אלהים אינו מעלים ומצמצם אלא לתחתונים
ולא לגבי הקב"ה מאחר שהוא ושמו אלהים אחד

at the end of *Deuteronomy* 4:39, that, ***"in the heavens above and in the earth
below, there is none else."***

The traditional interpretation of "there is none else," is that no other deity
exists besides G-d. In the *Tanya's* radical re-reading of the verse, *"there is none
else"* is understood in the most literal sense: *nothing* exists outside of G-d.

Above (in chapters 1-3) we understood this to be true because G-d creates
the world continually, and therefore the world has no independent existence of
its own. But our discussion of the Divine attributes (from chapter 4 onwards) has
added a complication, because, in hindsight, chapters 1-3 seem to be speaking
only from the perspective of *Havayah,* which continually provides creative energy (voiding the world of its independent existence). But from the perspective
of *Elokim*, which *hides* that creative force, it would seem that there is a separate
world. Isn't the whole purpose of *Elokim* energy to make separateness real?

Chapter 6 clarifies that *"even the name Elokim (gevurah), which diminishes
and hides G-d's light, is really kindness (chesed), like the name Havayah."* That
means even G-d's power of diminishment (*Elokim*) is
not absolute; its purpose/goal/inner identity is disclosure. So, ultimately, even from the perspective of
Elokim there is no separate world, because *Elokim* is
never completely devoid of *Havayah.*

PRACTICAL LESSONS

— פֵּירוּשׁ שֶׁגַּם הָאָרֶץ הַחוּמְרִית שֶׁנִּרְאֵית יֵשׁ גָּמוּר לְעַיִן כֹּל
**Meaning that even this physical earth which every-
one can see exists independently,** הִיא אַיִן וָאֶפֶס מַמָּשׁ
is, to G-d, *"null and void"* — לְגַבֵּי הַקָּדוֹשׁ בָּרוּךְ הוּא
(see *Isaiah* 40:17), כִּי שֵׁם אֱלֹהִים אֵינוֹ מַעֲלִים וּמְצַמְצֵם
אֶלָּא לַתַּחְתּוֹנִים — **because the Divine name *Elokim*
only hides and diminishes** G-d's light **from the lower
worlds,** וְלֹא לְגַבֵּי הַקָּדוֹשׁ בָּרוּךְ הוּא — **but it does not
hide** anything **from G-d,** מֵאַחַר שֶׁהוּא וּשְׁמוֹ אֱלֹהִים אֶחָד
— **since He is one with His name, *Elokim*.**

Even when G-d
hides Himself it is *an
expression of G-d*;
and, therefore, a type
of "revelation." G-d
is in the pain as well
as the pleasure.

If you were invited to give a twenty-minute talk summarizing five years of
your research findings to a lay audience, you would have to significantly "diminish" your understanding of the topic. But you don't actually become dumber
through the process, you simply "diminish" the ideas *for your audience.*

ולכן גם הארץ ומתחת לארץ הן אין ואפס ממש
לגבי הקב"ה ואינן נקראות בשם כלל אפילו בשם
עוד שהוא לשון טפל כמאמר רז"ל יהודה ועוד
לקרא וכגוף שהוא טפל לנשמה וחיות שבתוכו

In a similar way, G-d's "diminishment" is only from our perspective ("the audience"). Even after G-d's light is dimmed and hidden through His power of
gevurah, from His perspective, it is as if nothing has happened.

וְלָכֵן גַּם הָאָרֶץ וּמִתַּחַת לָאָרֶץ הֵן אַיִן וָאֶפֶס מַמָּשׁ לְגַבֵּי הַקָּדוֹשׁ בָּרוּךְ הוּא — **So even
the earth and below the earth, are** *"null and void"* **to G-d,** וְאֵינָן נִקְרָאוֹת בְּשֵׁם
כְּלָל — **and their** existence **is not** sufficiently independent for them to be **called
by their own name at all,** אֲפִילוּ בְּשֵׁם עוֹד — **even the name** *oid,* **"something
else."**

If *"Havayah is Elokim,"* even the world's separate identity (formed by *Elokim*),
contains the inner truth of *Havayah* that "there is nothing else" outside G-d.
Therefore, even "in the earth below," formed by *Elokim,* it is possible to "know"
and "take to heart... there is none else *(oid)*."

SECTION THREE: SECONDARY EXISTENCE

The verse states that the world does not have even a secondary existence,
"there is none else (oid)" besides G-d. The *Tanya* will now clarify the precise
meaning of the term *oid* ("something else").

שֶׁהוּא לְשׁוֹן טָפֵל — *Oid* **is a term that expresses a secondary status.**

Oid means that something exists, but its existence is secondary to something
else more important.

כְּמַאֲמַר רַבּוֹתֵינוּ זִכְרוֹנָם לִבְרָכָה יְהוּדָה וְעוֹד לִקְרָא — **As in the statement of our
Sages of blessed memory, "(How can you cite the law from) Judah** *in addition*
(ve-oid) to Scripture?" *(Kidushin* 6a).

The *Talmud* objected to a legal precedent from the province of Judah being
cited to support an explicit Scriptural ruling. If it is stated in Scripture, no further
proof is necessary.

This illustrates the meaning of the term *oid.* The legal precedent from the
province of Judah exists and is generally of value; but it simply pales into insignificance compared to a ruling of Scripture.

Another illustration of the term *oid* is the body compared to the soul.

וּכְגוּף שֶׁהוּא טָפֵל לַנְּשָׁמָה וְחַיּוּת שֶׁבְּתוֹכוֹ — **And like the body which is secondary
to the soul and the energy within it.**

[וז"ש אהללה ה' בחיי אזמרה לאלהי בעודי
שהחיים נמשכים משם הוי"ה והעוד שהוא הגוף   81A
הטפל משם אלהים] לפי שהנשמה אינה מהוה
הגוף מאין ליש אבל הקב"ה המהוה את הכל
מאין ליש הכל בטל במציאות אצלו כמו אור

The body is a tool of expression for the soul, and it has no purpose other than that. But the body still exists independently from the soul.

וְזֶהוּ שֶׁכָּתוּב אֲהַלְלָה ה' בְּחַיָּי אֲזַמְּרָה לֵאלֹהַי בְּעוֹדִי שֶׁהַחַיִּים נִמְשָׁכִים מִשֵּׁם הֲוָיָ"ה וְהָעוֹד] הַגּוּף הַטָּפֵל מִשֵּׁם אֱלֹהִים] [שֶׁהוּא — **Which is why the verse states,** *"Let me praise G-d (Havayah) with my life, let me sing to my G-d (Elokai) with my being (oidi)"* (*Psalms* 146:2), **since "life" comes from the name** *Havayah,* **whereas** *oid,* **the body, which is secondary, comes from the name** *Elokim.*

In this parenthetical note, the *Tanya* shows how our above explanation illuminates the meaning of *Psalms* 146:2. We praise G-d with our souls ("my life") and our bodies ("my being"). The soul, which reflects G-d's creative power, praises its corresponding Divine attribute, *Havayah.* The body, which is formed through diminishment and containment of Divine light, praises *Elokim.*

We return to our discussion of secondary existence. Why is the body "secondary" to the soul, and not "null and void" as the world is to G-d?

לְפִי שֶׁהַנְּשָׁמָה אֵינָהּ מְהַוָּה הַגּוּף מֵאַיִן לְיֵשׁ — **The body is not "null and void"** compared to the soul, **because the soul does not create the body, something-from-nothing,** אֲבָל הַקָּדוֹשׁ בָּרוּךְ הוּא הַמְהַוֶּה אֶת הַכֹּל מֵאַיִן לְיֵשׁ הַכֹּל בָּטֵל בִּמְצִיאוּת אֶצְלוֹ — **but in relation to G-d, who** *does* **create everything something-from-nothing, no thing has any independent existence,** כְּמוֹ אוֹר הַשֶּׁמֶשׁ בַּשֶּׁמֶשׁ — **like** our earlier example of **light rays inside the sun** (chapter 3).

In conclusion: When the verse states, "there is none else (oid)," it makes clear that the world does not even enjoy a secondary existence; rather, it is "null and void" to G-d.

SECTION FOUR: FOUR REASONS FOR VOIDING

18TH SIVAN REGULAR | 19TH SIVAN LEAP

We will now examine the beginning of the verse. Why was it necessary to state, *"And you shall know today and take to your heart, that G-d (Havayah) is G-d (Elokim) in the heavens above and in the earth below, there is none else"*?

וְלָכֵן הוּצְרַךְ הַכָּתוּב לְהַזְהִיר וְיָדַעְתָּ הַיּוֹם וַהֲשֵׁבֹתָ אֶל לְבָבֶךָ וְגוֹ' — **And this is why the verse had to instruct us,** *"And you shall know today and take to your heart, etc."*

השמש בשמש. ולכן הוצרך הכתוב להזהיר
וידעת היום והשבות אל לבבך וגו' שלא תעלה
על דעתך שהשמים וכל צבאם והארץ ומלואה
הם דבר נפרד בפני עצמו והקדוש ברוך הוא
ממלא כל העולם כהתלבשות הנשמה בגוף
ומשפיע כח הצומח בארץ וכח התנועה בגלגלים
ומניעם ומנהיגם כרצונו כמו שהנשמה מניעה את
הגוף ומנהיגתו כרצונה. אך באמת אין המשל
דומה לנמשל כלל כי הנשמה והגוף הם באמת נפרדי'
זה מזה בשרשם כי אין התהוות שרש הגוף ועצמותו

The verse stresses that we ought to make a special effort to "know" and "take to heart" that "there is none else." This is because significant contemplation is required to accept the counterintuitive notion that the world's existence is not even secondary to G-d, but "null and void."

PRACTICAL LESSONS

G-d's relationship to the world is not like your soul's relationship with your body. Your body only depends on your soul for life-energy; it does not depend on it for existence.

שֶׁלֹּא תַעֲלֶה עַל דַּעְתְּךָ שֶׁהַשָּׁמַיִם וְכָל צְבָאָם וְהָאָרֶץ וּמְלוֹאָה — הֵם דָּבָר נִפְרָד בִּפְנֵי עַצְמוֹ — That you shouldn't let yourself think that the heavens with all their contents, and the earth with all its contents, have their own separate, secondary existence, וְהַקָּדוֹשׁ בָּרוּךְ הוּא מְמַלֵּא — and G-d merely fills all the world, like the soul dresses in the body, כָּל הָעוֹלָם כְּהִתְלַבְּשׁוּת הַנְּשָׁמָה בַּגּוּף, וּמַשְׁפִּיעַ כֹּחַ הַצּוֹמֵחַ בָּאָרֶץ — and G-d merely implants the power of growth in a separately existing earth, וְכֹחַ הַתְּנוּעָה בַּגַּלְגַּלִים — and the power of movement in separately existing planets, וּמְנִיעָם וּמַנְהִיגָם כִּרְצוֹנוֹ — and He merely directs and controls these separately existing entities according to His will, כְּמוֹ שֶׁהַנְּשָׁמָה מְנִיעָה אֶת הַגּוּף וּמַנְהִיגָתוֹ כִּרְצוֹנָהּ — like the soul directs and controls the body according to its will.

You need to make a special effort to "know" and "take to heart" that this is not the case. Rather, "there is none else": the heavens and earth do not even have a secondary existence.

אַךְ בֶּאֱמֶת אֵין הַמָּשָׁל דּוֹמֶה לַנִּמְשָׁל כְּלָל — In truth, there is no comparison to be made here at all between soul/body and G-d/world, כִּי הַנְּשָׁמָה וְהַגּוּף הֵם בֶּאֱמֶת נִפְרָדִים זֶה מִזֶּה בְּשָׁרְשָׁם — because soul and body are truly separate entities, even in their origin, כִּי אֵין הִתְהַוּוּת שֹׁרֶשׁ הַגּוּף וְעַצְמוּתוֹ מִנִּשְׁמָתוֹ — as the soul is not the source of the body, and does not it bring it into being.

מנשמתו אלא מטפות אביו ואמו וגם אחרי כן אין
גידולו מנשמתו לבדה אלא על ידי אכילת ושתיית
אמו כל תשעה חדשים ואחר כך על ידי אכילתו
ושתייתו בעצמו מה שאין כן השמים והארץ שכל
עצמותם ומהותם נתהוה מאין ואפס המוחלט רק
בדבר ה' ורוח פיו ית' וגם עדיין נצב דבר ה'
לעולם ושופע בהם תמיד בכל רגע ומהוה

אֶלָּא מִטְפּוֹת אָבִיו וְאִמּוֹ — **Rather,** the body **comes from the seed of** the child's
father and mother, וְגַם אַחֲרֵי כֵן אֵין גִּידּוּלוֹ מִנִּשְׁמָתוֹ לְבַדָּהּ — **and even after** con-
ception, the fetus does **not grow merely through the soul's influence,** אֶלָּא עַל
יְדֵי אֲכִילַת וּשְׁתִיַּית אִמּוֹ כָּל תִּשְׁעָה חֳדָשִׁים — **but rather through what the mother
eats and drinks during all nine months** of her pregnancy, וְאַחַר כָּךְ עַל יְדֵי אֲכִילָתוֹ
וּשְׁתִיָּיתוֹ בְּעַצְמוֹ — **and after that** the child grows **from his** or her **own eating
and drinking.**

מַה שֶּׁאֵין כֵן הַשָּׁמַיִם וְהָאָרֶץ — **But that's not the case with the heavens and the
earth,** שֶׁכָּל עַצְמוּתָם וּמַהוּתָם נִתְהַוָּה מֵאַיִן וָאֶפֶס הַמּוּחְלָט — **whose entire being is
created from absolute nothing and void,** רַק בִּדְבַר ה' וְרוּחַ פִּיו יִתְבָּרֵךְ — **exclusively from "G-d's word"** and **"the breath of His mouth"** (*Psalms* 33:6).

Unlike the body, which is not brought into being by the soul, the "heavens
and earth" are "created exclusively from G-d's word." Therefore they have no
independent existence, not even a secondary one.

וְגַם עֲדַיִין נִצָּב דְּבַר ה' לְעוֹלָם — **For even now, "G-d's word stands forever** in the
heavens" (see *Psalms* 119:89), וְשׁוֹפֵעַ בָּהֶם תָּמִיד בְּכָל רֶגַע וּמְהַוֶּה אוֹתָם תָּמִיד מֵאַיִן

A CHASIDIC THOUGHT

From G-d's perspective, His infinite light is really
here the whole time; it has just become concealed
from us. G-d made a veil that fooled us, but it
didn't fool Him.

And that's good news. G-d's concealment is really *a matter of
perspective*, an eclipse of the mind rather than a true eclipse of
G-d—which means it's easier to reverse. If G-d had built real barriers they would be harder to smash down, but His concealment
is really a matter of perspective, and a perspective can always be
changed.

אותם תמיד מאין ליש כהתהוות האור מהשמש
בתוך גוף כדור השמש עצמו דרך משל ואם כן הם
בטלים באמת במציאות לגמרי לגבי דבר ה' ורוח
פיו ית' המיוחדים במהותו ועצמותו ית' כמו שיתבאר

לְיֵשׁ — and this energy **flows into** the heavens and earth **constantly, creating them constantly something-from-nothing, at every moment.**

As we have learned in chapters 1-3, the world's identity is voided by the need for a constant influx of creative power from G-d.

כְּהִתְהַוּוֹת הָאוֹר מֵהַשֶּׁמֶשׁ בְּתוֹךְ כַּדּוּר גּוּף הַשֶּׁמֶשׁ עַצְמוֹ דֶּרֶךְ מָשָׁל — This results in a complete voiding of the world's identity, **like** our earlier **illustration of the creation of sunlight within the sun's globe,** in chapter 3.

וְאִם כֵּן הֵם בְּטֵלִים בֶּאֱמֶת בִּמְצִיאוּת לְגַמְרֵי לְגַבֵּי דְּבַר ה' וְרוּחַ פִּיו יִתְבָּרֵךְ — This being the case, the independent identity of heavens and earth **is completely and utterly voided by** *"G-d's word"* and *"the breath of His mouth,"* הַמְיוּחָדִים בְּמַהוּתוֹ וְעַצְמוּתוֹ יִתְבָּרֵךְ — **which themselves are totally merged with** G-d's **very essence and being.**

The *Tanya* adds a fresh detail here, not mentioned in chapters 1-3, which contributes to the voiding of the world's identity. Namely, the Divine energies which create the world *"themselves are totally merged with G-d's very essence and being."*

PRACTICAL LESSONS

G-d's power of diminishment is only real *from our perspective*. It hides nothing from Him.

It's a bit like a snail's shell. To outsiders, the shell conceals what's inside; but to the snail, the shell is part of its body.

כְּמוֹ שֶׁיִּתְבָּאֵר לְקַמָּן — **As will be further explained below,** in chapters 11-12, כְּבִיטוּל אוֹר הַשֶּׁמֶשׁ בַּשֶּׁמֶשׁ — the emanations of G-d are **voided like sunlight within the sun.**

In summary: The *Tanya* has indicated four factors contributing to the voiding of the world's independent identity by G-d, which are not present in the soul/body relationship:

1.) G-d creates the world, unlike the soul which does not create the body.

2.) G-d creates the world *continually*.

3.) The world remains subsumed within G-d, like light rays within the sun.

4.) The Divine energy which creates the world is itself totally merged with G-d.

לקמן כביטול אור השמש בשמש רק שהן הן
גבורותיו במדת הגבורה והצמצום להסתיר ולהעלים
החיות השופע בהם שיהיו נראים השמים והארץ
וכל צבאם כאילו הם דבר בפני עצמו אך אין
הצמצום וההסתר אלא לתחתונים אבל לגבי הקדוש
ברוך הוא כולא קמיה כלא ממש חשיבי כאור
השמש בשמש ואין מדת הגבורה מסתרת חס ושלום
לפניו יתברך כי איננה דבר בפני עצמו אלא ה'
הוא האלהים:

81B

Why, then, does the world appear to us as if it does have an independent existence? The *Tanya* reminds us of the answer we have already learned.

רַק שֶׁהֵן הֵן גְּבוּרוֹתָיו — Only *"these are in fact, expressions of G-d's might (gevurah)"* (*Yalkut Shimoni,* par. 1071; cf. *Yoma* 69b), בְּמִדַּת הַגְּבוּרָה וְהַצִּמְצוּם לְהַסְתִּיר וּלְהַעֲלִים הַחַיּוּת הַשּׁוֹפֵעַ בָּהֶם — through His attribute of *gevurah* and diminishment, which hides and conceals the Divine energy which flows into the creations, שֶׁיִּהְיוּ נִרְאִים הַשָּׁמַיִם וְהָאָרֶץ וְכָל צְבָאָם כְּאִילוּ הֵם דָּבָר בִּפְנֵי עַצְמוֹ — so that *"the heavens, the earth and all their contents"* (Genesis 2:1) appear as if they exist independently from G-d.

אַךְ אֵין הַצִּמְצוּם וְהַהֶסְתֵּר אֶלָּא לַתַּחְתּוֹנִים — However this diminishment and con-cealment is only from the perspective of the lower worlds, אֲבָל לְגַבֵּי הַקָּדוֹשׁ בָּרוּךְ הוּא כּוּלָּא קַמֵּיהּ כְּלָא מַמָּשׁ חֲשִׁיבֵי — but from G-d's perspective, *"in His presence, everything is considered zero"* (Zohar 1, 11b), literally, כְּאוֹר הַשֶּׁמֶשׁ בַּשֶּׁמֶשׁ — like sunlight within the sun.

וְאֵין מִדַּת הַגְּבוּרָה מַסְתֶּרֶת חַס וְשָׁלוֹם לְפָנָיו יִתְבָּרֵךְ — And as we have learned ear-lier in this chapter, the Divine attribute of *gevurah* does not hide anything from Him, G-d forbid, כִּי אֵינֶנָּה דָּבָר בִּפְנֵי עַצְמוֹ — because it is not separate from Him, אֶלָּא ה' הוּא הָאֱלֹהִים — rather, *"Havayah is Elokim,"* and even within G-d's power of diminishment, disclosure is implicit.

פרק ז ובזה יובן מ"ש בזהר הקדוש דפסוק
שמע ישראל הוא יחודא עילאה
וברוך שם כבוד מלכותו לעולם ועד הוא יחודא

CHAPTER 7

UPPER/LOWER UNIFICATION

SECTION ONE: TWO LEVELS OF UNIFICATION

At the very beginning of this book, on the "Author's Title Page," we read that Part Two of the *Tanya* is *"based on the first paragraph of the Shema."* We learned in the "Author's Opening" that the purpose of this book is to give us at least *"a minimal understanding"* of the *Zohar's* commentary on this *mitzvah.* We now return to this topic.

וּבְזֶה יוּבַן מַה שֶּׁכָּתוּב בַּזֹּהַר הַקָּדוֹשׁ — **All this** discussion in the first six chapters **will** help us to **explain** the deeper meaning of **what is written in the holy** *Zohar* (1, 18a-b), דְּפָסוּק שְׁמַע יִשְׂרָאֵל הוּא יְחוּדָא עִילָאָה — **that the verse,** *"Hear O Israel, G-d is our G-d, G-d is one"* (Deuteronomy 6:4), **is "upper unification"** (*yichuda ila'ah*), וּבָרוּךְ שֵׁם כְּבוֹד מַלְכוּתוֹ לְעוֹלָם וָעֶד הוּא יְחוּדָא תַּתָּאָה — **and** the phrase we recite immediately afterwards, *"Blessed be the name of His glorious kingdom forever and ever,"* **is "lower unification"** (*yichuda tata'ah*).

Deuteronomy 6:4 is a declaration of faith recited twice daily according to Jewish Law. The simple meaning of *"G-d is one"* is: only one G-d exists, and there are no other gods, *i.e., exclusive monotheism.*

The previous six chapters have significantly deepened our understanding of G-d's "exclusive" status. Our continual stress has been that the world has no independent existence, and is voided by G-d's presence. The existence of G-d excludes *all other existence.*

As we noted in chapter 3, the precise name for this belief is *panentheism:* everything (*pan*) is within (*en*) G-d (*theism*). To be more precise, it is *apophatic panentheism,* ("apophatic" meaning "negation"), the belief that the existence of the universe is voided and negated within G-d's presence.

According to this deeper understanding, when we say *"G-d is one,"* we affirm that G-d is the only true existence and all other existence is voided within Him.

The *Zohar*, however, points to two different levels of G-d-consciousness, which it terms "upper unification" (*yichuda ila'ah*) and "lower unification" (*yichu-*

תתאה כי ועד הוא אחד בחלופי אתוון כי הנה
סיבת וטעם הצמצום וההסתר ההזה שהסתיר והעלים
הקדוש ברוך הוא את החיות של העולם כדי שיהיה

da tata'ah). We have not yet learned what these terms mean, and this will be the focus of our chapter. But what is already apparent is that, according to the *Zohar*, these two levels ought to be in our minds during the first two lines of the *Shema* declaration. When reciting *Deuteronomy* 6:4 we should contemplate "upper unification"; and when reciting the following line (*"Blessed be the name of His glorious kingdom forever and ever"*), we should contemplate "lower unification."

First we need to clarify: How does the phrase *"Blessed be the name of His glorious kingdom forever and ever"* imply G-d's unity?

כִּי וָעֶד הוּא אֶחָד בְּחִלּוּפֵי אַתְוָון — **Since, through exchanging letters,** the word **va-ed (*"and ever"*) can be changed into echad ("one").**

In the Kabbalistic understanding of Hebrew language, two different words may have a similar "energy" and meaning, a fact which can be decoded through the precise methodology of letter exchange (*chilufei osios*). Here the *Tanya* tells us that the word *va-ed* (the last word of the second line of the *Shema*), can be "decoded" to mean "one" through letter exchange; and that is how G-d's unity is indicated by the second line of *Shema*.

(The fact that letter exchange is required indicates that the unity is more veiled; in the Zohar's language it is "lower unity.")

How are the letters of the word *va-ed* (spelled *vav-ayin-daled*) exchanged to spell *echad* (*alef-ches-daled*)?

The *vav* is exchanged for an *alef* since they are both consonants which can be used to represent a vowel sound. (For this reason the letters *alef, hei, vav* and *yud* are all interchangeable.)

The *ayin* is exchanged for a *ches* since they are both guttural letters produced by the throat. (The guttural letters are *alef, ches, hei* and *ayin*.)

(See, at length, Rabbi Yoel Kahan, *Sefer Ha-Arachim Chabad*, volume 8 (Brooklyn: Kehos, 2009), pp. 257-330.)

SECTION TWO: G-D'S SOVEREIGNTY

In order to explain the two levels mentioned in the *Zohar*, the *Tanya* will first teach us a further lesson about the creation process.

הָעוֹלָם נִרְאָה דָּבָר נִפְרָד בִּפְנֵי עַצְמוֹ הִנֵּה הוּא יָדוּעַ
לַכֹּל כִּי תַּכְלִית בְּרִיאַת הָעוֹלָם הוּא בִּשְׁבִיל
הִתְגַּלּוּת מַלְכוּתוֹ יִתְבָּרֵךְ דְּאֵין מֶלֶךְ בְּלֹא עָם פֵּי' עִם
מִלְּשׁוֹן עוֹמְמוֹת שֶׁהֵם דְּבָרִים נִפְרָדִים וְזָרִים וּרְחוֹקִים

כִּי הִנֵּה סִיבַּת וְטַעַם הַצִּמְצוּם וְהַהֶסְתֵּר הַזֶּה — **Now** what was **the cause and reason for the diminishment and concealment** of G-d's creative energy? שֶׁהֶסְתִּיר — וְהֶעֱלִים הַקָּדוֹשׁ בָּרוּךְ הוּא אֶת הַחַיּוּת שֶׁל הָעוֹלָם — Why did **G-d conceal and hide the world's** source in Divine **energy,** כְּדֵי שֶׁיִּהְיֶה הָעוֹלָם נִרְאֶה דָּבָר נִפְרָד בִּפְנֵי עַצְמוֹ — causing the world to appear as an independent entity?

As we have learned, the diminishment was necessary to create the world. But now the *Tanya* asks, what was the reason why G-d created the world in the first place?

PRACTICAL LESSONS

The layer of Divine energy which is closest to the world is *malchus*. At that level G-d controls the universe directly, like a king.

כִּי תַּכְלִית — הִנֵּה הוּא יָדוּעַ לַכֹּל — **Now everyone is aware,** בְּרִיאַת הָעוֹלָם הוּא בִּשְׁבִיל הִתְגַּלּוּת מַלְכוּתוֹ יִתְבָּרֵךְ — that the purpose of the world's creation was to reveal G-d's sovereignty over it, דְּאֵין מֶלֶךְ בְּלֹא עָם — for *"there can be no king without a people"* (see *Rabbenu Bachaye, Genesis* 38:30).

G-d created the world so that He would be recognized by free-willed individuals. This is described in Jewish sources as a king/subject relationship, since the appointment of a king is dependent on his subjects (as opposed, for example, to a dictator, who rules without the people's consent).

The *Tanya* offers us a more nuanced reading of the saying, *"there can be no king without a people (um)."*

פֵּירוּשׁ עִם מִלְּשׁוֹן עוֹמְמוֹת — **The term** *um* ("people") here can be read as a derivative of *omemos,* "hidden," שֶׁהֵם דְּבָרִים נִפְרָדִים וְזָרִים וּרְחוֹקִים מִמַּעֲלַת הַמֶּלֶךְ — implying that the people **are separate, alien and distant from the king's level.**

Omemos is a term used to describe coals that are aflame, but whose light is obscured, hidden inside the coals (*Rashi, Pesachim* 75b). The similarity between *um* and *omemos* suggests that the people who appoint the king must be so distant from him in level that none of the king's qualities shine through them.

(The three terms "separate," "alien" and "distant" correspond here to the three spiritual worlds, *Beriah, Yetzirah* and *Asiyah—Likutei Levi Yitzchak.*)

ממעלת המלך כי אילו אפילו היו לו בנים רבים
מאד לא שייך שם מלוכה עליהם וכן אפילו על
שרים לבדם רק ברוב עם דווקא הדרת מלך ושם

The *Tanya* offers a further clarification of this point.

כִּי אִילוּ אֲפִילוּ הָיוּ לוֹ בָּנִים רַבִּים מְאֹד — **For even** if the king **were to have a huge number of children,** לֹא שַׁיָּיךְ שֵׁם מְלוּכָה עֲלֵיהֶם — **he could never be described as their "king,"** since his children are close in level to him, and are not "separate, alien or distant."

וְכֵן אֲפִילוּ עַל שָׂרִים לְבַדָּם — **Similarly,** he could not be described as a "king" **just over his ministers alone.**

The king's children, and even his staff, reflect some of the king's qualities and are therefore too close to constitute a populace.

רַק בְּרוֹב עָם דַּוְוקָא הַדְרַת מֶלֶךְ — **Rather it is specifically** *"In the multitude of people (um) is the king's glory"* (Proverbs 14:28).

Only the people who are "separate, alien and distant" from the king's level can appoint him and confer sovereign status upon him.

This helps us to understand that *"the purpose of the world's creation was to reveal G-d's sovereignty over it."* Unlike the spiritual worlds, which do reflect some of G-d's qualities, our physical world and all its contents are completely "separate, alien and distant" from G-d; the Divine light which creates them is totally hidden from them. Therefore only our physical world can act as the place

A CHASIDIC THOUGHT

Speech is called the attribute of *malchus*. This is because the king's servants can only obey his speech, as they cannot fathom his thought.

The king himself has no need for speech, but for the sake of the recipients, it was necessary for him to contract himself into a voice, and then into speech.

Nevertheless, everything is utter oneness, and all is the king alone; only the vessels are different from each other.

All of this is because the receivers cannot fathom the king's thought, and his voice could still not be understood, until he contained himself in speech.

(The Maggid of Mezritch—*Maggid Devarav le-Ya'akov*, sec. 60)

הַמּוֹרֶה עַל מִדַּת מַלְכוּתוֹ יִתְבָּרֵךְ הוּא שֵׁם אֲדֹנוּת

כִּי הוּא אָדוֹן כָּל הָאָרֶץ וְנִמְצָא כִּי מִדָּה זוֹ וְשֵׁם

זֶה הֵן הַמְהַוִּין וּמְקַיְּימִין הָעוֹלָם לִהְיוֹת עוֹלָם כְּמוֹת

שֶׁהוּא עַכְשָׁיו יֵשׁ גָּמוּר וְדָבָר נִפְרָד בִּפְנֵי עַצְמוֹ

וְאֵינוֹ בָּטֵל בִּמְצִיאוּת מַמָּשׁ כִּי בְּהִסְתַּלְּקוּת מִדָּה

זוֹ וְשֵׁם זֶה חַ"ו הָיָה הָעוֹלָם חוֹזֵר לִמְקוֹרוֹ בִּדְבַר ה' **82A**

where G-d's "sovereignty," His ability to enter into a king/subject relationship, can be revealed.

וְשֵׁם הַמּוֹרֶה עַל מִדַּת מַלְכוּתוֹ יִתְבָּרֵךְ הוּא שֵׁם אֲדֹנוּת — **And the Divine name which refers to G-d's sovereignty (***malchus***) and His direct, authoritative relationship with the world is the name *Adonai*** (enunciated *Adni* when not praying), literally "my Master," כִּי הוּא אָדוֹן כָּל הָאָרֶץ — **for He is** *"Master (Adon) of all the earth"* (*Psalms* 97:5; see *Bereishis Rabah* 17:4; *Shulchan Aruch, Orach Chaim* 5:1).

PRACTICAL LESSONS

G-d's *malchus* (sovereignty) is responsible for the world's sense of autonomy. If we didn't feel separate and in control of our lives G-d wouldn't be our King; He would be a Dictator.

In the Torah, G-d is referred to by a variety of different ent names depending on the activity He performs at any given moment. As the *Midrash* teaches:

"G-d said to Moshe: 'You wish to know My name! Well, I am called according to My actions…. When I am judging creations, I am called "Elokim," and when I am waging war against the wicked, I am called "G-d of Hosts." When I suspend judgment for a man's sins, I am called "Almighty G-d," and when I am merciful towards My world, I am called "Havayah"'" (*Shemos Rabah* 3:6).

The *Tanya* teaches us here that when G-d diminishes His light so that it will be imperceptible to the physical world, enabling Him to be in a king/subject relationship with them, He is referred to with the name *Adonai*.

וְנִמְצָא כִּי מִדָּה זוֹ וְשֵׁם זֶה הֵן הַמְהַוִּין וּמְקַיְּימִין הָעוֹלָם — **So it is this attribute** of sovereignty (*malchus*) expressed by **this name,** *Adonai*, **that brings the world into being and sustains it,** לִהְיוֹת עוֹלָם כְּמוֹת שֶׁהוּא עַכְשָׁיו — **to be a "world" as it exists in its current state,** יֵשׁ גָּמוּר וְדָבָר נִפְרָד בִּפְנֵי עַצְמוֹ — appearing as **a completely autonomous, independent entity,** וְאֵינוֹ בָּטֵל בִּמְצִיאוּת מַמָּשׁ — **without any loss of independent identity.**

כִּי בְּהִסְתַּלְּקוּת מִדָּה זוֹ וְשֵׁם זֶה חַס וְשָׁלוֹם — **For if this attribute** of sovereignty **expressed by this name,** *Adonai*, **were to depart, G-d forbid,** הָיָה הָעוֹלָם חוֹזֵר

ורוח פיו ית' ובטל שם במציאות ממש ולא היה
שם עולם עליו כלל והנה גדר ובחי' שם עולם
נופל על בחי' מקום ובחי' זמן דוקא בחי' מקום
הוא מזרח ומערב צפון דרום מעלה ומטה בחי'
זמן עבר הוה ועתיד. והנה כל בחי' אלו אין
להן שייכות במדות הקדושות העליונות כי אם
במדת מלכותו ית' לבדה שייך לומר שהוא ית'
מלך למעלה עד אין קץ ולמטה עד אין תכלית

בִּדְבַר ה' וְרוּחַ פִּיו יִתְבָּרֵךְ — לִמְקוֹרוֹ — **the world would return to its source** in G-d, — in **"G-d's word"** and **"the breath of His mouth,"** וּבָטֵל שָׁם בִּמְצִיאוּת מַמָּשׁ — **and there** in its Divine source, the world would have **no independent identity at all,** וְלֹא הָיָה שֵׁם עוֹלָם עָלָיו כְּלָל — **and it could not be called a "world" at all.**

20TH SIVAN REGULAR | 21ST SIVAN LEAP

G-d's attribute of *malchus* is responsible for concealing His presence so that the world can have a sense of autonomy.

But in addition to the (quantitative) concealment of G-d's presence, there is also a *qualitative* change in the attribute of *malchus*, which makes it different from the other Divine attributes, as the *Tanya* will now explain.

וְהִנֵּה גֶּדֶר וּבְחִינַת שֵׁם עוֹלָם נוֹפֵל עַל בְּחִינַת מָקוֹם וּבְחִינַת זְמַן דַּוְקָא — **Now anything called by the term "world" must be defined by the dimensions of space and time,** בְּחִינַת מָקוֹם הוּא מִזְרָח וּמַעֲרָב צָפוֹן דָּרוֹם מַעֲלָה וּמַטָּה — **"space" referring to east, west, north, south, up and down,** בְּחִינַת זְמַן עָבָר הֹוֶה וְעָתִיד — **and "time" referring to past, present and future,** וְהִנֵּה כָּל בְּחִינוֹת אֵלּוּ אֵין לָהֶן שַׁיָּיכוּת בְּמִדּוֹת הַקְּדוֹשׁוֹת הָעֶלְיוֹנוֹת — **but none of these qualities are applicable to any of the Divine attributes,** כִּי אִם בְּמִדַּת מַלְכוּתוֹ יִתְבָּרֵךְ לְבַדָּהּ — **except to G-d's attribute of** *malchus.*

Space and time are worldly, not G-dly, parameters. If G-d had not created the world, He would have no use for these phenomena. So it is only in His attribute of sovereignty, *which directly creates the world,* that time and space first appear in their spiritual form.

שַׁיָּיךְ לוֹמַר שֶׁהוּא יִתְבָּרֵךְ מֶלֶךְ — **Only in reference to G-d's attribute of** *malchus* **can you say "He is king"** over a certain place, לְמַעְלָה עַד אֵין קֵץ וּלְמַטָּה עַד — אֵין תַּכְלִית — **a sovereignty which extends throughout the universe,** *"upwards without limit and downwards without end"* (*Tikunei Zohar,* end of *Tikun* 57), וְכֵן לְד' סִטְרִין — **and just as His sovereignty extends up and down without limit, so too, it extends in all four** compass **directions.**

וכן לד' סטרין וכן בבחי' זמן ה' מלך ה' מלך ה'
ימלוך ונמצא שחיות המקום וכן חיות הזמן
והתהוותם מאין ליש וקיומם כל זמן קיומם הוא
ממדת מלכותו ית' ושם אדנות ב"ה ולפי שמדת

וְכֵן בִּבְחִינַת זְמַן — And likewise His sovereignty extends throughout time, past, present and future, ה' מֶלֶךְ ה' מָלָךְ ה' יִמְלוֹךְ — "G-d is King, G-d was King and G-d will be King" (Morning Liturgy).

The term "king" implies sovereignty at a certain place and time. In the case of G-d, His sovereignty is "everywhere" and "forever"; but that's still a reference to place and time, so it's referring to an attribute which can be spoken of in such terms.

וְנִמְצָא שֶׁחַיּוּת הַמָּקוֹם — It follows, then, that the energetic source of "space," וְהִתְהַוּוּתָם מֵאַיִן לְיֵשׁ — and the energetic source of "time," וְכֵן חַיּוּת הַזְּמַן — which bring space and time into being, וְקִיּוּמָם כָּל זְמַן קִיּוּמָם — and sustains them so long as they exist, הוּא מִמִּדַּת מַלְכוּתוֹ יִתְבָּרֵךְ — is the Divine attribute of sovereignty (malchus), וְשֵׁם אַדְנוּת בָּרוּךְ הוּא — and the Divine name Adonai.

In earlier chapters we learned that creation is powered by the Divine attributes of chesed and gevurah corresponding to the Divine names Havayah and Elokim. Yet here, in chapter 7, we are taught that creation is powered exclusively by the attribute of sovereignty (malchus) corresponding to the name Adonai.

How are these two teachings to be reconciled?

Malchus does not have any specific power of its own; it functions merely as a channel for the higher attributes. Practically speaking, it is malchus that directly creates and powers the universe; but it does so by drawing on the higher energies of chesed and gevurah. So creation results from a partnership between all the attributes and malchus.

There is a very important distinction, though, between chesed and gevurah themselves, and chesed and gevurah as expressed through malchus, a point which will shape the following discussion.

A CHASIDIC THOUGHT

"Creation" is really the process by which G-d becomes the universe.

As this process unfolds, there must be a stage at which Divine energy assumes some of the universe's diverse features, including the rigid boundaries of time and space. That stage is called malchus, or Divine "sovereignty."

מלכותו ית' מיוחדת במהותו ועצמותו ית' בתכלית

As far as *chesed* and *gevurah* are concerned, the world is totally insignificant. The powers of *chesed* and *gevurah* are not emanated by G-d for the sake of the world; they just represent G-d expressing Himself.

With regard to *malchus*, the opposite is true. The whole purpose of *malchus* is to make the world possible.

So if we were to ask the question: from G-d's perspective, does the world exist? The answer would be: It depends. From the perspective of *chesed* and *gevurah* (and the other attributes), the world is utterly insignificant and does not exist. But from the perspective of *malchus*, the world certainly does exist; that's why *malchus* is here in the first place, to make the world possible.

And, as we shall see later in the chapter, this is the key difference between the *Zohar's* terms "upper" and "lower unification." "Upper unification" is dominated by the perspective of the attributes above *malchus,* where the world's identity is totally voided by G-d. In "lower unification" the perspective shifts towards *malchus* itself, where the world exists, but is dependent on the Divine energy (of *malchus*) that sustains it.

SECTION THREE: UPPER UNIFICATION

A problem with what we have learned so far is: We are creations that are a product of *malchus*, and from the perspective of *malchus* the existence of the world is real, so how can we ever achieve the perspective that nothing exists outside G-d?

The deeper reality that the world's existence is "null and void" seems to be something experienced by the Divine attributes themselves, but not by *malchus* or the world created through it.

As we shall soon see, however, this is not the case, because *malchus* does not exist independently; it is enmeshed with the attributes above it, the level at which the universe's existence is totally null and void!

The degree of this enmeshment of *malchus* with the higher attributes is the context of the *Zohar's* terms "upper unification" and "lower unification." When *malchus* is deeply enmeshed with the higher attributes, in "upper unification," *malchus* too adopts an energy of transcendence, absorbing the reality that the world's existence is null and void. But when *malchus* is less enmeshed with the attributes, in a state of "lower unification," the confines of space and time become more apparent.

First, the *Tanya* will discuss "upper unification."

היחוד כמו שיתבאר הלכך גם בחי' המקום
והזמן בטילים במציאות ממש לגבי מהותו ועצמותו
ית' כביטול אור השמש בשמש וזהו שילוב שם
אדנות בשם הוי"ה כי שם הוי"ה מורה שהוא
למעלה מן הזמן שהוא היה הוה ויהיה ברגע א'

וּלְפִי שֶׁמִּדַּת מַלְכוּתוֹ יִתְבָּרֵךְ מְיוּחֶדֶת בְּמַהוּתוֹ וְעַצְמוּתוֹ יִתְבָּרֵךְ בְּתַכְלִית הַיִּחוּד כְּמוֹ
שֶׁיִּתְבָּאֵר — **And since, as we will explain, G-d's attribute of** *malchus* **is merged
in perfect union with** the upper attributes, which express **G-d's** transcendent
essence and being beyond the world, הִלְכָּךְ גַּם בְּחִינוֹת הַמָּקוֹם וְהַזְּמַן בְּטֵילִים
בִּמְצִיאוּת מַמָּשׁ לְגַבֵּי מַהוּתוֹ וְעַצְמוּתוֹ יִתְבָּרֵךְ — **therefore,** when *malchus* is deeply enmeshed with the higher attributes in "upper unification," then **space and
time,** which are created through *malchus,* **are also voided of their independent
identity by the** transcendent **essence and being of G-d,** כְּבִיטוּל אוֹר הַשֶּׁמֶשׁ
בַּשֶּׁמֶשׁ — **like** the identity of a ray of **sunlight is voided in the sun.**

From the perspective of *malchus* itself, the world exists. But when *malchus*
is deeply enmeshed with the Divine attributes above, in "upper unification,"
malchus acts as a channel for that higher reality, and the limitations of time and
space are flooded with the higher awareness that everything is voided in G-d's
presence.

To illustrate how this deep enmeshment takes place, the *Tanya* gives us an
illustration with a Divine name.

וְזֶהוּ שִׁילוּב שֵׁם אַדְנוּת בְּשֵׁם הֲוָיָ"ה — **This** "upper unification," the deep enmeshment of *malchus* with the higher attributes **is** represented by **the blending of
the name** *Adonai* **into the name** *Havayah,* spelling **יאהדונהי.**

The "Octogrammaton" (יאהדונהי) is a Divine name formed by alternating the
letters of *Havayah* (י-ה-ו-ה) and *Adonai* (אדני). As we have learned, *Adonai* is
a name associated with *malchus. Havayah,* in this case, represents the transcendent energies above *malchus.* In the Octogrammaton, both names are
blended together, symbolic of "upper unification" where *malchus* becomes
deeply enmeshed in the higher attributes.

The key here is the first letter. The Octogrammaton begins with a *yud* (from
Havayah), indicating that *Havayah* is the dominant energy and *Adonai* is subsumed and absorbed within it.

The *Tanya* explains why *Havayah* is a name appropriate for the attributes
above *malchus.*

כִּי שֵׁם הֲוָיָ"ה מוֹרֶה שֶׁהוּא לְמַעֲלָה מִן הַזְּמַן — **For** *Havayah* **refers** to G-d as He
transcends time, שֶׁהוּא הָיָה הֹוֶה וְיִהְיֶה בְּרֶגַע אֶחָד — **how He is past, present and**

כמ"ש [בר"מ פרשת פנחס] וכן למעלה מבחי' מקום
כי הוא מהוה תמיד את כל בחי' המקום כולו
מלמעלה עד למטה ולד' סטרין. והנה אף על פי

future all at once, [בְּרַעְיָא מְהֵימְנָא פָּרָשַׁת פִּנְחָס] כְּמוֹ שֶׁכָּתוּב — **as stated in** the *Zohar, **Raya Mehemna, Parshas Pinchas** 3, 257b.

The word *Havayah* is a composite of the three words *hayah* (past), *hoveh* (present) and *yihyeh* (future), indicating a perspective that transcends time.

כִּי הוּא מְהַוֶּה וְכֵן לְמַעְלָה מִבְּחִינַת מָקוֹם — **Similarly,** *Havayah* **transcends space,** תָּמִיד אֶת כָּל בְּחִינַת הַמָּקוֹם כּוּלוֹ — **since** *Havayah* **is the one which continual-ly,** though indirectly, **powers existence (*mehaveh*) to all dimensions of space,** מִלְמַעְלָה עַד לְמַטָּה וּלְד' סְטְרִין — **up, down, and the four** compass **directions.**

As we have seen, it is *malchus* (*Adonai*) that is the *direct* cause of creation. But since *malchus* has no power of its own, and draws all its energy from the attributes above (*Havayah*), the name *Havayah* is also described as having creative power. This is hinted to by the similarity of the words *Havayah* and *mehaveh* ("brings into being").

So, to sum up what we have just learned: "Upper unification" occurs when *malchus* is strongly enmeshed with the Divine attributes above it, and takes on their transcendent energy, from which point of view the universe is "null and void."

But even at "upper unification" the world does not cease to exist. The world/*malchus*, *while retaining its limitations*, gets an overwhelming sense of the higher truth that, in reality, it is null and void.

The point is captured by the *Talmud's* description of the Holy Ark in the Tem-ple, which *"took up no space"* (*Yoma* 21a). That didn't mean the Ark disap-peared; it still measured *"two and a half cubits long, and a cubit and a half wide"* (*Exodus* 25:10). But when the Ark was placed in the center of the Holy of Holies, it took up no space. (The Holy of Holies measured twenty by twenty cubits, but the measurement from each side of the Holy of Holies to the Ark was ten cubits. So the Ark effectively took up no space.) *Space itself collapsed into a consciousness of no-space.*

SECTION FOUR: "LOWER" UNIFICATION

21ST SIVAN REGULAR | 22ND SIVAN LEAP

Now we turn to "lower unification."

וְהִנֵּה אַף עַל פִּי שֶׁהוּא יִתְבָּרֵךְ לְמַעְלָה מֵהַמָּקוֹם וְהַזְמָן אַף עַל פִּי כֵן הוּא נִמְצָא גַּם לְמַטָּה בְּמָקוֹם וּזְמַן — **Now, even though G-d transcends space and time, He is nev-**

שֶׁהוּא יִת׳ לְמַעְלָה מֵהַמָּקוֹם וְהַזְּמַן אַף עַל פִּי כֵן
הוּא נִמְצָא גַּם לְמַטָּה בְּמָקוֹם וּזְמַן דְּהַיְינוּ
שֶׁמִּתְיַיחֵד בְּמִדַּת מַלְכוּתוֹ שֶׁמִּמֶּנָּה נִמְשָׁךְ וְנִתְהַוָּה
הַמָּקוֹם וְהַזְּמַן וְזֶהוּ יִחוּדָא תַּתָּאָה [שִׁילוּב הֲוָי״ה
בַּאֲדֹנוּת בְּ״ה] דְּהַיְינוּ שֶׁמַּהוּתוֹ וְעַצְמוּתוֹ יִתְבָּרֵךְ
הַנִּקְרָא בְּשֵׁם אֵין סוֹף בָּרוּךְ הוּא מְלֹא אֶת כָּל הָאָרֶץ

82B

ertheless present down here, within space and time, דְּהַיְינוּ שֶׁמִּתְיַיחֵד בְּמִדַּת
מַלְכוּתוֹ שֶׁמִּמֶּנָּה נִמְשָׁךְ וְנִתְהַוָּה הַמָּקוֹם וְהַזְּמַן — **spiritually, this means that** G-d **is
merged with His attribute of** malchus, **from which space and time are derived.**

וְזֶהוּ יִחוּדָא תַּתָּאָה — **And this is** what the Zohar means by **"lower unification."**

Unlike "upper unification," where the confines of space and time dissolve, in
"lower unification" they are very much apparent. The weaker enmeshment of
malchus with the higher attributes in "lower unification" results in an awareness
of G-d within space and time, but not to the extent that space and time lose
their boundaries.

A good illustration of "lower unification" is the phenomenon of a "miracle
within the natural order," such as the story of Purim in Megillas Esther. No laws
of physics are violated, but there is a strong sense of G-d's presence within the
normal boundaries of space and time.

PRACTICAL LESSONS

In "upper unification,"
G-d's unity transcends
and surpasses all
being. In "lower
unification," G-d's
unity embraces the
variety and richness
of the universe.

[שִׁילוּב הֲוָי״ה בַּאֲדֹנוּת בָּרוּךְ הוּא] — "Lower unification"
is indicated by the **enmeshment of the Divine name**
Havayah **into the name** Adonai, **spelling** אידהנויה.

In "lower unification," the perspective of malchus
(worldly limitation) predominates. This is symbolized
by the Divine name אידהנויה, which contains the letters of both Adonai (malchus) and Havayah (higher
attributes), but, in this combination, the first letter is
the alef of Adonai, indicating that the perspective of
malchus predominates (see Rabbi Shneur Zalman, Likutei Torah, Shir Ha-Shirim 65d).

The Tanya elaborates further on the perspective of
"lower unity."

דְּהַיְינוּ שֶׁמַּהוּתוֹ וְעַצְמוּתוֹ יִתְבָּרֵךְ הַנִּקְרָא בְּשֵׁם אֵין סוֹף בָּרוּךְ
הוּא — **This means that the very essence and being of**
G-d, **which we call the Blessed** Ein Sof **("Infinite One"),** מְלֹא אֶת כָּל הָאָרֶץ מַמָּשׁ
בִּזְמַן וּמָקוֹם — **actually fills the earth and is present in space and time.**

In "lower unification," the universe is acutely conscious of G-d's presence,
but space and time remain unchanged.

ממש בזמן ומקום כי בשמים ממעל ובארץ ולד'
סטרין הכל מלא מאור א"ס ב"ה בשוה ממש כי
כך הוא בארץ מתחת כמו בשמים ממעל ממש
כי הכל הוא בחי' מקום הבטל במציאות באור
אין סוף ברוך הוא המתלבש בו על ידי מדת
מלכותו המיוחדת בו ית' רק שמדת מלכותו היא

כִּי בַּשָּׁמַיִם מִמַּעַל וּבָאָרֶץ וְלד' סְטְרִין — **For** in "lower unification" we are aware that **"in the heavens above and in the earth** below" (Deuteronomy 4:39), **and in** all **four directions,** הַכֹּל מָלֵא מֵאוֹר אֵין סוֹף בָּרוּךְ הוּא בְּשָׁוֶה מַמָּשׁ — **everything is filled with the** Ohr Ein Sof, G-d's infinite, transcendent light, **equally so.**

In "lower unification" we are aware of the presence of G-d's transcendent light (Ohr Ein Sof) everywhere. This light is present everywhere equally, since, being transcendent, it is not affected by any worldly distinctions.

כִּי כָּךְ הוּא בָּאָרֶץ מִתַּחַת כְּמוֹ בַּשָּׁמַיִם מִמַּעַל מַמָּשׁ — In "lower unification" we are aware **that** Ohr Ein Sof is present **"in the earth below" just as in the "heavens above,"** כִּי הַכֹּל הוּא בְּחִינַת מָקוֹם — **for all** those distinctions of "below" and "above," **are aspects of "space,"** הַבָּטֵל בִּמְצִיאוּת בְּאוֹר אֵין סוֹף בָּרוּךְ הוּא — **and** we are aware that space is **voided of any identity by the** Ohr Ein Sof.

הַמִּתְלַבֵּשׁ בּוֹ עַל יְדֵי מִדַּת מַלְכוּתוֹ — And while we see that space and time exist, we are aware that Ohr Ein Sof is present here since it **"dressed" into space by means of the Divine attribute of** malchus, which recognizes the confines of space and time, הַמְיוּחֶדֶת בּוֹ יִתְבָּרֵךְ — **and** malchus **is merged with G-d's** higher attributes of transcendence, causing Ohr Ein Sof to fill the universe.

A CHASIDIC THOUGHT

Malchus is a paradox. It is close enough to the One to be a Divine attribute; but it is also close enough to the world to power multitudes of diversity.

Since it exists in a paradox, malchus cannot sit statically; it exists in dynamic tension. Sometimes malchus is closer to the One. Sometimes, while remaining bound with the One, it shifts to be a little closer to the world.

When malchus is closer to the One, its space/time contours become fluid and non-apparent. We call this state "upper unification."

When malchus shifts toward the world, its contours sharpen and act as a container for the infinite. We call this "lower unification."

מדת הצמצום וההסתר להסתיר אור אין סוף ב״ה
שלא יבטלו הזמן והמקום ממציאותם לגמרי ולא
יהיה שום בחי׳ זמן ומקום במציאות אפילו
לתחתונים. והנה במ״ש יובן מ״ש אני ה׳
לא שניתי פי׳ שאין שום שינוי כלל כמו שהיה
לבדו קודם בריאת העולם כך הוא לבדו אחר
שנברא וז״ש אתה הוא עד שלא נברא העולם

How, then, do space and time still exist?

רַק שֶׁמִּדַּת מַלְכוּתוֹ הִיא מִדַּת הַצִּמְצוּם וְהַהֶסְתֵּר — **Only, since the Divine attribute of** *malchus* **is a power of diminishment and concealment,** לְהַסְתִּיר אוֹר אֵין סוֹף — *malchus* **hides the** *Ohr Ein Sof* בָּרוּךְ הוּא שֶׁלֹּא יְבָטְלוּ הַזְּמַן וְהַמָּקוֹם מִמְּצִיאוּתָם לְגַמְרֵי — **so that "time" and "place" won't be completely voided of their independent existence,** וְלֹא יִהְיֶה שׁוּם בְּחִינַת זְמַן וּמָקוֹם בְּמְצִיאוּת אֲפִילוּ לַתַּחְתּוֹנִים — **which would deny the existence of "time" and "space" even to the lowest, physical world.**

All this represents the *"enmeshment of Havayah into Adonai."* The limitations of space and time remain plainly apparent, since *Adonai* (*malchus*) predominates. Nevertheless, within space and time we are deeply aware that the *Ohr Ein Sof* is everywhere, since *Adonai* has absorbed *Havayah*.

SECTION FIVE: G-D REMAINS ALONE

22ND SIVAN REGULAR | 23RD SIVAN LEAP

The notion that the world's existence is voided in G-d's presence is largely an innovation of Chasidic thought (with some precedent in the Kabbalah), but it is hinted in some classic texts, as we shall now see. (These sources were also cited in the first book of *Tanya*, chapter 20.)

וְהִנֵּה בְּמַה שֶׁנִּתְבָּאֵר יוּבַן מַה שֶׁכָּתוּב אֲנִי ה׳ לֹא שָׁנִיתִי — **Now, based on what we have explained above we will be able to** better understand the verse, *"I, G-d, have not changed"* (*Malachi* 3:6), פֵּירוּשׁ שֶׁאֵין שׁוּם שִׁינוּי כְּלָל — **which means that** G-d's status of being alone in the universe **has not changed at all** through the creation process, כְּמוֹ שֶׁהָיָה לְבַדּוֹ קוֹדֶם בְּרִיאַת הָעוֹלָם כָּךְ הוּא לְבַדּוֹ אַחַר שֶׁנִּבְרָא — **just as He was alone before the creation of the world, so too, He is alone, now, after the creation.**

וְזֶהוּ שֶׁאוֹמְרִים אַתָּה הוּא עַד שֶׁלֹּא נִבְרָא הָעוֹלָם אַתָּה הוּא כו׳ — **And that is the meaning of what we say,** *"You were alone before the world was created; You*

אתה הוא כו' בלי שום שינוי בעצמותו ולא

are alone since the world has been created" (Morning Liturgy), בְּלִי שׁוּם שִׁינּוּי בְּעַצְמוּתוֹ — **without any change in His self.**

From all that we have learned, both in Chapter Seven and in the preceding chapters, the voiding of the world's existence can be understood on four different levels.

1.) That the world exists, but since its continued existence is constantly dependent on "G-d's word" it has no independent existence (as we learned in Chapters 1-2). This is the perspective from G-d's attribute of *malchus,* which dims and molds Divine energy so that it can power the universe.

2.) At the other extreme, from the perspective of G-d's transcendent attributes above *malchus,* there is no significance to the world whatsoever. The world does exist, but its identity is completely voided like a ray of light in the globe of the sun (as we learned in Chapter 3).

Between these perspectives, there are two intermediate levels, where *malchus* partially adopts, to differing extents, the view of the transcendent attributes.

3.) If the energy of *malchus* is merely open and receptive to the transcendent attributes, we have the weaker enmeshment of "lower unification." Here, the confines of space and time become conscious of the limitless energy of the transcendent attributes.

4.) If there is a stronger enmeshment, and *malchus* significantly loses its identity in the higher attributes ("upper unification"), then the world/*malchus,* while retaining its limitations, gets an overwhelming sense of the higher truth that, in reality, it is null and void.

According to *any* of these four perspectives, it could be said that *"I, G-d, have not changed,"* i.e., that the world is not significant enough to actually exist as a separate entity from G-d. The creation of the world did not change G-d's status of being alone in the universe.

SECTION SIX: G-D'S KNOWLEDGE

In this section, the *Tanya* addresses another factor which, at first glance, seems to affect G-d's status of being utterly "alone" and "without change": G-d's knowledge.

When you acquire information, something has been added to you. So you might imagine that when G-d knows something, there is some sort of "addition" to Him too. Obviously, this would be happening *within G-d,* and His knowledge

בדעתו כי בידיעת עצמו יודע כל הנבראים שהכל

would not be a separate thing from Him, but you still might argue that G-d is now not "alone" any more, as He has been "joined" by His knowledge of the universe!

This question was discussed extensively by *Rambam* (Maimonides) in his works, and the *Tanya* cites *Rambam's* explanation here.

וְלֹא בְּדַעְתּוֹ — G-d remains alone and that status is **not** affected **by His knowledge** of the universe, כִּי בִּידִיעַת עַצְמוֹ יוֹדֵעַ כָּל הַנִּבְרָאִים — **because by knowing Himself He knows all the creations** (*Mishneh Torah, Laws of Foundations of the Torah* 2:9).

In Part One of the *Tanya*, Chapter 42, this point has already been discussed. G-d knows everything, not through an active process of *acquiring* knowledge, but,

"like a person knows and feels everything that's happening and occurring in each of the 248 limbs of his body like cold or heat or even, to give an extreme example, heat in his toenail when it's scorched by fire, and a person also intuitively knows the status of the actual limbs themselves, in their core, and all that is affected in them, he knows and feels automatically in his brain, without having to consciously 'collect' the information."

"In a vaguely comparable fashion to this example of 'automatic' knowing from within, G-d knows everything that's happening to all the creations, upper and lower, since the life energy of all creations flows from Him, as the verse states, 'for from You, all things come' (1 Chronicles 29:14)."

A CHASIDIC THOUGHT

"Be conscious that everything—whether it be planetary space, the angelic world or the celestial throne room—all is like zero before G-d."

"For all these things exist merely within the vacated space of G-d's diminished light. Everything came into being merely from G-d's speech."

"Why, then, should you be drawn after anything desirable in any of those worlds, when it's all just a word of G-d? It's better to attach yourself to the main thing, to G-d, who is beyond the worlds, than to be attached to something secondary" (The *Ba'al Shem Tov—Tzava'as Ha-Rivash* 84).

ממנו ובטל במציאות אצלו וכמ"ש הרמב"ם ז"ל
שהוא היודע והוא הידוע והוא הדיעה עצמה הכל
אחד ודבר זה אין כח בפה לאמרו ולא באזן
לשמעו ולא בלב האדם להכירו על בוריו כי
הקב"ה מהותו ועצמותו ודעתו הכל אחד ממש
מכל צד ופינה בכל דרך יחוד ואין דעתו דבר
נוסף על מהותו ועצמותו כמו שהוא בנפש האדם
שדעתה דבר נוסף על מהותה ומורכב בה שהרי

שֶׁהַכֹּל מִמֶּנּוּ וּבָטֵל בִּמְצִיאוּת אֶצְלוֹ — **Since everything is from Him, and voided of any separate identity in His presence,** it is as if the world is an "extension" of Him, so, *"by knowing Himself He knows all the creations."*

The *Tanya* cites a further discussion of this idea in the works of *Rambam*.

וּכְמוֹ שֶׁכָּתַב הָרַמְבַּ"ם זִכְרוֹנוֹ לִבְרָכָה — **And, as *Rambam* of blessed memory writes,** שֶׁהוּא הַיּוֹדֵעַ וְהוּא הַיָּדוּעַ וְהוּא הַדֵּיעָה עַצְמָה הַכֹּל אֶחָד — that *"G-d is the 'knower,' the 'known' and the 'knowledge' itself, all are one,"* וְדָבָר זֶה אֵין כֹּחַ **"but the mouth** בַּפֶּה לְאָמְרוֹ וְלֹא בָאֹזֶן לְשָׁמְעוֹ וְלֹא בַלֵּב הָאָדָם לְהַכִּירוֹ עַל בּוּרְיוֹ — **has no power to express this idea, nor the ear to hear it, nor the heart of man to recognize it properly"** (*Laws of Foundations of the Torah ibid.,* 10).

G-d is not separate from His knowledge We, however, have no frame of reference to truly understand this phenomenon, since human knowledge is always separate and acquired.

Nevertheless, *Rambam* stresses that man cannot "recognize it *properly,"* suggesting that we can have *some* appreciation of this idea, but not a substantial one (*Notes on Tanya*).

To help us have more insight, the *Tanya* elaborates on this concept further.

כִּי הַקָּדוֹשׁ בָּרוּךְ הוּא מַהוּתוֹ וְעַצְמוּתוֹ וְדַעְתּוֹ הַכֹּל אֶחָד מַמָּשׁ — **For G-d is totally one with His essence, being and knowledge,** מִכָּל צַד וּפִינָה בְּכָל דֶּרֶךְ יְחוּד — **from every possible point of view, and with every type of unity,** וְאֵין דַּעְתּוֹ דָּבָר נוֹסָף **essence and being,** עַל מַהוּתוֹ וְעַצְמוּתוֹ — **and His knowledge is not something additional to His** כְּמוֹ שֶׁהוּא בְּנֶפֶשׁ הָאָדָם שֶׁדַּעְתָּהּ דָּבָר נוֹסָף עַל מַהוּתָהּ וּמוּרְכָּב בָּה — **as is the case with man's soul, where knowledge is something extrinsic to the soul itself, grafted on to it** (*Rambam ibid.*)

The *Tanya* demonstrates why human knowledge is always acquired and external.

שֶׁהֲרֵי כְּשֶׁהָאָדָם לוֹמֵד וְיוֹדֵעַ אֵיזֶה דָּבָר כְּבָר הָיְתָה בּוֹ נַפְשׁוֹ הַמַּשְׂכֶּלֶת בְּטֶרֶם שֶׁלָּמַד וְיָדַע — **For when a person is about to learn and know something, he already pos-**

83A

כשהאדם לומד ויודע איזה דבר כבר היתה בו
נפשו המשכלת בטרם שלמד וידע ואחר שלמד
וידע ניתוספה ידיעה זו בנפשו וכן מידי יום ביום
ימים ידברו ורוב שנים יודיעו חכמה ואין זו אחדות
פשוטה אלא מורכבת אבל הקב"ה הוא אחדות
פשוט בלי שום הרכבה וצד ריבוי כלל ואם כן ע"כ
מהותו ועצמותו ודעתו הכל דבר אחד ממש בלי
שום הרכבה ולפיכך כשם שאי אפשר לשום נברא
בעולם להשיג מהות הבורא ועצמותו כך אי אפשר
להשיג מהות דעתו רק להאמין באמונה שהיא
למעלה מהמשכל ומהשגה שהקב"ה יחיד ומיוחד הוא

sesses soul-intelligence before he learns and knows that thing, וְאַחַר שֶׁלָּמַד
וְיָדַע נִיתוֹסְפָה יְדִיעָה זוֹ בְּנַפְשׁוֹ — and after he learns and knows it, that information becomes incorporated into his soul, וְכֵן מִידֵי יוֹם בְּיוֹם יָמִים יְדַבֵּרוּ וְרוֹב שָׁנִים
יוֹדִיעוּ חָכְמָה — and this remains true, as days pass and the person acquires
wisdom throughout his or her life, **"Let days speak, and let great age make
wisdom known"** (Job 32:7).

PRACTICAL LESSONS

Humans change
when they acquire
knowledge.
G-d doesn't.

וְאֵין זו אַחְדוּת פְּשׁוּטָה אֶלָּא מוּרכֶּבֶת — This human
knowledge is not a non-composite unification of
knower and knowledge, but a grafting of knowledge
upon knower.

אֲבָל הַקָּדוֹשׁ בָּרוּךְ הוּא הוּא אַחְדוּת פָּשׁוּט — But when
G-d knows something, knower and knowledge are
non-composite and one, בְּלִי שׁוּם הַרכָּבָה וְצַד רִיבּוּי כְּלָל
— there is no mixture of multiple components at all,
וְאִם כֵּן עַל כָּרְחָךְ מַהוּתוֹ וְעַצְמוּתוֹ וְדַעְתוֹ הַכֹּל דָּבָר אֶחָד
מַמָּשׁ בְּלִי שׁוּם הַרכָּבָה — so it must be the case that
G-d's essence and being and His knowledge all exist
as one, non-composite unity, literally.

וּלְפִיכָךְ כְּשֵׁם שֶׁאִי אֶפְשָׁר לְשׁוּם נִבְרָא בָּעוֹלָם לְהַשִּׂיג מַהוּת הַבּוֹרֵא וְעַצְמוּתוֹ כָּךְ אִי
אֶפְשָׁר לְהַשִּׂיג מַהוּת דַּעְתּוֹ — Therefore, it is impossible for any worldly mortal to
really understand G-d's knowledge, just as it is impossible to understand the
Creator Himself (Mishneh Torah, Laws of Teshuvah 5:5).

רַק לְהַאֲמִין בֶּאֱמוּנָה שֶׁהִיא לְמַעְלָה מֵהַשֵּׂכֶל וּמֵהַשָּׂגָה — We can **only** accept this
truth **with faith, a belief that transcends intellect and understanding,** שֶׁהַקָּדוֹשׁ

ודעתו הכל אחד ממש ובידיעת עצמו מכיר ויודע
כל הנמצאים עליונים ותחתונים עד שלשול קטן
שבים ועד יתוש קטן שיהיה בטבור הארץ אין דבר
נעלם ממנו ואין ידיעה זו מוסיפה בו ריבוי והרכבה
כלל מאחר שאינה רק ידיעת עצמו ועצמותו ודעתו
הכל אחד ולפי שזה קשה מאד לצייר בשכלנו ע"כ
אמר הנביא כי גבהו שמים מארץ כן גבהו דרכי
מדרכיכם ומחשבותי ממחשבותיכם וכתיב החקר
אלוה תמצא וגו' וכתיב העיני בשר לך אם כראות
אנוש תראה שהאדם רואה ויודע כל הדברים בידיעה

בָּרוּךְ הוּא יָחִיד וּמְיוּחָד הוּא וְדַעְתּוֹ הַכֹּל אֶחָד מַמָּשׁ — that G-d is *"the one and only one"* (*Deuteronomy Rabah,* 2:31), He is literally one with His knowledge.

וּבִידִיעַת עַצְמוֹ מַכִּיר וְיוֹדֵעַ כָּל הַנִּמְצָאִים עֶלְיוֹנִים וְתַחְתּוֹנִים — And that, through knowing Himself, He automatically knows and recognizes everything that exists in the upper and lower worlds, עַד שְׁלְשׁוּל קָטָן שֶׁבַּיָּם — right down to *"a tiny worm in the sea"* (*Shulchan Aruch, Yoreh De'ah* 4:6), וְעַד יַתוֹשׁ קָטָן שֶׁיִּהְיֶה בְּטַבּוּר הָאָרֶץ אֵין דָּבָר נֶעְלָם מִמֶּנּוּ — and down to *"the smallest mosquito in the belly of the earth... nothing is hidden from Him"* (*Mishneh Torah, Laws of Foundations of the Torah* 2:9).

וְאֵין יְדִיעָה זוֹ מוֹסִיפָה בּוֹ רִיבּוּי וְהַרְכָּבָה כְּלָל — This knowledge introduces no multiplicity or compositeness whatsoever within G-d, מֵאַחַר שֶׁאֵינָהּ רַק יְדִיעַת עַצְמוֹ — because He is merely knowing Himself, since He וְעַצְמוּתוֹ וְדַעְתּוֹ הַכֹּל אֶחָד is one with His knowledge.

Again, the *Tanya* returns to our difficulty in fully understanding this idea, as *Rambam* stated that man cannot *"recognize it properly."*

וּלְפִי שֶׁזֶּה קָשֶׁה מְאֹד לְצַיֵּיר בְּשִׂכְלֵנוּ — But since this is so difficult to picture in our minds, עַל כֵּן אָמַר הַנָּבִיא כִּי גָבְהוּ שָׁמַיִם מֵאָרֶץ כֵּן גָּבְהוּ דְרָכַי מִדַּרְכֵיכֶם — וּמַחְשְׁבוֹתַי מִמַּחְשְׁבוֹתֵיכֶם — therefore the prophet said, *"As the heavens are higher than the earth, so are My ways higher than your ways and My thoughts than your thoughts"* (*Isaiah* 55:9; cited in *Laws of Teshuvah,* ibid.), וּכְתִיב הַחֵקֶר אֱלוֹהַּ תִּמְצָא וְגו' — and the verse states, *"Can you find what G-d has probed? etc.,"* (*Job* 11:7; cited in *Laws of Foundations of the Torah,* 1:9), וּכְתִיב הַעֵינֵי בָשָׂר לָךְ אִם כִּרְאוֹת אֱנוֹשׁ תִּרְאֶה — and the verse states, *"Do You have the eyes of mortal flesh, do You see as man would see?"* (*Job* 10:4), שֶׁהָאָדָם רוֹאֶה וְיוֹדֵעַ כָּל הַדְּבָרִים בִּידִיעָה שֶׁחוּץ מִמֶּנּוּ — for man sees and knows all

שחוץ ממנו והקב"ה בידיעת עצמו עכ"ל [ע"ש בה'
יסודי התורה והסכימו עמו חכמי הקבלה כמבואר
בפרדס מהרמ"ק ז"ל]:

things with a knowledge which is apart from himself, וְהַקָּדוֹשׁ בָּרוּךְ הוּא בִּידִיעַת
עַצְמוֹ — but G-d knows everything **by knowing Himself.**

These verses express the subtle balance between our general inability to understand G-d's unity, alongside some limited success if we do apply ourselves to the task. *"Can you find what G-d has probed?"* suggests that you will not "find" and *fully* succeed in this endeavor, but you might have some limited success. As the *Rambam* has stressed, "this is *so very difficult* to picture in our minds," but not "impossible" (*Notes on Tanya*).

עַד כָּאן לְשׁוֹנוֹ — **Here ends our citation** of *Rambam's* discussion of this matter.

[עַיֵּן שָׁם בְּהִלְכוֹת יְסוֹדֵי הַתּוֹרָה — **See** *Laws of Foundations of the Torah ibid.;* *Guide For the Perplexed* 3:20-21, וְהִסְכִּימוּ עִמוֹ חַכְמֵי הַקַּבָּלָה כְּמְבוֹאָר בַּפַּרְדֵּס מֵהָרְמַ"ק זִכְרוֹנוֹ לִבְרָכָה] — **and,** in this instance, **the sages of the Kabbalah concurred** with *Rambam,* **as Rabbi Moshe Cordovero explains in** *Pardes* (4:4).

Rambam followed the school of Jewish Philosophy (*Chakirah*) that was often at odds with Kabbalah (on which the *Tanya's* theology is based), but in this case they were in agreement. (This point is discussed further in the Author's Note to Chapter Two of the *Tanya*, Part One.)

וְהִנֵּה מכאן יש להבין שגגת מקצת חכמים בעיניהם
ה' יכפר בעדם ששגו וטעו בעיונם בכתבי

IS THE TZIMTZUM LITERAL?

SECTION ONE: THE DISPUTE OVER TZIMTZUM

23RD SIVAN REGULAR | 24TH SIVAN LEAP

The following pages, until the end of this chapter, were included in the original manuscript version of the *Tanya*, circulated by the author during 1792-96 (see "Translator's Introduction," *The Practical Tanya, Part One,* p. xiii). However, the author omitted this addendum from the printed edition, which first appeared in 1796, presumably so as not to further antagonize those who had opposed the Chasidic movement (in part, due to some of the ideas presented here). The passage was omitted from the subsequent twenty-nine printings of the *Tanya,* until the Vilna edition of 1900, in which it was re-incorporated as an addendum to Chapter 7. (For details of the Vilna edition, see ibid. pp. xxi-xxii.)

וְהִנֵּה מִכָּאן יֵשׁ לְהָבִין שִׁגְגַת מִקְצָת חֲכָמִים בְּעֵינֵיהֶם — **From the discussion above** in Section Six **you will understand the error of a few** scholars, *"wise in their own eyes"* (*Isaiah* 5:21), ה' יְכֻפֵּר בַּעֲדָם — *"May G-d pardon them!"* (see 2 *Chronicles* 30:18), שֶׁשָּׁגוּ וְטָעוּ בְּעִיּוּנָם בְּכִתְבֵי הָאֲרִ"י זִכְרוֹנוֹ לִבְרָכָה — who were authentic Kabbalists but, nevertheless, **inadvertently erred in their analysis of the writings of Rabbi Yitzchak Luria of blessed memory.**

Rabbi Yitzchak Luria (*Arizal,* 1534–1572) was the most innovative and influential of the early modern kabbalists, and his teachings became the foundation of all subsequent Jewish mystical discourse. A central symbol of Arizal's Kabbalah is the *tzimtzum,* a primordial "diminishment" of the Divine Infinite, to make "space" for finite worlds.

The following is one version of Arizal's teaching of *tzimtzum,* as recorded by his student, Rabbi Chaim Vital.

"Know that before emanations were produced and creatures were created, there was an undifferentiated, supernal light that filled all existence. There was no empty space.... When it arose in His abstract will to create worlds and produce emanations... the Ein Sof (Infinite) then diminished (tzimtzem) itself...

הָאֲרִיזַ"ל וְהֵבִינוּ עִנְיַן הַצִּמְצוּם הַמּוּזְכָּר שָׁם כִּפְשׁוּטוֹ
שֶׁהַקַּבַּ"ה סִילֵק עַצְמוֹ וּמַהוּתוֹ ח"ו מֵעוֹהַ"ז רַק שֶׁמַּשְׁגִיחַ

removing itself on all sides from around the central point. Then there was an empty space, a complete vacuum... in such a manner that empty space was a circle completely equidistant all around" (Etz Chaim 1:2).

וְהֵבִינוּ עִנְיַן הַצִּמְצוּם הַמּוּזְכָּר שָׁם כִּפְשׁוּטוֹ — Certain scholars **understood the concept of** *tzimtzum* (diminishment of the Divine) **mentioned there** in *Arizal's* writings, **in a literal way (*ki-peshuto*),** שֶׁהַקָּדוֹשׁ בָּרוּךְ הוּא סִילֵק עַצְמוֹ וּמַהוּתוֹ חַס וְשָׁלוֹם מֵעוֹלָם הַזֶּה — **meaning that** they understood that, in the act of *tzimtzum,* **G-d Himself** *actually* **departed from** the place where He later created **this world, G-d forbid.**

The first and most prominent author to argue forcefully that the *tzimtzum* was to be interpreted literally was Raphael Immanuel Chai Ricchi (1688–1743), an Italian Kabbalist who later settled in Safed, Israel. Rabbi Ricchi became an authority on Arizal's Kabbalah through his influential work *Mishnas Chasidim* (Amsterdam, 1727), a systematic summary of Arizal's writings. *Mishnas Chasidim* was a highly authoritative work, relied upon many times by the author of *Tanya* himself.

In *Yosher Levav* (Amsterdam, 1737), Rabbi Ricchi offered a lengthy argument why the *tzimtzum* must be read literally. His central proof for this position was, *"so that you do not come to tarnish G-d's honor and think that G-d is actually present in the low, dishonorable, physical and even disgusting things, G-d forbid, because without tzimtzum (taken literally), there would be no place empty of His self" (Yosher Levav, Batei Ha-lev* 1:12).

Why did the *Tanya* reject those who adopted *Yosher Levav's* position so strongly, even writing, *"May G-d pardon them"*?

As we shall see in the next section, the question of whether the *tzimtzum* is literal is a matter of central importance, since it touches on two principles of faith. This point was stressed by Rabbi Yosef Irgas (1685-1730), a contemporary

A CHASIDIC THOUGHT

The story of the *tzimtzum* aims to answer the question: If all is One, why don't we experience it that way? Why does the universe appear so fragmented?

But if the answer to that question is *too good*, we have made fragmentation real; we have sacrificed the One. So we mustn't take the *tzimtzum* literally.

מלמעלה בהשגחה פרטית על כל היצורים כולם 83B
אשר בשמים ממעל ועל הארץ מתחת והנה מלבד

of Rabbi Ricchi and a strong advocate for the non-literal reading of *tzimtzum.* After offering ten arguments why the *tzimtzum* must be read non-literally, Rabbi Irgas concludes: *"Anyone who understands tzimtzum literally will come to make many mistakes and will come to contradict many of the principles of faith"* (Rabbi Yosef Irgas, *Shomer Emunim, vikuach sheni,* sec. 35).

The rejection of a literal reading of *tzimtzum* is something Rabbi Shneur Zalman received from his teacher, the Magid of Mezritch. Rabbi Hillel Malisov of Paritch (1795-1864), one of Rabbi Shneur Zalman's prominent disciples, noted that his master had, *"heard in Mezritch... not to understand the tzimtzum literally"* (Rabbi Hillel Malisov, *Likutei Biurim* to Rabbi Dov Ber of Lubavitch, *Sha'ar Ha-Yichud, Kehos* 1995, p. 180).

In one of Rabbi Shneur Zalman's discourses, the emphasis on sharply rejecting a literal reading of *tzimtzum* is attributed to the *Ba'al Shem Tov* himself. He states that *tzimtzum "needs to be understood well and thoroughly, divorced from any physical connotation, for the Ba'al Shem Tov protested against those who studied Kabbalah and did not know to interpret [its symbols] non-physically"* (*Ma'amarei Admor Ha-Zaken, Inyanim* p. 318).

In the view of those who interpreted the *tzimtzum* literally, how does G-d interact with the world if He has actually removed Himself from it?

רַק שֶׁמַּשְׁגִּיחַ מִלְמַעְלָה בְּהַשְׁגָּחָה פְּרָטִית — Those who interpret the *tzimtzum* literally understand that G-d is not Himself present in the world but **merely supervises from above, through Divine providence,** עַל כָּל הַיְצוּרִים כּוּלָּם אֲשֶׁר בַּשָּׁמַיִם מִמַּעַל וְעַל הָאָרֶץ מִתָּחַת — **over every single creation, "*in the heavens above and in the earth below*"** (*Deuteronomy* 4:39).

Those who took the *tzimtzum* literally did not believe that G-d had abandoned the world. In this view, while G-d is seen to have removed His *sacred presence* from the mundane physical world, He is still understood to be supervising and controlling its every detail (*Yosher Levav,* ibid. 13).

This point, whether G-d's presence is to be found within mundane physical objects (discussed at length later in this chapter), was one of the key points of contention between the early Chasidic movement and its opponents (*misnagdim*). It was one of the reasons why *Tzava'as Ha-Rivash,* an early compilation of the teachings of the *Ba'al Shem Tov* and Maggid of Mezritch, was publicly burned by the *misnagdim.*

The concept was also referred to by Rabbi Eliyahu the *Ga'on* of Vilna (1720-1797), the most authoritative Torah scholar in Europe at the time, in his 1796 public proclamation against the Chasidic movement. Responding to *Tzava'as*

שא"א כלל לומר ענין הצמצום כפשוטו שהוא ממקרי
הגוף על הקב"ה הנבדל מהם ריבוא רבבות הבדלות

Ha-Rivash's statement, *"Everything in the universe contains holy sparks... even sticks and stones"* (ibid., par. 141), the *Ga'on* wrote that Chasidim *"misinterpret the Torah... and proclaim of every stick and every stone, 'These are your gods, Israel!'* (*Exodus* 32:8)," words proclaimed by the worshipers of the Golden Calf! (The letter is reproduced in Mordechai Wilensky, *Chasidim u-Misnagdim,* vol. 1, pp. 188–189).

Since the two ideas (interpreting the *tzimtzum* non-literally, and the presence of the Divine in "sticks and stones") are closely linked, we would expect to find that the *Ga'on* understood the *tzimtzum* more literally. While this is not stated explicitly in his writings (he never uses the terms "literal" or "non-literal"), some of the *Ga'on's* statements imply that he did embrace a literal reading. The strongest such indication is his description of the Divine re-emergence after the *tzimtzum* (known as the *kav,* or "line") as mere Divine "providence" and not the presence of G-d Himself (*Likutei Ha-Gra,* appended to *Sifra De-Tzinusa im biur Ha-Gra,* Vilna 1912, p. 38a). This, as the *Tanya* stated above, is a hallmark of the literalist camp. In another text, the Vilna Ga'on describes the *tzimtzum* as a "removal" of the Divine, a term used by those who interpret the doctrine literally (*Asarah Klalim, Klal* 2, in Yosef Avivi, *Kabalas Ha-Gra,* Jerusalem 1993).

It is no wonder, then, that Rabbi Shneur Zalman chose to omit this entire "addendum" from the printed version of the *Tanya,* since it contains a lengthy explanation of how G-d is present in physical objects, even "stones." The ideas here had clearly resulted in much hardship for Chasidim, as they had contributed to the *Ga'on's* intense hostility to Chasidism. (The Ga'on had just publicly declared, a few months before the *Tanya* was sent to print, *"Anyone who is called a Jew, whose heart is touched by fear of G-d, it is incumbent upon him to repulse them and persecute them [the Chasidim] with every kind of persecution and subjugate them wherever the hand of a Jew can reach"*—letter of *Rosh Chodesh Sivan* 1796, Wilensky, pp. 183-4.)

Furthermore, since the *Ga'on* appears to have been sympathetic towards the view that the *tzimtzum* was literal, sharp criticism of that position here in the *Tanya* could have easily been interpreted as an attack by the author on the *Ga'on* himself!

This was unlikely to have been the author's intention as, generally speaking, Rabbi Shneur Zalman's approach to navigating opposition to his movement was one of moderation, and restraint from retaliation when attacked. It would also be highly out of character for Rabbi Shneur Zalman to charge the *Ga'on* with heresy, when in other writings he accords him the utmost respect.

עַד אֵין קֵץ אַף גַּם זֹאת לֹא בְדַעַת יְדַבְּרוּ מֵאַחַר
שֶׁהֵם מַאֲמִינִים בְּנֵי מַאֲמִינִים שֶׁהַקָּבָּ"ה יוֹדֵעַ כָּל
הַיְצוּרִים שֶׁבָּעוֹהָ"ז הַשָּׁפֵל וּמַשְׁגִּיחַ עֲלֵיהֶם וְעַ"כ אֵין
יְדִיעָתוֹ אוֹתָם מוֹסִיפָה בּוֹ רִיבּוּי וְחִידוּשׁ מִפְּנֵי שֶׁיּוֹדֵעַ

Rather, the author's intention here, as in the rest of *Tanya*, appears to have been scholarly rather than polemical. He sought to explain the fundamental world-view of Chasidism, that all objects, even sticks and stones, are saturated with the Divine presence. And since Rabbi Shneur Zalman's writings are characterized by placing Chasidism in the context of Arizal's Kabbalah, he chose to make clear that the Chasidic worldview is based on a rejection of a literal reading of Arizal's *tzimtzum*.

SECTION TWO: PROOFS THAT THE TZIMTZUM IS NOT LITERAL

Having stated that Chasidism is based on a rejection of a literal reading of *tzimtzum*, the *Tanya* offers two arguments to support the non-literal approach.

וְהִנֵּה מִלְּבַד שֶׁאִי אֶפְשָׁר כְּלָל לוֹמַר עִנְיַן הַצִּמְצוּם כִּפְשׁוּטוֹ — **Now besides the fact that taking the *tzimtzum* literally is totally unacceptable** according to *Rambam's* Third Principle of Faith, שֶׁהוּא מִמִּקְרֵי הַגּוּף עַל הַקָּדוֹשׁ בָּרוּךְ הוּא — **since** a literal reading of *tzimtzum* **attributes corporeal qualities to G-d,** הַנִּבְדָּל מֵהֶם רִיבּוֹא רְבָבוֹת הַבְדָּלוֹת עַד אֵין קֵץ — **who is endlessly and infinitely removed from them** (*Rambam, Laws of Foundations of the Torah* 1:7, 11).

Rabbi Shneur Zalman argues that a literal reading of *tzimtzum* contravenes the logic underlying *Rambam's* Third Principle of Faith, that G-d is incorporeal. Having a body means you are found in one place, and not in another. If G-d can literally remove Himself from a physical space, it means that G-d is subject to properties of the physical world, which in turn implies corporeality.

Another objection to the position arises from *Rambam's* comments cited in Section Six above, that G-d knows the world through knowing Himself.

אַף גַּם זֹאת לֹא בְדַעַת יְדַבֵּרוּ — **Also,** those who say the *tzimtzum* is literal *"speak without knowledge"* (*Job* 34:35), מֵאַחַר שֶׁהֵם מַאֲמִינִים בְּנֵי מַאֲמִינִים שֶׁהַקָּדוֹשׁ — **for they,** too, are *"believers, the children of believers"* (*Talmud, Shabbos* 97a), בָּרוּךְ הוּא יוֹדֵעַ כָּל הַיְצוּרִים שֶׁבָּעוֹלָם הַזֶּה הַשָּׁפֵל — that G-d *"knows all things formed"* (Liturgy, High Holidays), **in this lowly world,** וּמַשְׁגִּיחַ עֲלֵיהֶם — **and He supervises** all worldly things, so He must also know them in order to supervise them, וְעַל כָּרְחָךְ אֵין יְדִיעָתוֹ אוֹתָם מוֹסִיפָה בּוֹ רִיבּוּי וְחִידוּשׁ — **and you have to admit that through knowing them, no addition or change is imposed on Him,**

הכל בידיעת עצמו הרי כביכול מהותו ועצמותו
ודעתו הכל א' וז"ש בתקונים תיקון נ"ז דלית אתר
פנוי מיניה לא בעילאין ולא בתתאין ובר"מ פ' פנחס
איהו תפיס בכולא ולית מאן דתפיס ביה כו' איהו

מִפְּנֵי שֶׁיּוֹדֵעַ הַכֹּל בִּידִיעַת עַצְמוֹ — because, as we learned above from *Rambam*,
He knows them all through knowing Himself, הֲרֵי כִּבְיָכוֹל מַהוּתוֹ וְעַצְמוּתוֹ וְדַעְתּוֹ
הַכֹּל אֶחָד — and, so to speak, His essence and being is one with His knowledge.

In Chapter Seven, Section Six, we learned *Rambam's* explanation that G-d is
not separate from His knowledge. If G-d had literally removed Himself from the
world, there would be a split between His knowledge and Himself: His knowledge would extend down here to the world, a place where He Himself would
not be present. Consequently, He would know something outside of Him. This
contradicts *Rambam's* statement that G-d knows the world through knowing
Himself.

The *Tanya* has therefore raised two objections to interpreting the *tzimtzum*
literally: 1.) It violates the principle that G-d has no body; 2.) It introduces a dual-
ism between G-d and His knowledge.

SECTION THREE: G-D'S RELATIONSHIP WITH THE WORLD

As we have seen, the view that the *tzimtzum* was not literal translates into a
belief that the Divine is present in all things, "even sticks and stones." In the
following section, the *Tanya* elaborates on this point, based on passages from
the Zohar.

וְזֶהוּ שֶׁכָּתוּב בַּתִּקּוּנִים תִּיקוּן נ"ז — This is the meaning of what is written in *Tikunei Zohar, Tikun 57* (91b), דְּלֵית אֲתַר פָּנוּי מִינֵיהּ לָא בְּעִילָאִין וְלָא בְּתַתָּאִין — that
"no place is devoid of Him, neither in the higher worlds or the lower worlds."

The Zohar's statement, "No place is devoid of Him," is supportive of a non-literal reading of the *tzimtzum,* as it suggests that every place in the universe is
saturated with the Divine.

The *Tanya* now cites a passage from the *Zohar* which discusses this idea in
more detail.

וּבְרַעְיָא מְהֵימְנָא פָּרָשַׁת פִּנְחָס — And in the *Zohar, Raya Mehemna,* in the portion
of *Pinchas* it is written, אִיהוּ תָּפִיס בְּכוּלָא וְלֵית מַאן דְּתָפִיס בֵּיהּ כו' — "He grasps

סוכ״ע כו׳ ולית מאן דנפיק מרשותי׳ לבר איהו
ממכ״ע כו׳ איהו מקשר ומיחד זינא לזיניה עילא
ותתא ולית קורבא בד׳ יסודין אלא בקב״ה כד איהו

all, but none grasp Him, etc.," אִיהוּ סוֹבֵב כָּל עָלְמִין כוּ׳ — *"He encompasses all worlds, etc.,"* וְלֵית מַאן דְּנָפֵיק מֵרְשׁוּתֵיה לְבַר — *"and nothing departs outside His domain,"* אִיהוּ מְמַלֵּא כָּל עָלְמִין כוּ׳ — *"He fills all worlds, etc.,"* אִיהוּ מְקַשֵּׁר וּמְיַחֵד זִינָא לְזִינֵיה עֵילָא וְתַתָּא — *"He binds and unites one form to another, upper and lower,"* וְלֵית קוּרְבָא בְּד׳ יְסוֹדִין אֶלָּא בְּקוּדְשָׁא בְּרִיךְ הוּא כַד אִיהוּ בֵּינַיְיהוּ — *"and there is no interaction between the four elements without the presence of the Blessed Holy One in them,"* עַד כָּאן לְשׁוֹנוֹ — *end of quote* from the *Zohar* (3, 225a).

The *Tanya* will offer us an extended commentary on this passage from the *Zohar*.

Two general points require elaboration:

1. *"None grasp Him"* — Why is G-d's light/energy not influenced by the world?

2. *"He grasps all"* — How does G-d's light/energy create and influence ("grasp") the world?

Within each of these areas, two specific explanations are required, corresponding to G-d's two types of light/energy:

a.) The transcendent, undiminished light/energy which "encompasses all worlds."

b.) The immanent, vastly diminished light which "fills all worlds."

Putting all this together, we have four issues to clarify:

1a.) Why is G-d's transcendent, undiminished light/energy which "encompasses all worlds" not "grasped" by the world?

1b.) Why is G-d's immanent, diminished light/energy which "fills all worlds" not "grasped" by the world with which it interacts and which it "fills"?

2a.) How does G-d's transcendent, undiminished light/energy which "encompasses all worlds" nevertheless influence and create ("grasp") the world which it transcends?

2b.) How does G-d's immanent, diminished light/energy which "fills all worlds" influence and create ("grasp") the world which it fills?

Through the remainder of this chapter, the *Tanya* will address each of these four questions systematically.

בינייהו עכ"ל. ור"ל לית מאן דתפיס בי' שאין מי
שיתפוס בהשגת שכלו מכל שכלים העליונים במהותו
ועצמותו של הקב"ה כמ"ש בתקונים סתימא דכל
סתימין ולית מחשבה תפיסא בך כלל וגם בתחתונים

SECTION FOUR: "NONE GRASP HIM"

First we will turn to question 1a.) Why is G-d's transcendent, undiminished light/
energy which "encompasses all worlds" not "grasped" by the world?

וְרוֹצֶה לוֹמַר לֵית מַאן דְּתָפִיס בֵּיהּ — **The meaning of** *"none grasp Him,"* as applied
to G-d's transcendent light which "encompasses all worlds," שֶׁאֵין מִי שֶׁיִּתְפּוֹס
is — בְּהַשָּׂגַת שִׂכְלוֹ מִכָּל שְׂכָלִים הָעֶלְיוֹנִים בְּמַהוּתוֹ וְעַצְמוּתוֹ שֶׁל הַקָּדוֹשׁ בָּרוּךְ הוּא
that even **among all the celestial** (angelic) **intellects, not one can grasp the
essence and being of G-d with their minds,** כְּמוֹ שֶׁכָּתוּב בַּתִּקוּנִים סְתִימָא דְכָל
סְתִימִין וְלֵית מַחֲשָׁבָה תְּפִיסָא בָּךְ כְּלָל — **as the** *Tikunei Zohar* **(17a) states** that G-d
is, *"Hidden of all hidden; no thought can grasp You at all."*

G-d's transcendence, how He "encompasses all worlds," obviously cannot
be grasped by us, but it cannot even be grasped by the celestial intellects.

That is fairly straightforward. Now, we turn to a more taxing question: 1b.) Why
is G-d's immanent, diminished light/energy which "fills all worlds" not "grasped"
by the very worlds with which it interacts and which it "fills"?

אַף עַל גַּב דְּאִיהוּ מְמַלֵּא כָּל עָלְמִין — **And even in the lower worlds,** וְגַם בַּתַּחְתּוֹנִים
— while *"He fills all worlds,"* and you would think this would render G-d "grasp-
able," nevertheless, even here, *"none grasp Him."*

When we say that G-d "fills" the world, it refers to how His presence is felt and
expressed *through* each detail of the world. That's because the Divine light/
energy which "fills" the world has been sufficiently diminished to be compatible
with the world's existence.

You might imagine that since this light/energy is heavily diminished, it could
be fully "grasped." However, the *Tanya* now explains why this is not the case.

A CHASIDIC THOUGHT

Be conscious of the Creator, *"the whole earth is
full of His glory" (Isaiah* 6:3). The *Shechinah* (Divine presence) is constantly at your side. Look at
the *Shechinah* next to you as you would look at
physical objects.

(The *Ba'al Shem Tov—Tzava'as Ha-Rivash* 133)

אע"ג דאיהו ממכ"ע אינו כנשמת האדם תוך גופו
שהיא נתפסת תוך הגוף עד שמתפעלת ומקבלת
שינויים משינויי הגוף וצערו מהכאות או קרירות או
חמימות האש וכיוצא משא"כ בהקב"ה שאינו מקבל
שום שינוי משינויי עוה"ז מקיץ לחורף ומיום ללילה
כדכתיב גם חשך לא יחשיך ממך ולילה כיום יאיר
לפי שאינו נתפס כלל תוך העולמות אע"ג דממלא

אֵינוֹ כְּנִשְׁמַת הָאָדָם תּוֹךְ גּוּפוֹ — The way in which G-d fills the worlds **is not like the soul's presence in the body,** שֶׁהִיא נִתְפֶּסֶת תּוֹךְ הַגּוּף — where the soul is "grasped" by the body, עַד שֶׁמִּתְפָּעֶלֶת וּמְקַבֶּלֶת שִׁינוּיֵי מְשִׁינוּיֵי הַגּוּף — such that the soul is influenced by, and fluctuates with, changes in the body, וְצַעֲרוֹ מֵהַכָּאוֹת אוֹ קְרִירוּת אוֹ חֲמִימוּת הָאֵשׁ וְכַיּוֹצֵא — and the soul is pained by the body's injuries, or intense cold or heat from fire, *etc.*

מַה שֶׁאֵין כֵּן בְּהַקָּדוֹשׁ בָּרוּךְ הוּא שֶׁאֵינוֹ מְקַבֵּל שׁוּם שִׁינוּי מְשִׁינוּיֵי עוֹלָם הַזֶּה — That's not the case with G-d, who is unchanged by any fluctuation in this world, מִקַּיץ כְּדִכְתִיב — from summer to winter, and from day to night, לְחוֹרֶף וּמִיּוֹם לְלַיְלָה — **as the verse states,** גַּם חֹשֶׁךְ לֹא יַחְשִׁיךְ מִמֶּךָ וְלַיְלָה כַּיּוֹם יָאִיר — *"Darkness itself will not darken for You, and the night will light up like the day"* (Psalms 139:12).

לְפִי שֶׁאֵינוֹ נִתְפַּס כְּלָל תּוֹךְ הָעוֹלָמוֹת אַף עַל גַּב דִּמְמַלֵּא לוֹן — **That's because He is not "grasped" at all by the worlds, even though He "fills" them.**

For the soul to engage with the body it must interact with and "fill" the body. This opens a two-way channel: the soul influences the body, but the body also affects the soul. While G-d's light/energy that "encompasses all worlds" clearly remains aloof, you might imagine that His light/energy which "fills all worlds" *is* affected by the world. After all, the whole purpose of the diminishment of this light was to interact with and "fill" the worlds.

The *Tanya* informs us here that this is not the case. The soul may be influenced by the body, but the soul is not G-d. When G-d's light/energy interacts and engages with ("fills") the world, it is not "grasped" or influenced by it.

SECTION FIVE: "HE ENCOMPASSES ALL WORLDS"

24TH SIVAN REGULAR | 26TH SIVAN LEAP

We have explained the first half of the Zohar's comment, why *"none grasp Him,"* both with respect to G-d's transcendent light/energy (1a) and His immanent light/energy (1b).

לון וזהו ג"כ ענין סוכ"ע פי' ד"מ כשאדם מתבונן
באיזה דבר חכמה בשכלו או דבר גשמי במחשבתו   84A
אזי שכלו ומחשבתו מקיפים על הדבר ההוא המצויר
במחשבתו או בשכלו אך אין מקיפים על הדבר ההוא

Now we turn to the second part of the Zohar's words, *"He grasps all."* First we will clarify this statement in regard to G-d's transcendent light/energy, which "encompasses all worlds." We need to explain: 2a.) How does G-d's transcendent light/energy which "encompasses all worlds" nevertheless influence and create ("grasp") the worlds which it transcends?

וְזֶהוּ גַם כֵּן עִנְיַן סוֹבֵב כָּל עָלְמִין — The *Zohar's* statement *"He grasps all,"* **will help us to clarify why** G-d's transcendent light/energy is referred to by the term, **"encompasses all worlds."**

Above we learned that, when speaking of G-d's transcendent light/energy, even among the celestial intellects, *"none grasp Him."* You might think, then, that G-d's transcendent energy is so aloof that it has no connection whatsoever with our universe.

To counteract this notion, the *Zohar* refers to this light/energy as one which *encompasses* all worlds. The term "encompasses" implies that we do have a relationship with the transcendent light/energy, as the *Tanya* will now explain.

פֵּירוּשׁ דֶּרֶךְ מָשָׁל — A relationship where one entity "encompasses" the other **means, to give an example,** כְּשֶׁאָדָם מִתְבּוֹנֵן בְּאֵיזֶה דְּבַר חָכְמָה בְּשִׂכְלוֹ אוֹ דָּבָר **ple,** גַּשְׁמִי בְּמַחֲשַׁבְתּוֹ — **when a person contemplates a certain idea in his mind, or a physical object in his thoughts,** אֲזַי שִׂכְלוֹ וּמַחֲשַׁבְתּוֹ מַקִּיפִים עַל הַדָּבָר הַהוּא הַמְצוּיָּר בְּמַחֲשַׁבְתּוֹ אוֹ בְּשִׂכְלוֹ — **then his mind, his thoughts, "encompass" that** idea or object, **which is pictured in his thoughts or his mind.**

PRACTICAL LESSONS

G-d fills the universe, and yet at the same time, He transcends it. He is not caught up by changes in the world; but He is still intimately involved in the world, providing energy for each creation to flower.

Is your mind aloof from the ideas that it contemplates? Of course not. In fact the very opposite is true, your mind is deeply engaged in the ideas it thinks about. But your mind is also "bigger" than its own ideas and "encompasses" them.

This illustration helps us to appreciate how G-d's transcendent light/energy is far greater than the world, but nevertheless engages with it.

But the *Tanya* highlights a weakness in the analogy.

ממש בפועל ממש. אבל הקב"ה דכתיב ביה כי לא
מחשבותי מחשבותיכם וגו' מחשבתו וידיעתו שיודע
כל הנבראים מקפת כל נברא ונברא בפו"מ שהרי
היא היא חיותו והתהוותו מאין ליש בפועל ממש.
וממלא כל עלמין היא בחי' החיות המתלבשת תוך
עצם הנברא שהיא מצומצמת בתוכו בצמצום רב

אַךְ אֵין מַקִּיפִים עַל הַדָּבָר הַהוּא מַמָּשׁ — **Though,** of course, a person's mind **isn't literally encompassing that object** which it is thinking about, בְּפוֹעַל מַמָּשׁ — his mind isn't **actually** encompassing the object.

The term "encompass," which implies being engulfed in space, isn't completely accurate for the example of contemplating an object. If you think about a chair which is in front of you, the *idea* of the chair is encompassed by your mind, but the actual chair remains in front of you.

אֲבָל הַקָּדוֹשׁ בָּרוּךְ הוּא דִכְתִיב בֵּיהּ כִּי לֹא מַחְשְׁבוֹתַי מַחְשְׁבוֹתֵיכֶם וְגוֹ' — **But with G-d,** of whom it is written, *"My thoughts are not your thoughts, etc.,"* (Isaiah 55:9), מַחֲשַׁבְתּוֹ וִידִיעָתוֹ שֶׁיּוֹדֵעַ כָּל הַנִּבְרָאִים מַקֶּפֶת כָּל נִבְרָא וְנִבְרָא בְּפוֹעַל מַמָּשׁ — **His "thoughts" and His "mind," through which He knows all creations, actually encompass every single creation,** שֶׁהֲרֵי הִיא הִיא חַיּוּתוֹ וְהִתְהַוּוּתוֹ מֵאַיִן לְיֵשׁ בְּפוֹעַל מַמָּשׁ — for G-d's thought of the object **is in fact the very energy which sustains its existence, something-from-nothing, literally.**

The chair only exists because G-d thinks about it. Therefore, it is truly "encompassed" by Him.

SECTION SIX: "HE FILLS ALL WORLDS"

27TH SIVAN LEAP

We are left with the fourth question above: 2b.) How does G-d's immanent, diminished light/energy which "fills all worlds" influence and create ("grasp") the world which it fills?

Our discussion in Section Five has also left us with a further issue that requires clarification. If G-d's transcendent light/energy is like the "thought" of creation, which actually powers and "encompasses" it, why is a further light/energy (which "fills all worlds") necessary? Don't we already have a direct, creative, Divine power?

וּמְמַלֵּא כָּל עָלְמִין הִיא בְּחִינַת הַחַיּוּת הַמִּתְלַבֶּשֶׁת תּוֹךְ עֶצֶם הַנִּבְרָא — G-d's light which **"fills all worlds" is the energy which is embodied within the particular creation,** שֶׁהִיא מְצוּמְצֶמֶת בְּתוֹכוֹ בְּצִמְצוּם רַב כְּפִי עֵרֶךְ מַהוּת הַנִּבְרָא — **that is greatly**

כְּפִי עֵרֶךְ מַהוּת הַנִּבְרָא שֶׁהוּא בַּעַל גְּבוּל וְתַכְלִית
בְּכַמּוּתוֹ וְאֵיכוּתוֹ דְּהַיְינוּ מַעֲלָתוֹ וַחֲשִׁיבוּתוֹ כְּגוֹן הַשֶּׁמֶשׁ
שֶׁגּוּפוֹ יֵשׁ לוֹ גְּבוּל וְתַכְלִית בְּכַמּוּתוֹ שֶׁהוּא כְּמוֹ קס"ז

diminished within it, the level of **diminishment depending on the particular qualities of** the individual **created thing.**

At the level of the light/energy which "encompasses all worlds," the universe exists *at G-d's level,* abstract and infinite. The light/energy which "fills all worlds" provides a creative force *at the universe's level,* which is tangible and finite.

The light/energy which "encompasses all worlds" is like G-d's creative *thought*; the light/energy which "fills all worlds" is like G-d's creative *speech,* which gives a more specific and "real" articulation of His thought.

Both energies work together. If the universe would be created only from the light/energy which "encompasses all worlds," it would have no real form or limits. But the light/energy which "fills all worlds" alone cannot create the universe, just as you would have nothing to speak about if you did not think first.

This provides the basic answer to our question: 2b.) How does G-d's immanent, diminished light/energy which "fills all worlds" influence and create ("grasp") the world which it fills? The answer we have just learned is that this light/energy influences and creates by becoming *"embodied within the particular creation."* The light/energy is "tailor-made" to the creation through being *"heavily diminished within it. The level of diminishment depends on the particular qualities of the individual created thing."*

In order to understand this concept more clearly, the *Tanya* will elaborate at some length. First we need to understand why each creation is different, requiring it to have its own type of light/energy to create it.

שֶׁהוּא בַּעַל גְּבוּל וְתַכְלִית בְּכַמּוּתוֹ וְאֵיכוּתוֹ — Every created entity **is totally finite, both in its size and quality,** דְּהַיְינוּ מַעֲלָתוֹ וַחֲשִׁיבוּתוֹ — its "quality" **meaning its value and worth.**

At the most basic level, the creations differ from each other in two variables: quantity and quality. The *Tanya* offers a simple illustration.

A CHASIDIC THOUGHT

In G-d's transcendent light, *sovev,* I am *emptied* of my being and merge with the One.

G-d's immanent light, *memalei,* fills every detail of my being. The One is expressed in the many.

פְּעָמִים כְּגוֹדֶל כַּדּוּר הָאָרֶץ וְאֵיכוּתוֹ וּמַעֲלָתוֹ הוּא אוֹרוֹ
ג"כ יֵשׁ לוֹ גְּבוּל עַד כַּמָּה יוּכַל לְהָאִיר כִּי לֹא יָאִיר
לְבִלְתִּי תַכְלִית מֵאַחַר שֶׁהוּא נִבְרָא וְכֵן כָּל הַנִּבְרָאִים
הֵם בַּעֲלֵי גְּבוּל וְתַכְלִית כִּי מֵהָאָרֶץ לָרָקִיעַ מַהֲלָךְ ת"ק
שָׁנָה כו'. וְאִ"כ הַחַיּוּת הַמְלוּבֶּשֶׁת בָּהֶם הִיא בִּבְחִי'
צִמְצוּם רַב וְעָצוּם כִּי צְרִיכָה תְּחִלָּה לְהִתְצַמְצֵם
צִמְצוּמִים רַבִּים וַעֲצוּמִים עַד שֶׁיִּתְהַוֶּה מִכֹּחָהּ וְאוֹרָהּ
עֶצֶם הַנִּבְרָאִים כְּמוֹת שֶׁהֵם בַּעֲלֵי גְּבוּל וְתַכְלִית כִּי

כְּגוֹן הַשֶּׁמֶשׁ שֶׁגוּפוֹ יֵשׁ לוֹ גְּבוּל וְתַכְלִית בְּכַמּוּתוֹ שֶׁהוּא כְּמוֹ קס"ז פְּעָמִים כְּגוֹדֶל כַּדּוּר הָאָרֶץ — **For example, the "quantity" of the sun is that its body is around 167 times the size of the earth** (*Rambam*, introduction to *Commentary on the Mishnah*), גַּם כֵּן וְאֵיכוּתוֹ וּמַעֲלָתוֹ הוּא אוֹרוֹ — **and its "quality" and "value" is its light,** יֵשׁ לוֹ גְּבוּל עַד כַּמָּה יוּכַל לְהָאִיר — **and its power of illumination also has a limit,** כִּי לֹא יָאִיר לְבִלְתִּי תַכְלִית מֵאַחַר שֶׁהוּא נִבְרָא — **since it cannot shine endlessly, for it is a** finite **creation.**

The sun is limited in its dimensions (quantity) and its function (quality). It also has a limited time during which it can fulfill its function.

וְכֵן כָּל הַנִּבְרָאִים הֵם בַּעֲלֵי גְּבוּל וְתַכְלִית — **Similarly, all creations are totally finite,** כִּי מֵהָאָרֶץ לָרָקִיעַ מַהֲלָךְ ת"ק שָׁנָה כו' — **as the** *Talmud* **indicates by stating that a journey "from earth to heaven takes five hundred years"** (*Talmud, Chagigah* 13a), **and no more.**

The hallmark of Divine light/energy that "*fills* all worlds" is that it adopts some of the limitations of the finite entity that it fills, in order to become properly "embodied" in it.

וְאִם כֵּן הַחַיּוּת הַמְלוּבֶּשֶׁת בָּהֶם הִיא בִּבְחִינַת צִמְצוּם רַב וְעָצוּם — **This being the case, the** Divine **energy embodied in** all creations must be **greatly and formidably diminished,** כִּי צְרִיכָה תְּחִלָּה לְהִתְצַמְצֵם צִמְצוּמִים רַבִּים וַעֲצוּמִים עַד שֶׁיִּתְהַוֶּה מִכֹּחָהּ — וְאוֹרָהּ עֶצֶם הַנִּבְרָאִים כְּמוֹת שֶׁהֵם בַּעֲלֵי גְּבוּל וְתַכְלִית — **because** G-d's infinite light **must first be diminished repeatedly and formidably to the point where its power/light can bring about totally finite creations, the state in which they are now.**

SECTION SEVEN: THE SOURCE OF "HE FILLS ALL WORLDS"

25TH SIVAN REGULAR | 28TH SIVAN LEAP

G-d did not make a direct transition from the light/energy which "encompasses all worlds" to the energies that "fill all worlds" in their present condition. He first

מקור החיות הוא רוח פיו של הקב"ה המתלבש
בעשרה מאמרות שבתורה ורוח פיו ית' היה יכול
להתפשט לאין קץ ותכלית ולברוא עולמות אין
קץ ותכלית לכמותם ואיכותם ולהחיותם עדי עד ולא
הי' נברא עוה"ז כלל (שכמו שהקב"ה נקרא א"ס כך
כל מדותיו ופעולותיו דאיהו וגרמוהי חד היינו החיות

produced an intermediate phase, which was *the source* of the energy which now "fills all worlds."

In the intermediate phase, the Divine light/energy was diminished in the direction of the world's limitations, but it was not diminished enough to power all the detailed creations found in the universe.

This intermediate phase is the energy of the ten creative statements of genesis (discussed in chapter 1), an immanent "fills all worlds"-type of energy, which was still not sufficiently diminished and differentiated to power the detailed world as we know it.

כִּי מְקוֹר הַחַיּוּת הוּא רוּחַ פִּיו שֶׁל הַקָּדוֹשׁ בָּרוּךְ הוּא הַמִּתְלַבֵּשׁ בַּעֲשָׂרָה מַאֲמָרוֹת שֶׁבַּתּוֹרָה — **For the source of** this **energy,** which now "fills all worlds," **is the "breath of G-d's mouth" which is "dressed" in the ten** creative **statements of the** genesis story in the **Torah.**

וְרוּחַ פִּיו יִתְבָּרֵךְ הָיָה יָכוֹל לְהִתְפַּשֵׁט לְאֵין קֵץ וְתַכְלִית וְלִבְרוֹא עוֹלָמוֹת אֵין קֵץ וְתַכְלִית לִכְמוּתָם וְאֵיכוּתָם וּלְהַחֲיוֹתָם עֲדֵי עַד — If not for subsequent diminishment, **the** "breath of G-d's mouth" from the genesis story **could have extended infinitely and endlessly, creating worlds infinite and endless in quantity and quality, sustaining them forever,** וְלֹא הָיָה נִבְרָא עוֹלָם הַזֶּה כְּלָל — **and our** limited **world would not have been created at all.**

If the universe had been created from the energy of the ten statements of genesis *without any further diminishment,* the Divine creative power would not have absorbed enough limitation to create real finitude. There would be some form ("quantity and quality"), but in infinite proportions.

In a parenthetical note, the *Tanya* explains why the initial emergence of G-d's "speech," the source of the light/energy which "fills all worlds," still remains infinite.

(שֶׁכְּמוֹ שֶׁהַקָּדוֹשׁ בָּרוּךְ הוּא נִקְרָא אֵין סוֹף — **For just as G-d is called "without end"** (*Ein Sof*), כָּךְ כָּל מִדּוֹתָיו וּפְעוּלוֹתָיו, — **so too, all His attributes and** direct **actions are,** by their nature, without end, דְּאִיהוּ וְגַרְמוֹהִי חַד — **for** *"He and the attributes that He causes are one"* (*Tikunei Zohar* 3b), His attributes are infinite like Him.

הַיְינוּ הַחַיּוּת הַנִּמְשֶׁכֶת מִמִּדּוֹתָיו — **Therefore the energy which flows from**

הנמשכת ממדותיו שהן חסד ורחמים ושאר מדותיו
הקדושות ע"י התלבשותן שמתלבשות ברוח פיו
כי הוא אמר ויהי ועולם ע"י חסד יבנה בדבר ה'
ורוח פיו הנעשה כלי ולבוש לחסד זה כהדין קמצא
דלבושיה מיניה וביה) אלא שצמצם הקב"ה האור

His attributes, שֶׁהֵן חֶסֶד וְרַחֲמִים וּשְׁאָר מִדּוֹתָיו הַקְּדוֹשׁוֹת — **which are chesed,
rachamim and His other holy attributes,** is also infinite.

Any direct action of G-d, even if that action is to make a finite world, will be
infinite, because G-d Himself is infinite.

עַל יְדֵי הִתְלַבְּשׁוּתָן שֶׁמִּתְלַבְּשׁוֹת בְּרוּחַ פִּיו — **And when** the infinite energy of
these attributes **"dresses"** in Divine speech, *"the breath of His mouth,"* כִּי הוּא
אָמַר וַיֶּהִי — in order to create the world, *"For He spoke, and it came to be'"*
(*Psalms* 33:9), וְעוֹלָם עַל יְדֵי חֶסֶד יָבָּנֶה — **and then, by means of** His (infinite)
attribute of *"chesed the world was built"* (*ibid.* 89:3), בִּדְבַר ה' וְרוּחַ פִּיו הַנַּעֲשֶׂה
כְּלִי וּלְבוּשׁ לְחֶסֶד זֶה — since *"G-d's speech," "the breath of His mouth,"* was
rendered an instrument and "garment" for His attribute of *chesed.*

G-d's "speech" in the ten statements of genesis is a vehicle of expression
for G-d's creative energy. Since that creative energy is the *infinite* attribute of
chesed, the vehicle itself cannot completely veil that infinitude. The result is
a somewhat immanent and "applied" light/energy, that is more concrete and
tends more towards finitude than the abstract light/energy which "surrounds all
worlds"; but it is still infinite nonetheless.

(כְּהָדֵין קַמְצָא דִּלְבוּשֵׁיהּ מִינֵיהּ וּבֵיהּ) — The energy of the ten statements is infinite,
like the attributes that power it, similar to *"the snail, whose garment, the shell
that hides it, is part of its body"* (*Genesis Rabah* 21:5; see *Tanya, Part One,* end
of Chapter 21).

While the purpose of the ten statements is to veil and diminish the light/ener-
gy of the attributes, they remain one organic entity. Since the speech is Divine,
it does not fully veil the infinite properties of the attributes which power it.

Therefore, further diminishments were required.

SECTION EIGHT: TRANSITION FROM INFINITE TO FINITE

As we have seen, the ten statements alone did not represent a sufficient diminishment to create a finite world.

אֶלָּא שֶׁצִּמְצֵם הַקָּדוֹשׁ בָּרוּךְ הוּא הָאוֹר וְהַחַיּוּת — **Rather,** in order that the world
should be created with limits, **G-d** further **diminished the light and energy** of

וְהַחִיּוּת שֶׁיּוּכַל לְהִתְפַּשֵּׁט מֵרוּחַ פִּיו וְהַלְבִּישׁו תּוֹךְ
צֵירוּפֵי אוֹתִיּוֹת שֶׁל עֲשָׂרָה מַאֲמָרוֹת וְצֵירוּפֵי צֵירוּפֵיהֶן
בְּחִלּוּפֵי וּתְמוּרוֹת הָאוֹתִיּוֹת עַצְמָן וּבְחֶשְׁבּוֹנָן וּמִסְפָּרָן
שֶׁכָּל חִלּוּף וּתְמוּרָה מוֹרֶה עַל יְרִידַת הָאוֹר וְהַחִיּוּת
מִמַּדְרֵגָה לְמַדְרֵגָה דְּהַיְינוּ שֶׁיּוּכַל לִבְרוֹא וּלְהַחִיּוֹת
בְּרוּאִים שֶׁמַּדְרֵגוֹת אֵיכוּתָם וּמַעֲלָתָם הִיא פְּחוּתָה
מִמַּדְרֵגוֹת אֵיכוּת וּמַעֲלַת הַבְּרוּאִים הַנִּבְרָאִים מֵאוֹתִיּוֹת
וְתֵיבוֹת עַצְמָן שֶׁבָּעֲשָׂרָה מַאֲמָרוֹת שֶׁבָּהֶן מִתְלַבֵּשׁ

the ten statements, שֶׁיּוּכַל לְהִתְפַּשֵּׁט מֵרוּחַ פִּיו — so that light and energy could **leave** the infinite level of *"the breath of His mouth,"* וְהִלְבִּישׁו תּוֹךְ צֵירוּפֵי אוֹתִיּוֹת שֶׁל עֲשָׂרָה מַאֲמָרוֹת — **and become veiled**/diminished to a finite level, and this was achieved **through** applying **letter-combinations to the** text of the **ten statements.**

As we have learned, the ten statements themselves represented an infinite light, too boundless to become embodied in most finite creations. A further level of diminishment was required, and this is represented by the various letter re-arrangements that were applied to the ten statements, discussed above in chapter 1.

The *Tanya* reminds us why letter re-arrangements represent a diminishment of light/energy.

וְצֵירוּפֵי צֵירוּפֵיהֶן בְּחִלּוּפֵי וּתְמוּרוֹת הָאוֹתִיּוֹת עַצְמָן וּבְחֶשְׁבּוֹנָן וּמִסְפָּרָן — The light/energy of the ten statements was diminished from infinite to finite by veiling through **multiple combinations** achieved **by switching and exchanging the actual letters, and** also by exchanging them based on **their numerical value,** שֶׁכָּל חִלּוּף וּתְמוּרָה מוֹרֶה עַל יְרִידַת הָאוֹר וְהַחִיּוּת מִמַּדְרֵגָה לְמַדְרֵגָה — **each** letter **combination and exchange** indicating **that** G-d's **light and energy has been diminished from one level to the next.**

Like a code or anagram which confuses the meaning of a word, letter re-arrangements of the ten statements effectively dimmed its light.

דְּהַיְינוּ שֶׁיּוּכַל לִבְרוֹא וּלְהַחִיּוֹת בְּרוּאִים שֶׁמַּדְרֵגַת אֵיכוּתָם וּמַעֲלָתָם הִיא פְּחוּתָה מִמַּדְרֵגַת אֵיכוּת וּמַעֲלַת הַבְּרוּאִים הַנִּבְרָאִים מֵאוֹתִיּוֹת וְתֵיבוֹת עַצְמָן שֶׁבָּעֲשָׂרָה מַאֲמָרוֹת — The purpose of these diminishments through letter exchanges **is so that creations could be made and sustained at a** finite **level/quality/value lower than the**

PRACTICAL LESSONS

The letters which G-d produced to create the world were too luminous for us. That's why more veiling was required, through letter switching and substitution.

הקב"ה בכבודו ובעצמו שהן מדותיו והחשבון מורה
על מיעוט האור והחיות מיעוט אחר מיעוט עד שלא
נשאר ממנו אלא בחי' אחרונה שהוא בחי' החשבון
ומספר כמה מיני כחות ומדרגות כלולות באור וחיות
הזה המלובש בצירוף זה של תיבה זו (ואחר כל
הצמצומי' האלה וכיוצא בהן כאשר גזרה חכמתו ית'
הוא שהי' יכול האור והחיות להתלבש גם בתחתוני'

infinite **level/quality/value of creations** if **made** directly **from the actual letters and words of the ten statements,** before any exchanges.

שֶׁבָּהֶן מִתְלַבֵּשׁ הַקָּדוֹשׁ בָּרוּךְ הוּא בִּכְבוֹדוֹ וּבְעַצְמוֹ — For in the ten statements, **the** infinite **Blessed Holy One Himself is** directly **"dressed,"** שֶׁהֵן מִדּוֹתָיו — since the ten statements **are** direct expressions of **His** ten **attributes,** so the result would be infinite creations.

29TH SIVAN LEAP

וְהַחֶשְׁבּוֹן מוֹרֶה עַל מִיעוּט הָאוֹר וְהַחַיּוּת — **Whereas** when letters are derived through **numerical** exchanges, **it shows that** G-d's **light and energy has been reduced,** עַד שֶׁלֹא נִשְׁאַר — **one downgrade after another,** מִיעוּט אַחַר מִיעוּט מִמֶּנּוּ אֶלָּא בְּחִינָה אַחֲרוֹנָה — **to the point where only a minimal amount** of light and energy **remains,** שֶׁהוּא בְּחִינַת הַחֶשְׁבּוֹן וּמִסְפָּר — **indicated by its numerical value,** כַּמָּה מִינֵי כֹחוֹת וּמַדְרֵגוֹת כְּלוּלוֹת בָּאוֹר וְחַיּוּת הַזֶּה — **which merely tells you the quantity of powers/levels included in this light/energy,** הַמְלוּבָּשׁ בְּצֵירוּף זֶה שֶׁל תֵּיבָה זוֹ — **which is embodied in this particular** letter **combination or word.**

A numerical exchange represents a greater diminishment than a letter exchange. When a letter is converted to a number, its meaning is completely lost.

SECTION NINE: AN EXAMPLE OF A LETTER COMBINATION

To illustrate the point further, the *Tanya* offers an example of how the light/energy which "fills all worlds" of one particular creation arises. We are taught the case of a stone. (This had been the Ba'al Shem Tov's emphasis, *"Everything in the universe contains holy sparks... even stones."*)

(וְאַחַר כָּל הַצִמְצוּמִים הָאֵלֶּה וְכַיּוֹצֵא בָהֶן — And after all these diminishments *etc.,* הוּא שֶׁהָיָה יָכוֹל הָאוֹר — **as** G-d's **wisdom had decreed,** כַּאֲשֶׁר גָּזְרָה חָכְמָתוֹ יִתְבָּרֵךְ וְהַחַיּוּת לְהִתְלַבֵּשׁ גַּם בַּתַּחְתּוֹנִים כְּמוֹ אֲבָנִים וְעָפָר הַדּוֹמֵם — **it became possible for** G-d's **light and energy to become embodied even in** objects within **the lower worlds, such as motionless stones and dirt.**

כמו אבנים ועפר הדומם כי אבן ד"מ שמה מורה
כי שרשה משם העולה ב"ן במספרו ועוד אלף נוספת
משם אחר (לישעם) [נר' דצ"ל לטעם] הידוע ליוצרה.
והנה שם ב"ן בעצמו הוא בעולמות עליונים מאד
רק שע"י צמצומי' רבים ועצומים ממדרגה למדרגה
ירד ממנו חיות מועט במאד מאד עד שיוכל

The Hebrew word for stone is *even,* spelled *alef-beis-nun.* The *Tanya* now traces the origin of these three letters in their creative source.

כִּי אֶבֶן דֶּרֶךְ מָשָׁל שְׁמָה מוֹרָה כִּי שָׁרְשָׁה מִשֵּׁם הָעוֹלֶה בַּ"ן בְּמִסְפָּרוֹ — **For the word EVeN ("stone"), for example, indicates that its** spiritual **root is in the** Divine **name whose numerical value is 52 (Ba"N).**

When written in *plene* or "expanded" form (where each of the four letters is spelled out in full, as if it were a word), the Tetragrammaton can be spelled in many different ways. For example, the "word" *hei* could be spelled *hei-alef, hei-hei,* or *hei-yud. Vav* could be spelled *vav-alef-vav, vav-yud-vav,* or *vav-vav.* This creates the possibility for spelling the Tetragrammaton in 27 different ways, with 13 different numerical values!

Particular significance is attributed to the *plene* spellings with the values of 72 (A"B), 63 (Sa"G), 45 (Ma"H) and 52 (Ba"N).

The name whose value is 52 (Ba"N) is spelled *yud-vav-daled, hei-hei, vav-vav, hei-hei.*

The *Tanya* suggests here that the light/energy of the stone originated in the Divine name Ba"N. This accounts for the fact that e*VeN* and Ba"N share the letters *beis* and *nun.*

Where is the third letter of *even,* the *alef,* derived from?

וְעוֹד אֶלֶף נוֹסֶפֶת מִשֵּׁם אַחֵר לְטַעַם הַיָּדוּעַ לְיוֹצְרָהּ — **BaN spells EVeN when another letter alef is added, from another** unidentified **Divine name, for a reason known** only **to G-d.**

How does the infinite vitality of a Divine name end up as the minuscule life-energy of a motionless, physical stone?

וְהִנֵּה שֵׁם בַּ"ן בְּעַצְמוֹ הוּא בְּעוֹלָמוֹת עֶלְיוֹנִים מְאֹד — **Now the** Divine **name Ba"N itself is** an energy **from a very lofty spiritual world,** רַק שֶׁעַל יְדֵי צִמְצוּמִים רַבִּים וַעֲצוּמִים מִמַּדְרֵגָה לְמַדְרֵגָה יָרַד מִמֶּנּוּ חִיּוּת מוּעֶטֶת בִּמְאֹד מְאֹד עַד שֶׁתּוּכַל לְהִתְלַבֵּשׁ בְּאֶבֶן — **and it is only through many profound diminishments that it can be**

PRACTICAL LESSONS

Even something as mundane as a stone begins its existence as the name of G-d.

לְהִתְלַבֵּשׁ בָּאֶבֶן וְזוֹ הִיא נֶפֶשׁ הַדּוֹמֵם הַמְחַיֶּה וּמְהַוֶּה
אוֹתוֹ מֵאַיִן לְיֵשׁ בְּכָל רֶגַע וּכְמַשַׁ"ל וְזוֹ הִיא בְּחִי'
85A מִמְמַכַ"ע מַשַׁא"כ בְּחִי' סוֹכַ"ע) וְכָל כֹּחַ וּמַדְרֵגָה יָכוֹל
לִבְרוֹא בְּרוּאִים כְּפִי בְּחִי' מַדְרֵגָה זוֹ גַּם כֵּן לְאֵין קֵץ
וְתַכְלִית בְּכַמּוּתָם וְאֵיכוּתָם לְהַחֲיוֹת עֲדֵי עַד מֵאַחַר

downgraded to the extremely minuscule energy that is capable of being embodied in a stone.

וְזוֹ הִיא נֶפֶשׁ הַדּוֹמֵם הַמְחַיֶּה וּמְהַוֶּה אוֹתוֹ מֵאַיִן לְיֵשׁ בְּכָל רֶגַע — **But this** heavily diminished energy, rooted in Ba"N, **is the "soul" of the motionless** stone, **which energizes it and brings it into existence, something-from-nothing, at every moment,** וּכְמוֹ שֶׁנִּתְבָּאֵר לְעֵיל — **as was explained above** (chapter 1).

וְזוֹ הִיא בְּחִינַת מְמַלֵּא כָל עָלְמִין — **And we are,** of course, **referring here to** what the *Zohar* calls the light **which "fills all worlds,"** מַה שֶּׁאֵין כֵּן בְּחִינַת סוֹבֵב כָּל (עָלְמִין) — **not the** light which **"encompasses all worlds."**

SECTION TEN: WHY EVEN FINITE ENERGY IS INFINITE

We have learned that both the Divine light/energy that "encompasses" all worlds and the *source of* the light/energy which "fills all worlds" are infinite. The light/energy which "fills all worlds," however, is finite, so as to be compatible with finite creations. But that finitude does not emerge directly from G-d; rather it is achieved through the veiling of His light/energy through letter combinations.

In this concluding passage, the *Tanya* adds a further nuance to this idea. Even this final, finite light, is not *entirely* finite.

וְכָל כֹּחַ וּמַדְרֵגָה יָכוֹל לִבְרוֹא בְּרוּאִים — **And** even after this final diminishment through letter combinations, **each power/level** of G-d's energy **can create** finite **creations,** כְּפִי בְּחִינַת מַדְרֵגָה זוֹ — and those creations will be no higher than **the level of that** diminished light/energy which creates them.

The limitations of the light/energy are real. The light/energy which creates a stone cannot power a plant, and certainly not an animal.

Where do we see that the light/energy retains some aspect of infinitude?

גַּם כֵּן לְאֵין קֵץ וְתַכְלִית בְּכַמּוּתָם וְאֵיכוּתָם — **But on that** particular **level of quantity/quality of creation,** which the diminished light/energy is capable of creating, it can do so **endlessly and limitlessly,** לְהַחֲיוֹת עֲדֵי עַד — **giving energy** to them **forever.**

שהוא כח ה' המתפשט ונאצל מרוח פיו ואין מעצור
כו'. אך שלא יהי' איכותם במעלה גדולה כ"כ
כאיכות ומעלת ברואים שיוכלו להבראות מבחי' כח
ומדריגת האותיות עצמן:

The light/energy which creates a stone is limited to powering stones. However, it can create an infinite number of stones, for eternity.

מֵאַחַר שֶׁהוּא כֹּחַ ה' הַמִּתְפַּשֵּׁט וְנֶאֱצַל מֵרוּחַ פִּיו — **Because** this light/energy **is a Divine power** which ultimately is something which **emerged and emanated from** *"the spirit of His mouth,"* וְאֵין מַעֲצוֹר כוּ' — and *"there is no restraint to His spirit"* (see *Proverbs* 25:28).

Even in its most diminished form, the light which "fills all worlds" retains some infinitude, since, ultimately, it is a Divine power.

אַךְ שֶׁלֹּא יִהְיֶה אֵיכוּתָם בְּמַעֲלָה גְדוֹלָה כָּל כָּךְ כְּאֵיכוּת וּמַעֲלַת בְּרוּאִים שֶׁיּוּכְלוּ לְהִבָּרְאוֹת מִבְּחִינַת כֹּחַ וּמַדְרֵיגַת הָאוֹתִיּוֹת עַצְמָן — **But the quality/value** of these creations made from diminished light **will not be as great as the quality/value of creations that could be made from the level of power in the** original **letters themselves** in the ten statements.

The formidable diminishments of the letter combinations only impose limitations on quality and value. They do not limit the amount of creations that any Divine power is capable of producing.

פרק ח והנה   מ"ש הרמב"ם ז"ל שהקב"ה מהותו
ועצמותו ודעתו הכל אחד ממש
אחדות פשוטה ולא מורכבת כלל כן הענין ממש

CHAPTER 8

THE UNITY WITHIN G-D

SECTION ONE: G-D IS ONE WITH HIS POWERS AND NAMES

26TH SIVAN REGULAR | 30TH SIVAN LEAP

The previous seven chapters were devoted to explaining how the creation of the world imposed no "addition" to G-d (since the world enjoys no *true, independent* existence), so that G-d remains essentially alone, just as before He created the world.

In the following chapters we will discuss another dimension of G-d's unity, the absolute oneness that exists *within* G-d. We will seek to explain why the numerous Divine attributes, intellectual and emotional, do not in any way compromise G-d's oneness. (We touched upon this idea in Chapter 7, but now we will explore it more thoroughly.)

וְהִנֵּה מַה שֶּׁכָּתַב הָרַמְבַּ"ם זִכְרוֹנוֹ לִבְרָכָה — **Now as for what *Rambam* of blessed memory wrote,** cited above in Chapter 7, שֶׁהַקָּדוֹשׁ בָּרוּךְ הוּא מַהוּתוֹ וְעַצְמוּתוֹ וְדַעְתּוֹ הַכֹּל אֶחָד מַמָּשׁ — **that G-d is totally one with His essence, being and knowledge,** אַחְדוּת פְּשׁוּטָה וְלֹא מוּרְכֶּבֶת כְּלָל — **in an absolute and non-composite unity,** כֵּן הָעִנְיָן מַמָּשׁ בְּכָל מִדּוֹתָיו שֶׁל הַקָּדוֹשׁ בָּרוּךְ הוּא — **the same is true, literally, of** *all* **G-d's attributes.**

Fresh milk, for example, appears as a pure and simple, white liquid. In reality, it is a complex mix of carbohydrates, protein, fat and minerals; it is *composite*. When we say that G-d's unity is non-composite, we mean that He is not a harmonious blend of different intellectual and emotional energies. He is just one thing: G-d.

But that doesn't contradict the fact that G-d really does have intellectual and emotional energies.

How G-d can be absolutely one, and yet contain different Divine energies, is ultimately something you just have to accept on faith; but in the next few chapters the *Tanya* will try to make at least some sense of the idea.

בכל מדותיו של הקב"ה ובכל שמותיו הקדושים
והכינויים שכינו לו הנביאים וחז"ל כגון חנון ורחום
וחסיד וכיוצא בהן וכן מה שנקרא חכם דכתיב
וגם הוא חכם וגו' וכן רצונו כי רוצה ה' את יראיו
וחפץ חסד הוא ורוצה בתשובתם של רשעים ואינו
חפץ במיתתם וברשעתם וטהור עינים מראות ברע

First we will define the scope of G-d's unity. We have learned that it includes G-d's intellectual and emotional attributes. What else does it include?

G-d — וּבְכָל שְׁמוֹתָיו הַקְּדוֹשִׁים וְהַכִּינוּיִּים שֶׁכִּינוּ לוֹ הַנְּבִיאִים וַחֲכָמֵינוּ זִכְרוֹנָם לִבְרָכָה is absolutely one, not only with His attributes, but also with **all the names and** other **terms which the prophets and sages, of blessed memory, used in reference** to G-d.

G-d's names refer to G-d Himself. Therefore they must also be one with Him.

The *Tanya* offers some examples of what is meant by *"terms which the prophets and sages used in reference to G-d."*

כְּגוֹן חַנּוּן וְרַחוּם וְחָסִיד וְכַיּוֹצֵא בָּהֶן — Such as *"Gracious and Compassionate One"* (*Joel* 2:13; *Talmud, Shevu'os* 38a), *"Kind One"* (*Jeremiah* 3:12; *Talmud, Rosh Ha-Shanah* 17b), **and other such** terms, וְכֵן מַה שֶׁנִּקְרָא חָכָם דִּכְתִיב וְגַם הוּא חָכָם וְגו' — **and similarly,** this applies to G-d **being referred to as "Wise," as the verse states,** *"He is wise too"* (*Isaiah* 31:2).

וְכֵן רְצוֹנוֹ — **And the same** absolute non-composite unity **is true of His will** and desires.

While your desires are an expression of who you are, they are not you. In the case of G-d, that's not true. He *is* absolutely one with His desire.

The reference to "G-d's desires" includes both a.) what G-d wants to happen and b.) what He doesn't want, as the *Tanya* now illustrates.

כִּי רוֹצֶה ה' אֶת יְרֵאָיו — For *"G-d desires those that revere Him,"* (*Psalms* 147:11), וְרוֹצֶה בִּתְשׁוּבָתָם שֶׁל — and *"He desires kindness"* (*Michah* 7:18), וְחָפֵץ חֶסֶד הוּא רְשָׁעִים וְאֵינוֹ חָפֵץ בְּמִיתָתָם וּבְרִשְׁעָתָם — He *"desires the repentance of the wicked, and does not desire their death"* or their wickedness (*Liturgy, Yom Kippur, Ne'ilah*), וּטְהוֹר עֵינַיִם מֵרְאוֹת בְּרָע — and He prefers not to see evil, as the verse states *"You are of purer eyes than to behold evil"* (*Habakkuk* 1:13).

The *Tanya* sums up what G-d's unity incorporates.

PRACTICAL LESSONS

G-d's many attributes are one with Him. You can't understand this truth cognitively, but you can know it intuitively.

אין רצונו וחכמתו ומדת חסדו ורחמנותו ושאר
מדותיו מוסיפים בו ריבוי והרכבה ח"ו במהותו ועצמותו
אלא עצמותו ומהותו ורצונו וחכמתו ובינתו ודעתו
ומדת חסדו וגבורתו ורחמנותו ותפארתו הכלולה
מחסדו וגבורתו וכן שאר מדותיו הקדושות הכל
אחדות פשוטה ממש שהיא היא עצמותו ומהותו
וכמו"ש הרמב"ם ז"ל שדבר זה אין כח בפה לאמרו
ולא באזן לשמעו ולא בלב האדם להכירו על בוריו
כי האדם מצייר בשכלו כל המושכלות שרוצה
להשכיל ולהבין הכל כמות שהם בו כגון שרוצה

אֵין רְצוֹנוֹ וְחָכְמָתוֹ וּמִדַּת חַסְדּוֹ וְרַחֲמָנוּתוֹ וּשְׁאָר מִדּוֹתָיו מוֹסִיפִים בּוֹ רִיבּוּי וְהַרְכָּבָה חַס וְשָׁלוֹם בְּמַהוּתוֹ וְעַצְמוּתוֹ — **His will, wisdom, attributes of kindness/compassion, and His other attributes** are totally one with Him, and **they do not impose any multiplicity or compositeness on His actual self, G-d forbid,** אֶלָּא עַצְמוּתוֹ וּמַהוּתוֹ וּרְצוֹנוֹ וְחָכְמָתוֹ וּבִינָתוֹ וְדַעְתּוֹ וּמִדַּת חַסְדּוֹ וּגְבוּרָתוֹ וְרַחֲמָנוּתוֹ וְתִפְאַרְתּוֹ הַכְּלוּלָה מֵחַסְדּוֹ וּגְבוּרָתוֹ וְכֵן שְׁאָר מִדּוֹתָיו הַקְּדוֹשׁוֹת הַכֹּל אַחְדוּת פְּשׁוּטָה מַמָּשׁ — **rather, His actual being and self, His will, His *chochmah* (inquiry), His *binah* (cognition), His *da'as* (recognition), His attributes of kindness, severity, and compassion/*tiferes* (harmony, which balances His kindness and His severity), and all His other sacred attributes, are all one non-composite unity, literally,** שֶׁהִיא הִיא עַצְמוּתוֹ וּמַהוּתוֹ — **identical with His very being and self.**

The *Tanya* reminds us of *Rambam's* statement, cited in Chapter 7, that this idea is ultimately not something we can fully comprehend.

וּכְמוֹ שֶׁכָּתַב הָרַמְבַּ"ם זִכְרוֹנוֹ לִבְרָכָה — **And, as *Rambam* of blessed memory wrote,** שֶׁדָּבָר זֶה אֵין כֹּחַ בַּפֶּה לְאָמְרוֹ וְלֹא בָאֹזֶן לְשָׁמְעוֹ וְלֹא בְּלֵב הָאָדָם לְהַכִּירוֹ עַל בּוּרְיוֹ — **"the mouth has no power to express this idea, nor the ear to hear it, nor the heart of man to recognize it properly"** (*Laws of Foundations of the Torah* 2:10).

SECTION TWO: HOW HUMANS THINK ABOUT UNITY

The reason why we find it difficult to understand how G-d could have a variety of different powers and names, and yet be "absolutely one," is because we are picturing G-d in human terms.

כִּי הָאָדָם מְצַיֵּר בְּשִׂכְלוֹ כָּל הַמּוּשְׂכָּלוֹת שֶׁרוֹצֶה לְהַשְׂכִּיל וּלְהָבִין הַכֹּל כְּמוֹת שֶׁהֵם בּוֹ — **Because when a person pictures in his mind phenomena that he wishes to understand,** he pictures those phenomena **as they occur within himself.**

לצייר בשכלו מהות הרצון או מהות חכמה או בינה
או דעת או מהות מדת חסד ורחמים וכיוצא בהן   85B
הוא מצייר כולן כמות שהן בו אבל באמת הקדוש
ב"ה הוא רם ונשא וקדוש שמו כלומר שהוא קדוש
ומובדל ריבוא רבבות עד אין קץ ותכלית מדרגות
הבדלות למעלה מעלה מערך וסוג ומין כל התשבחות
והמעלות שיוכלו הנבראים להשיג ולצייר בשכלם

כְּגוֹן שֶׁרוֹצֶה לְצַיֵּיר בְּשִׂכְלוֹ מַהוּת הָרָצוֹן אוֹ מַהוּת חָכְמָה אוֹ בִּינָה אוֹ דַעַת אוֹ מַהוּת מִדַּת חֶסֶד וְרַחֲמִים וְכַיּוֹצֵא בָהֶן — **For example, if you want to picture the phenomenon of will, or the phenomena of *chochmah, binah* or *da'as,* or the attributes of kindness, severity or compassion, *etc.,* הוּא מְצַיֵּיר כּוּלָן כְּמוֹת שֶׁהֵן בּוֹ — you picture them as they occur in yourself,** אֲבָל בֶּאֱמֶת הַקָּדוֹשׁ בָּרוּךְ הוּא הוּא רָם **but, in truth, this is not an effective way to understand these phenomena within G-d, who is** *"high, exalted and whose name is holy"* (*Isaiah* 57:15), כְּלוֹמַר שֶׁהוּא קָדוֹשׁ וּמוּבְדָּל רִיבּוֹא רְבָבוֹת עַד אֵין קֵץ וְתַכְלִית מַדְרֵגוֹת הַבְדָּלוֹת **— *i.e.,* He is "holy" (which means "removed"), with innumerable, endless and limitless degrees of separations,** לְמַעְלָה מַעְלָה מֵעֵרֶךְ וְסוֹג וּמִין כָּל הַתִּשְׁבָּחוֹת וְהַמַּעֲלוֹת שֶׁיּוּכְלוּ הַנִּבְרָאִים לְהַשִׂיג וּלְצַיֵּיר בְּשִׂכְלָם **— utterly beyond the quality/order/kind of praises/virtues that we creations can grasp or picture in our minds.**

27H SIVAN REGULAR

To explain why G-d cannot be understood in human terms, the *Tanya* will draw on our discussion in Part One, Chapter Three. There we learned that the creative process, both in G-d and in humans, flows through a precise pathway of energies. First an idea appears in the imaginative, potential space of *chochmah* (inquiry), from where it passes to *binah* (cognition) to be processed and *da'as* (recognition) to be applied.

This creates emotional energies, which generally fall into three categories of love, fear, and compassion.

For the rest of this chapter the *Tanya* will revisit this process as it occurs in humans and the world. In the following chapter, we will learn how it differs within G-d.

PRACTICAL LESSONS

You can't picture G-d in human terms because the highest energy frequency in our universe doesn't even reach G-d's lowest energy frequency, so to speak.

כִּי הַמַּעֲלָה וּמַדְרֵגָה הָרִאשׁוֹנָה אֵצֶל הַנִּבְרָאִים הִיא
הַחָכְמָה שֶׁלָּכֵן נִקְרֵאת רֵאשִׁית כִּי בֶּאֱמֶת הִיא רֵאשִׁית
וּמְקוֹר כָּל הַחַיּוּת בַּנִּבְרָאִים כִּי מֵהַחָכְמָה נִמְשָׁכוֹת
בִּינָה וָדַעַת וּמֵהֶן נִמְשָׁכוֹת כָּל הַמִּדּוֹת שֶׁבַּנֶּפֶשׁ
הַמַּשְׂכֶּלֶת כְּמוֹ אַהֲבָה וָחֶסֶד וְרַחֲמִים וְכַיּוֹצֵא בָהֶן
וְכַנִּרְאֶה בְּחוּשׁ שֶׁהַקָּטָן שֶׁאֵין בּוֹ דַעַת הוּא בְּכַעַס
תָּמִיד וְאַכְזָרִי וְגַם אַהֲבָתוֹ הִיא לִדְבָרִים קְטַנִּים שֶׁאֵין
רָאוּי לְאָהֲבָם מִפְּנֵי שֶׁאֵין בּוֹ דַעַת לֶאֱהוֹב דְּבָרִים
הָרְאוּיִּים לְאָהֲבָם שֶׁהָאַהֲבָה כְּפִי הַדַּעַת וּמֵהַמִּדּוֹת
שֶׁבַּנֶּפֶשׁ נִמְשָׁכוֹת בָּהּ תֵּיבוֹת וְאוֹתִיּוֹת הַמַּחֲשָׁבָה

כִּי הַמַּעֲלָה וּמַדְרֵגָה הָרִאשׁוֹנָה אֵצֶל הַנִּבְרָאִים הִיא הַחָכְמָה — **For the highest level/quality in the created world is chochmah,** שֶׁלָּכֵן נִקְרֵאת רֵאשִׁית — **which is why Scripture refers to it as *"beginning"*** (*Psalms* 111:1).

The key point of departure between G-d's unity and the world's is at the level of *chochmah*. G-d transcends *chochmah,* the world does not. That's because everything in the universe can be traced to *chochmah,* as the *Tanya* now explains.

כִּי בֶּאֱמֶת הִיא רֵאשִׁית וּמְקוֹר כָּל הַחַיּוּת בַּנִּבְרָאִים — **Since** *chochmah* **really is the "beginning" and source of all energy in the created world,** כִּי מֵהַחָכְמָה נִמְשָׁכוֹת בִּינָה וָדַעַת — **since** *binah* **and** *da'as* **are derived from** *chochmah* **(see Part One, Chapter 3),** וּמֵהֶן נִמְשָׁכוֹת כָּל הַמִּדּוֹת שֶׁבַּנֶּפֶשׁ הַמַּשְׂכֶּלֶת — **and from them all human emotional energies arise within the intelligent soul,** כְּמוֹ אַהֲבָה וָחֶסֶד וְרַחֲמִים וְכַיּוֹצֵא בָהֶן — **such as love, kindness, compassion,** *etc.*

The *Tanya* reminds us of an illustration of this point that we learned in Part One, Chapter 6.

וְכַנִּרְאֶה בְּחוּשׁ שֶׁהַקָּטָן שֶׁאֵין בּוֹ דַעַת הוּא בְּכַעַס תָּמִיד וְאַכְזָרִי — **This is plainly obvious with children, whose** *da'as* **is immature, so they get in a temper all the time and are vindictive,** וְגַם אַהֲבָתוֹ הִיא לִדְבָרִים קְטַנִּים שֶׁאֵין רָאוּי לְאָהֲבָם — **they also love trivial things which are not worthy of love,** מִפְּנֵי שֶׁאֵין בּוֹ דַעַת לֶאֱהוֹב — **because they don't have** sufficiently developed *da'as* דְּבָרִים הָרְאוּיִּים לְאָהֲבָם — **to love things that are worthy of love,** שֶׁהָאַהֲבָה כְּפִי הַדַּעַת — **for love is a function of** *da'as.*

We now review the process through which thoughts emerge from these soul powers.

וּמֵהַמִּדּוֹת שֶׁבַּנֶּפֶשׁ נִמְשָׁכוֹת בָּהּ תֵּיבוֹת וְאוֹתִיּוֹת הַמַּחֲשָׁבָה שֶׁהַנֶּפֶשׁ מְחַשֶּׁבֶת — **And from the soul's emotional energies, words/letters of thought emerge in the**

שֶׁהַנֶּפֶשׁ מְחַשֶּׁבֶת בְּדָבָר שֶׁאוֹהֶבֶת אוֹ אֵיךְ לִפְעוֹל
הַחֶסֶד וְרַחֲמִים וְכֵן בִּשְׁאָר מִדּוֹת וּבְכָל מַחֲשָׁבָה
שֶׁבָּעוֹלָם מְלוּבֶּשֶׁת בָּהּ אֵיזוֹ מִדָּה הַמְּבִיאָה לַחְשׁוֹב
מַחֲשָׁבָה זוֹ וּמִדָּה זוֹ הִיא חַיּוּתָהּ שֶׁל מַחֲשָׁבָה זוֹ
וּמֵאוֹתִיּוֹת הַמַּחֲשָׁבָה נִמְשָׁכוֹת אוֹתִיּוֹת הַדִּבּוּר וְהֵן
חַיּוּתָן מַמָּשׁ וְהַדִּבּוּר מֵבִיא לִידֵי מַעֲשֵׂה הַצְּדָקָה וָחֶסֶד
כְּגוֹן הַמֶּלֶךְ שֶׁמְּצַוֶּה לַעֲבָדָיו לִיתֵּן וְגַם כְּשֶׁהָאָדָם עוֹשֶׂה
בְּעַצְמוֹ אֵיזֶה דָּבָר הֲרֵי כֹּחַ הַנֶּפֶשׁ וְחַיּוּתָהּ הַמִּתְלַבֵּשׁ
בַּעֲשִׂיָּה זוֹ הוּא כְּאַיִן מַמָּשׁ לְגַבֵּי כֹּחַ הַנֶּפֶשׁ וְחַיּוּתָהּ

soul as it thinks, בְּדָבָר שֶׁאוֹהֶבֶת — words about the thing you love, אוֹ אֵיךְ לִפְעוֹל הַחֶסֶד וְרַחֲמִים — or words describing how to carry out kindness or compassion, וְכֵן בִּשְׁאָר מִדּוֹת — and likewise with all the other emotions.

The soul-powers, and the thoughts which they lead to, remain energetically linked.

Any — וּבְכָל מַחֲשָׁבָה שֶׁבָּעוֹלָם מְלוּבֶּשֶׁת בָּהּ אֵיזוֹ מִדָּה הַמְּבִיאָה לַחְשׁוֹב מַחֲשָׁבָה זוֹ thought that occurs is fueled by an emotional energy from the soul which causes you to think that thought, וּמִדָּה זוֹ הִיא חַיּוּתָהּ שֶׁל מַחֲשָׁבָה זוֹ — and that emotional energy powers the thought.

We now review the process through which speech emerges from thought and the energetic connection between them.

וּמֵאוֹתִיּוֹת הַמַּחֲשָׁבָה נִמְשָׁכוֹת אוֹתִיּוֹת הַדִּבּוּר — And from letters/words in thought, spoken letters/words emerge, וְהֵן חַיּוּתָן מַמָּשׁ — the thought fully powering the speech.

Speech then leads to action.

וְהַדִּבּוּר מֵבִיא לִידֵי מַעֲשֵׂה הַצְּדָקָה וָחֶסֶד — Then, in this example of an emotion/thought/spoken word of kindness, the speech leads to the act of charity or kindness, כְּגוֹן הַמֶּלֶךְ שֶׁמְּצַוֶּה לַעֲבָדָיו לִיתֵּן — such as a king instructing his servants to donate.

(The Tanya brings this particular example, as it is a case where we can be sure speech will lead to immediate action.)

וְגַם כְּשֶׁהָאָדָם עוֹשֶׂה בְּעַצְמוֹ אֵיזֶה דָּבָר — And even when a person does a particular act himself, without speaking to instruct another to do it, that doesn't mean that the act is connecting directly to the soul and receiving more energy, הֲרֵי כֹּחַ הַנֶּפֶשׁ וְחַיּוּתָהּ הַמִּתְלַבֵּשׁ בַּעֲשִׂיָּה זוֹ הוּא כְּאַיִן מַמָּשׁ לְגַבֵּי כֹּחַ הַנֶּפֶשׁ וְחַיּוּתָהּ הַמִּתְלַבֵּשׁ בְּדִבּוּר הָאָדָם — rather, the soul energy invested in this person's act pales into insignificance when compared with the soul energy invested in his speech.

המתלבש בדבור האדם וכערך ומשל הגוף לנשמה
וכן ערך אותיות הדבור לאותיות המחשבה וכן ערך
אותיות המחשבה למהות המדה המלובשת בה
ומחיה אותה וכן ערך מהות וחיות המדה לגבי
החכמה ובינה ודעת שכללותן הוא השכל שממנו
נמשכה מדה זו וכל זה בנפש האדם ונפש כל
הברואים שבכל העולמות עליונים ותחתונים שבכולם
החכמה היא ראשית ומקור החיות:

Skipping thought and speech doesn't mean that an act is more in contact with the soul's energy. Action always occurs at a more diminished level of soul-energy, regardless of whether it is preceded by thought/speech or not.

The rule is: Action always has an immeasurably lesser degree of soul energy than speech, and speech an immeasurably lesser degree of soul energy than thought, as the *Tanya* now states.

וּכְעֶרֶךְ וּמְשַׁל הַגּוּף לַנְּשָׁמָה — The downgrade in energy from speech to action **is to the same extent, for example, that the body**'s energy pales into insignificance when compared **with the soul.**

וְכֵן עֶרֶךְ אוֹתִיּוֹת הַדִּבּוּר לְאוֹתִיּוֹת הַמַּחֲשָׁבָה — **The same is true when comparing the letters of speech with the letters of thought;** the energy of the former pales into insignificance when compared with the latter.

Thought is likewise a highly diminished energy when compared with the raw soul energies.

וְכֵן עֶרֶךְ אוֹתִיּוֹת הַמַּחֲשָׁבָה לְמַהוּת הַמִּדָּה הַמְלוּבֶּשֶׁת בָּה וּמְחַיָּה אוֹתָהּ — **And the same is true when comparing the letters of thought with the actual emotional soul-energy which produces** the thought **and energizes it;** the former pales into insignificance when compared with the latter.

וְכֵן עֶרֶךְ מַהוּת וְחִיּוּת הַמִּדָּה לְגַבֵּי הַחָכְמָה וּבִינָה וָדַעַת שֶׁכְּלָלוּתָן הוּא הַשֵּׂכֶל שֶׁמִּמֶּנּוּ נִמְשְׁכָה מִדָּה זוֹ — **And the same is true when comparing that actual emotional soul-energy with the** soul's *chochmah, binah* and *da'as,* **the intellectual soul-powers that produce the emotional soul-energy,** the former similarly pales into insignificance when compared with the latter.

וְכָל זֶה בְּנֶפֶשׁ הָאָדָם — **The above description is how the human soul functions,** וְנֶפֶשׁ כָּל הַבְּרוּאִים שֶׁבְּכָל הָעוֹלָמוֹת עֶלְיוֹנִים וְתַחְתּוֹנִים — **as well as the souls of all creatures, in the upper and lower worlds,** שֶׁבְּכוּלָם הַחָכְמָה הִיא רֵאשִׁית וּמְקוֹר הַחַיּוּת — **for all of them,** *chochmah* **is the "beginning" and source of all energy.**

All subsequent manifestations of energy pale into insignificance when compared with *chochmah*.

This concludes our discussion of the world's relationship with *chochmah*. In the following chapter we will explore how G-d relates to *chochmah* in a radically different fashion.

A CHASIDIC THOUGHT

Chochmah energizes the letters of my thought, but it is not bound by their rigid form. My *chochmah* can be expressed through language, but its pure energy can't be fully embodied in words.

In the formlessness of chochmah all ideas exist in unity, a gushing fountain of inspiration.

Nothing in the universe is like *chochmah*. All thoughts, words and things are bound by precise contours; *chochmah* is not. That's why *chochmah* is the beginning of everything, it can flow into any form and give it energy.

פרק ט אבל   לגבי הקדוש ברוך הוא מדרגת
החכמה שהיא תחלת מחשבה

CHAPTER 9

SPECTRUM OF CONSCIOUSNESS

SECTION ONE: PRELINGUAL/LINGUAL/POSTLINGUAL FORMS

28TH SIVAN REGULAR | 1ST TAMMUZ LEAP

Chapter 9 presents the "second half" of the insight presented in Chapter 8, concerning unity *within* G-d. The two chapters aim to contrast the inner experience of human beings with the inner experience of G-d. In the case of humans, the *experience* and the *person* are separate; experience is something that happens to you. With G-d, however, there are no separations and all is one. Anything that happens within Him, so to speak, any Divine "experiences" of intellect or emotion, must be seamlessly merged with His essence.

As we have seen, this idea is captured by *Rambam's* statement that G-d is simultaneously the "knower," the "power to know," and the "known" (*Laws of Foundations of the Torah* 2:10); and by the words of the *Tikunei Zohar*, "He and the attributes that He causes are one" (*Tikunei Zohar* 3b).

Ultimately, we cannot adequately fathom how no separation exists between G-d and His attributes, and the matter is left to faith. But in these chapters the *Tanya* offers us at least some insight to grapple with the issue.

Chapter 8 described the spectrum of all levels of internal experience, according to the *Tanya's* psychology. These can be summed up in three categories:

1.) *Prelingual*: soul activity which occurs before words crystallize in the mind.

2.) *Lingual:* language which occurs on the higher level of thoughts, or the lower level of spoken words.

3.) *Post-lingual:* actions that result from stages '1' and '2.'

Prelingual activity occurs at two levels:

1. *Intellectual powers of the soul.* This is not a conscious experience of thought, but the prelingual mental "apparatus" which is the soul's operating system. It is shaped and "programmed" by all data that it has received.

וראשיתה היא סוף מעשה אצלו דהיינו שנחשבת
כאילו היא בחי' ומדרגת עשייה לגבי הקדוש ב"ה

2. *Emotional powers of the soul.* These are the inherent biases ("like" or "dis-like") within the soul, which directly produce conscious thoughts. The biases of the emotional powers themselves are shaped by the intellectual powers.

In Chapter 8 we learned that the source of all these experiences/energies is *chochmah,* the highest prelingual power. As a result, we live in a post-*chochmah* world, and our perceptions are shaped by that limitation. Whatever our internal experience might be, prelingual, lingual, or post-lingual, it is a product of *chochmah.*

In Chapter 9 we will learn that, for G-d, *chochmah* has quite a different order of significance. While for us it is the source of all being, for G-d it is of negligible value.

אֲבָל לְגַבֵּי הַקָּדוֹשׁ בָּרוּךְ הוּא מַדְרֵגַת הַחָכְמָה — **But compared to G-d Himself, the level of** *chochmah,* שֶׁהִיא תְּחִלַּת מַחֲשָׁבָה וְרֵאשִׁיתָהּ — **which is the initial** *"beginning of thought"* (*Liturgy, Friday Night, Lecha Dodi*), הִיא סוֹף מַעֲשֶׂה אֶצְלוֹ — **to Him,** *chochmah* **is** *"the action at the end"* (*ibid.*).

In the *Lecha Dodi,* we say, *"The action at the end is in thought at the beginning."* Literally this means that any action that you perform is the "end" of a process which can be traced back to an initial thought. But here the *Tanya* borrows the phrase to contrast our perception of *chochmah* with G-d's. For us, *chochmah* is the "beginning of thought," a very high-consciousness, prelingual power; whereas for G-d it is a very low-consciousness power, like a mere physical action.

דְּהַיְינוּ שֶׁנֶּחֱשֶׁבֶת כְּאִילוּ הִיא בְּחִינַת וּמַדְרֵגַת עֲשִׂיָּיה לְגַבֵּי הַקָּדוֹשׁ בָּרוּךְ הוּא — **Meaning that, to G-d,** His own *chochmah* **is so low and far removed from His es-sence that it is considered** very low-consciousness, **like "action."**

The *Tanya* illustrates this point with a citation from Scripture.

כְּדִכְתִיב כּוּלָם בְּחָכְמָה עָשִׂיתָ — **As the verse states,** *"You made them all with chochmah"* (*Psalms* 104:24).

At the literal level, this verse praises G-d for crafting everything in the universe with the highest degree of intelligence associated with *chochmah.* But

PRACTICAL LESSONS

The spectrum from action to *chochmah* spans: a.) two lingual levels, speech/thought; and b.) two prelingual levels, emotions/intellect.

Each of these represents a massive shift, energetically speaking, to an entirely different plane.

כדכתיב כולם בחכמה עשית והיינו לומר שכערך
החיות שבעשיה גופנית וגשמיית לערך חיות החכמה
שהיא ראשית ומקור החיות באדם וכל הברואים
גשמיים שהוא כאין כאין לגבי חיות שבאותיות הדבור
שהוא כאין לגבי החיות שבאותיות המחשבה שהוא
כאין לגבי חיות ומעלת המדות שמהן נמשכה
מחשבה זו שהוא כאין לגבי חיות ומעלת ומדרגת

the *Tanya* here inverts the meaning: the verse is teaching us *G-d's perception of chochmah.* When G-d uses *chochmah,* it is not a high-level experience, but a very low-level one, similar to action for us. In the Chasidic interpretation, the Psalmist exclaims: *Chochmah* is our most elevated, prelingual power, yet for You it is at the opposite end of the spectrum, post-lingual, like action!

וְהַיְינוּ לוֹמַר שֶׁכְּעֵרֶךְ הַחַיּוּת שֶׁבַּעֲשִׂיָּה גוּפָנִית וְגַשְׁמִיִּית — **Meaning that when we compare the** spiritual **energy manifest within the performance of a physical act** a person performs **with his body,** לְעֵרֶךְ חַיּוּת הַחָכְמָה — **compared to the** spiritual **energy manifest within *chochmah,*** the spiritual energy manifest in the physical act is virtually zero, being separated from *chochmah* by many levels of separation.

Chochmah, being the highest, prelingual power, has the most soul-energy. Action, being post-lingual, has the least soul-energy.

The *Tanya* will now elaborate on this point in some detail. First we will clarify that *chochmah* has the most spiritual energy (see Part One, p. 217).

שֶׁהִיא רֵאשִׁית וּמְקוֹר הַחַיּוּת בָּאָדָם — *Chochmah* has the most energy **since it is the initial source of all man's** spiritual **energy,** וְכָל הַבְּרוּאִים גַּשְׁמִיִּים — **and** it is likewise **the** spiritual **energy of all physical creations.**

Now we turn to explain why action has the least spiritual energy.

שֶׁהוּא כְּאַיִן לְגַבֵּי חַיּוּת שֶׁבְּאוֹתִיּוֹת הַדִּבּוּר — The (post-lingual) spiritual energy manifest within the performance of a physical act, **pales into insignificance when compared with the** (lingual) spiritual **energy manifest in spoken language,** שֶׁהוּא כְּאַיִן לְגַבֵּי חַיּוּת שֶׁבְּאוֹתִיּוֹת הַמַּחֲשָׁבָה — **and** the spiritual energy manifest in spoken language **pales into insignificance when compared with the** spiritual **energy manifest in** unspoken **language in one's thoughts,** שֶׁהוּא כְּאַיִן לְגַבֵּי חַיּוּת וּמַעֲלַת הַמִּדּוֹת שֶׁמֵּהֶן נִמְשְׁכָה מַחֲשָׁבָה זוֹ — **and** the spiritual energy manifest in unspoken language in one's thoughts **pales into insignificance when compared with the** (prelingual) spiritual **energy manifest in the emotional powers of the soul, which give rise to these thoughts,** שֶׁהוּא כְּאַיִן לְגַבֵּי חַיּוּת וּמַעֲלַת וּמַדְרֵגַת הַחָכְמָה בִּינָה וָדַעַת מְקוֹר הַמִּדּוֹת — **and** the spiritual energy manifest in

החכמה בינה ודעת מקור המדות כן ממש ערך
מדרגת ומעלת החכמה שהיא ראשית ומקור החיות
שבכל העולמות לגבי הקדוש ב"ה בכבודו ובעצמו
המרומם והמתנשא ריבוא רבבות מדרגות רוממות
יותר מרוממות מדרגת החכמה על בחי' חיות שבעשייה
שהיא רוממות חמש מדרגות לבד שהן מדרגות בחי'

the emotional powers of the soul **pales into insignificance when compared with** the soul's intellectual powers, *chochmah, binah and da'as,* **which are the source of the emotional powers.**

The spectrum from action to *chochmah* spans two lingual levels (speech/thought) and two prelingual levels (emotions/intellect). Each of these represents a massive shift, energetically speaking, to an entirely different plane.

To say "action is lower than *chochmah*" is an understatement. It is *several orders of existence lower*, each of which pales into insignificance compared to the other.

SECTION TWO: CAN G-D'S TRANSCENDENCE BE DESCRIBED?

We are in the process of explaining the verse, *"You made them all with chochmah,"* which the *Tanya* has interpreted to mean: For G-d, the energy of *choch mah* (which for us is the super-high energetic source of the universe) is so low, it's like the bottom of the consciousness spectrum: post-lingual action.

In Section One we explained why action is placed so low on the human energetic/consciousness scale. Here in Section Two the *Tanya* will explain why for G-d the reverse is true: He looks at *chochmah* as we look at action.

כֵּן מַמָּשׁ — **So too, literally,** עֵרֶךְ מַדְרֵגַת וּמַעֲלַת הַחָכְמָה — **the level/quality of** *chochmah,* שֶׁהִיא רֵאשִׁית וּמְקוֹר הַחַיּוּת שֶׁבְּכָל הָעוֹלָמוֹת — **which is the prima-ry source of** spiritual **energy for all the worlds,** לְגַבֵּי הַקָּדוֹשׁ בָּרוּךְ הוּא בִּכְבוֹדוֹ וּבְעַצְמוֹ — pales into insignificance **compared to G-d Himself, in His essence,** הַמְרוֹמָם וְהַמִּתְנַשֵּׂא רִיבּוֹא רְבָבוֹת מַדְרֵגוֹת רוֹמְמוּת — **who is millions of levels of transcendence above and beyond** *chochmah,* יוֹתֵר מֵרוֹמְמוּת מַדְרֵגַת הַחָכְמָה עַל — **more than the** number of **levels by which,** in human בְּחִינַת חַיּוּת שֶׁבָּעֲשִׂיָּיה — experience, the spiritual energy in *chochmah* transcends the spiritual **energy in action.**

The "distance" (degree of transcendence) from G-d's essence down to *chochmah* is far greater that the "distance" from *chochmah* down to human action. That is because G-d transcends *chochmah* with "*millions of degrees of transcendence,*" whereas the "distance" from *chochmah* to human action,

עשייה ודבור ומחשבה ומדות ושכל אבל הקדוש ב"ה
רם ומתנשא ממדרגת החכמה רבבות מדרגות כאלו
עד אין קץ רק מפני שאין בנבראים כח להשיג רק
ההשתלשלות ממדרגת חכמה שהיא ראשיתם למדרגת
עשיה השפלה לכך אנו אומרים שלגבי הקדוש ב"ה
נחשבת מדרגת החכמה כמדרגת עשיה ממש דהיינו
לומר שהוא רם ונשא ונעלה עילוי רב מאד מאד

86B

שֶׁהִיא רוֹמְמוּת חָמֵשׁ מַדְרֵגוֹת לְבָד — **is just *five* degrees of transcendence.**

שֶׁהֵן מַדְרֵגוֹת בְּחִינוֹת עֲשִׂיָּה וְדִבּוּר וּמַחֲשָׁבָה וּמִדּוֹת וְשֵׂכֶל. — **Namely, the levels of:**
a.) **action,** b.) **speech,** c.) **thought,** d.) **emotional powers** and e.) **intellectual
powers.**

אֲבָל הַקָּדוֹשׁ בָּרוּךְ הוּא רָם וּמִתְנַשֵּׂא מִמַּדְרֵגַת הַחָכְמָה רִבְבוֹת מַדְרֵגוֹת כָּאֵלּוּ עַד אֵין קֵץ
— **G-d, on the other hand, is millions of such degrees of transcendence, if not
an infinite number, above and beyond the level of *chochmah*.**

29TH SIVAN REGULAR | 2ND TAMMUZ LEAP

But if this is the case, equating G-d's view of *chochmah* to our view of action is
a misleading understatement. How could the *Tanya* compare a relationship of
millions of degrees of separation (G-d to *chochmah*) to one of just five degrees
of separation (*chochmah* to action)?

רַק מִפְּנֵי שֶׁאֵין בַּנִּבְרָאִים כֹּחַ לְהַשִּׂיג רַק הַהִשְׁתַּלְשְׁלוּת מִמַּדְרֵגַת חָכְמָה שֶׁהִיא רֵאשִׁיתָם
— **Only,** the comparison is reasonable **since we creations can only under-
stand levels which have been downgraded from *chochmah,* which is their
initial** source, לְמַדְרֵגַת עֲשִׂיָּה הַשְּׁפֵלָה — **down to the humble level of** physical
action, לְכָךְ אָנוּ אוֹמְרִים שֶׁלְּגַבֵּי הַקָּדוֹשׁ בָּרוּךְ הוּא נֶחְשֶׁבֶת מַדְרֵגַת הַחָכְמָה כְּמַדְרֵגַת
עֲשִׂיָּה מַמָּשׁ — **therefore, we say that, compared to G-d, the level of *chochmah*
is really as low as action.**

The "distance" from *chochmah* down to physical action is, for us, the *full spectrum* of consciousness: our highest prelingual power to our lowest, post-lingual
one. While admittedly it is a far less "distance" than the infinite chasm separating G-d from *chochmah,* but it's the best illustration we have.

דְּהַיְינוּ לוֹמַר שֶׁהוּא רָם וְנִשָּׂא וְנַעֲלֶה עִילּוּי רַב מְאֹד מְאֹד מִמַּדְרֵגַת הַחָכְמָה — Our comparison **implies that He is very, very much above and beyond the level of
chochmah, transcending it exceedingly.**

Our comparison doesn't seek to equate the distance between G-d/*chochmah* and *chochmah*/human action. It's an imprecise comparison, but it's the
best we have, because prior to *chochmah,* finitude didn't exist.

ממדרגת החכמה ולא שייך כלל לייחס אצלו שום
ענין המתייחס לחכמה אפילו בדרך מעלה ועילוי
רב כגון לומר עליו שא"א לשום נברא עליונים

In summary: *Tanya* has given us an inadequate but nevertheless use-ful illustration to help us picture G-d's transcendence. We should carefully contemplate the metaphysical gap separating the highest and lowest en-tities in the universe (*chochmah* and action), stage by stage (through five major shifts), and then we should try to picture that the gap separating G-d from the highest entity in the universe vastly transcends that.

What, though, is the point of this exercise? Can't we just say more simply that G-d can't be understood and transcends the world?

That would, of course, be true. But if G-d transcends anything we can imagine, we get closer to an appreciation of Him by first expanding our imagination as much as possible, *and then transcending that.* To say that G-d is more powerful than a large ox is true, but not very inspiring, since G-d is not transcending very much. By expanding our perception to its limits, and then transcending it, we get the closest appreciation of G-d hu-manly possible.

SECTION THREE: A PRACTICAL RAMIFICATION

The above discussion leads us to a practical conclusion of what we can or cannot say about G-d.

וְלֹא שַׁיָּיךְ כְּלָל לְיַיחֵס אֶצְלוֹ שׁוּם עִנְיָן הַמִּתְיַיחֵס לְחָכְמָה — G-d transcends *chochmah* to the extent that no quality which is attributed to *chochmah* can be attributed to Him, אֲפִילוּ בְּדֶרֶךְ מַעֲלָה וְעִילוּי רַב — even if it's a very great quality and virtue.

Utter transcendence, practically speaking, means that two entities have nothing in common. The Divine power of *chochmah,* while extremely lofty, can be approached with human symbolism and language. G-d's essence, on the other hand, cannot, since it *infinitely* transcends *chochmah.*

כְּגוֹן לוֹמַר עָלָיו שֶׁאִי אֶפְשָׁר לְשׁוּם נִבְרָא עֶלְיוֹנִים וְתַחְתּוֹנִים לְהַשִּׂיג חָכְמָתוֹ — For example, while it sounds like a wonderful praise, it's inappropriate to say of G-d that no created intellect, in the upper or lower worlds, can compre-hend His *chochmah,* אוֹ מַהוּתוֹ — or grasp the nature of His essence.

It is inappropriate to *praise* G-d's transcendence of *chochmah* as some-thing that humans can't comprehend, as the *Tanya* now explains.

ותחתונים להשיג חכמתו או מהותו כי ענין ההשגה
מתייחס ונופל על דבר חכמה ושכל לומר שאפשר
להשיגו או אי אפשר להשיגו מפני עומק המושג
אבל הקדוש ברוך הוא שהוא למעלה מן השכל
והחכמה לא שייך כלל לומר בו שאי אפשר להשיגו
מפני עומק המושג כי אינו בבחי' השגה כלל והאומר
עליו שאי אפשר להשיגו הוא כאומר על איזו חכמה
רמה ועמוקה שאי אפשר למשה בידים מפני עומק

כִּי עִנְיַן הַהַשָּׂגָה מִתְיַחֵס וְנוֹפֵל עַל דְּבַר חָכְמָה וְשֵׂכֶל — It's inappropriate to praise G-d's transcendence of *chochmah* as something that humans can't comprehend, **since "comprehension" refers to something** *already in the realm* **of wisdom and intellect,** לוֹמַר שֶׁאֶפְשָׁר לְהַשִּׂיגוֹ — and once something is in the realm of the intellect, we can **say** either **that it's possible to comprehend it,** אוֹ אִי אֶפְשָׁר לְהַשִּׂיגוֹ מִפְּנֵי עוֹמֶק הַמּוּשָּׂג — **or that it's impossible to comprehend it, because it's too profound.**

אֲבָל הַקָּדוֹשׁ בָּרוּךְ הוּא שֶׁהוּא לְמַעְלָה מִן הַשֵּׂכֶל וְהַחָכְמָה — **But in reference to G-d, who transcends** the realm of **intellect and wisdom,** לֹא שַׁיָּיךְ כְּלָל לוֹמַר בּוֹ שֶׁאִי אֶפְשָׁר **לְהַשִּׂיגוֹ מִפְּנֵי עוֹמֶק הַמּוּשָּׂג — you can't say of Him that, "He's too deep a concept to be understood,"** כִּי אֵינוֹ **בִּבְחִינַת הַשָּׂגָה כְּלָל — because He's not something which can *at all* be grasped with intellect** to begin with.

The *Tanya* offers us an illustration of how the notion of intellect is an inappropriate and ludicrous tool to relate to G-d's essence.

וְהָאוֹמֵר עָלָיו שֶׁאִי אֶפְשָׁר לְהַשִּׂיגוֹ — **So to say of Him** that, **"You can't comprehend Him,"** הוּא כְּאוֹמֵר עַל אֵיזוֹ חָכְמָה רָמָה וַעֲמוּקָה שֶׁאִי אֶפְשָׁר לְמַשֵּׁשָׁה בְּיָדַיִם מִפְּנֵי עוֹמֶק הַמּוּשָּׂג — **is like saying about a sublime and profound idea that, "The concept is so deep you can't touch it with your hands."**

לְפִי שֶׁחוּשׁ הַמִּשּׁוּשׁ אֵינוֹ מִתְיַחֵס וְנוֹפֵל אֶלָּא עַל עֲשִׂיָּיה גַשְׁמִית הַנִּתְפֶּסֶת בְּיָדַיִם — **Anyone hearing this will laugh at you,** שֶׁכָּל הַשּׁוֹמֵעַ יִצְחַק לוֹ — **because a sense of touch is only appropriate in reference to the motor functions of the hands in physical action.**

הַמּוּשָׂג שֶׂכֶל הַשּׁוֹמֵעַ יִצְחַק לוֹ לְפִי שֶׁחוּשׁ הַמִּישׁוּשׁ
אֵינוֹ מִתְיַיחֵס וְנוֹפֵל אֶלָּא עַל עֲשִׂיָּיה גַּשְׁמִית הַנִּתְפֶּסֶת
בַּיָּדַיִם וְכָכָה מַמָּשׁ נֶחְשֶׁבֶת לְגַבֵּי הַקָּבָּ"ה מַדְרֵגַת
הַשֵּׂכֶל וְהַהַשָּׂגָה כַּעֲשִׂיָּה גַּשְׁמִית מַמָּשׁ וַאֲפִילוּ הַשָּׂגַת
שְׂכָלִים שֶׁבָּעוֹלָמוֹת עֶלְיוֹנִים וַאֲפִילוּ מַדְרֵגַת חָכְמָה
עִילָּאָה הַמְחַיָּה אֶת כּוּלָם כְּדִכְתִיב כּוּלָּם בְּחָכְמָה
עָשִׂיתָ. וּמָה שֶׁהַקָּדוֹשׁ בָּרוּךְ הוּא נִקְרָא חָכָם בַּכָּתוּב

וְכָכָה מַמָּשׁ נֶחְשֶׁבֶת לְגַבֵּי הַקָּדוֹשׁ בָּרוּךְ הוּא מַדְרֵגַת הַשֵּׂכֶל וְהַהַשָּׂגָה כַּעֲשִׂיָּה גַּשְׁמִית מַמָּשׁ — **In precisely the same way, the realm of intellect is, compared to G-d, literally like physical action.**

Human intellect is an inadequate tool to speak of G-d's transcendence. It is therefore no praise of G-d to say that He cannot be "comprehended." The two terms simply don't belong together in the same sentence.

וַאֲפִילוּ הַשָּׂגַת שְׂכָלִים שֶׁבָּעוֹלָמוֹת עֶלְיוֹנִים — And this holds true **even for the** disembodied **intellects** of the angels **in the upper worlds.**

It is similarly no praise of G-d to say that the angels can't comprehend Him. Angelic wisdom, though far greater than human wisdom, is an equally inadequate tool to approach G-d.

וַאֲפִילוּ מַדְרֵגַת חָכְמָה עִילָּאָה הַמְחַיָּה אֶת כּוּלָם — **And even the level of Divine "supernal** chochmah," **which energizes everything** in the universe, is inadequate to grasp G-d Himself.

Even the *Divine* intellect is an inadequate tool for G-d to grasp His own essence. Intellect, even if it is Divine, is ultimately a *form*, and G-d in His essence is utterly formless.

כְּדִכְתִיב כּוּלָּם בְּחָכְמָה עָשִׂיתָ — G-d vastly transcends His own intellect, **as the verse states,** *"You made them all with chochmah,"* suggesting that, from His perspective, His own intellectual power of *chochmah* is on the diminished level of action (as above).

SECTION FOUR: THE EMANATION STORY

In the previous section we learned how G-d is disidentified with His *chochmah*, vastly transcending it. The *Tanya* now questions this conclusion.

וּמָה שֶׁהַקָּדוֹשׁ בָּרוּךְ הוּא נִקְרָא חָכָם בַּכָּתוּב — **And as for the fact that Scripture identifies G-d with His** *chochmah*, **calling Him a** *"Chacham"* (Isaiah 31:2), וְגַם חֲכָמֵינוּ זִכְרוֹנָם לִבְרָכָה כִּינּוּ לוֹ מַדְרֵגַת וּמַעֲלַת הַחָכְמָה — **and our Sages, of**

וְגַם חז"ל כִּינוּ לוֹ מַדְרֵגַת וּמַעֲלַת הַחָכְמָה הַיְינוּ מִשּׁוּם
שֶׁהוּא מְקוֹר הַחָכְמָה שֶׁמִּמֶּנּוּ ית' נִמְשָׁךְ וְנֶאֱצָל מַהוּת
מַדְרֵגַת חָכְמָה עִילָאָה שֶׁבָּעוֹלָם הָאֲצִילוּת וְכֵן רַחוּם
וְחָסִיד עַל שֵׁם שֶׁהוּא מְקוֹר הָרַחֲמִים וְהַחֲסָדִים וְכֵן
שְׁאָר הַמִּדּוֹת שֶׁכּוּלָן נִמְשְׁכוּ וְנֶאֶצְלוּ מִמֶּנּוּ יִתְבָּרֵךְ
וְדֶרֶךְ וְעִנְיַן הַהַמְשָׁכָה וְהָאֲצִילוּת אֵיךְ וּמַה יָדוּעַ

blessed memory, also referred to Him as having the level/quality of *chochmah* (see *Talmud, Berachos* 58a), **nevertheless, as we shall see, this does not contradict what we have learned above.**

A name doesn't merely tell us one quality that a person possesses, it says who they are. If G-d totally transcends His *chochmah*, why does Scripture and the Talmud *name* G-d with this quality?

The *Tanya* answers:

הַיְינוּ מִשּׁוּם שֶׁהוּא מְקוֹר הַחָכְמָה — **What** Scripture and the Sages **meant was that** G-d **is *the source of chochmah*,** שֶׁמִּמֶּנּוּ יִתְבָּרֵךְ נִמְשָׁךְ וְנֶאֱצָל מַהוּת מַדְרֵגַת חָכְמָה עִילָאָה שֶׁבָּעוֹלָם הָאֲצִילוּת — **that the level of "supernal** *chochmah*" **(in the World of** *Atzilus***) emerges and emanates** *from* **G-d Himself.**

וְכֵן רַחוּם וְחָסִיד עַל שֵׁם שֶׁהוּא מְקוֹר הָרַחֲמִים וְהַחֲסָדִים — **Similarly,** they referred to Him as **"Compassionate One" and "Kind One" since He is the** emanating *source* of compassion and kindness.

וְכֵן שְׁאָר הַמִּדּוֹת שֶׁכּוּלָן נִמְשְׁכוּ וְנֶאֶצְלוּ מִמֶּנּוּ יִתְבָּרֵךְ — **And the same is true of all the other Divine attributes, that they all emerge and emanate** *from* **G-d.**

The key to understanding this relationship, between G-d's attributes and His essence, is one of emerging through *emanation*.

The Kabbalists often explained this phenomenon through the symbol of light emerging from a light-source. One ray of sunlight, for example, tells you a lot about the sun; it reflects the sun's qualities, although in a diminished way. On the other hand, the value of that one ray is basically zero compared to the sun itself.

So in an emanator/emanated relationship: a.) the emanator vastly transcends the emanated, such that the latter has no value compared to the former. b.) the emanated nevertheless closely reflects something of the emanator, albeit in diminished form.

That is the best way to picture G-d's relationship with His attributes.

וְדֶרֶךְ וְעִנְיַן הַהַמְשָׁכָה וְהָאֲצִילוּת אֵיךְ וּמַה יָדוּעַ — **And the precise method and scheme through which this emanation and flow occurs, is known,**

87A למשכילים* והנה אין לנו
עסק בנסתרו' אך הנגלות
לנו להאמין אמונה שלימה
דאיהו וגרמוהי חד דהיינו

הגה"ה

(סוד הצמצום באור א"ס ב"ה וצמצום
א"ק וסוד הדיקנא שסוד כל הצמצומים
לצמצם האור שיתלבש בבחי' כלים די"ס

לַמַּשְׂכִּילִים — **to scholars** of the Kabbalah.*

The Kabbalah depicts our monotheistic faith (that G-d is one with His attributes) through a *story of emanation.* The way in which G-d's light emerges from its source, and passes through a myriad of transformations, before eventually becoming the Divine attributes, is described in incredible detail in the Kabbalah.

וְהִנֵּה אֵין לָנוּ עֵסֶק בַּנִּסְתָּרוֹת — **Now, it is not our business to delve into** *"hidden matters,"* אַךְ הַנִּגְלוֹת לָנוּ — but, *"the revealed ones belong to us"* (*Deuteronomy* 29:28), דְּאִיהוּ לְהַאֲמִין אֱמוּנָה שְׁלֵימָה — namely, **to believe with perfect faith,** וְגַרְמוֹהִי חַד — that *"He and* the attributes that **He causes are one"** (*Tikunei Zohar* 3b).

הַגָהָה — *NOTE**

30TH SIVAN REGULAR | 3RD TAMMUZ LEAP

The Kabbalah describes this process of emanation in three general phases.

סוֹד הַצַּמְצוּם בְּאוֹר אֵין סוֹף בָּרוּךְ הוּא — a.) **The mystical secret of the** *tzimtzum* (diminishment) of the *Ohr Ein Sof* ("Infinite Light"),

וְצִמְצוּם אָדָם קַדְמוֹן — b.) **The** *tzimtzum* of *Adam Kadmon* ("Primordial Man").

וְסוֹד הַדִּיקְנָא — c.) **The mystical secret of the** *Dikna* ("Divine **Beard").**

Unlike Maimonides, the Kabbalists were not opposed to using human images to depict Divine emanations. The Kabbalah describes in detail how, from the formless Infinite Light (*Ohr Ein Sof*), lights emerged that resembled human forms ("Primordial Man" and "Beard"). This gradual acquisition of subtle form through the diminishment of Divine light is the Kabbalah's "story of emanation" which ends in the formation of Divine attributes.

שֶׁסוֹד כָּל הַצַּמְצוּמִים לְצַמְצֵם הָאוֹר שֶׁיִּתְלַבֵּשׁ בִּבְחִינוֹת כֵּלִים — **And the secret** purpose **of all "diminishments" was to dim the** Divine **light so as to** be compatible with, and **"dress" in, the "vessels,"** דְּי' סְפִירוֹת — of each of **the ten** *sefiros.*

Within the Divine attributes themselves, relatively formless Divine energy ("lights") enter and are dressed in Divine energies that possess a more distinct

מדותיו של הקדוש ב"ה
ורצונו וחכמתו ובינתו ודעתו
עם מהותו ועצמותו המרוממים

והנה אחר שנתלבש אור א"ס בבחי'
כלים דחב"ד אז שייך לומר מ"ש הרמב"ם
הוא היודע והוא המדע והוא הידוע
ובידיעת עצמו וכו' לפי שבחי' כלים

"It is not our business to delve into hidden matters" is a phrase often employed by Rabbinic authors who opposed the study of Kabbalah. This was, of course, not the view of the author of *Tanya*, whose discourses contain far more Kabbalistic references than his contemporaries. Rabbi Shneur Zalman in fact instructed his followers to "study a little from the *Zohar* every day, and on the Sabbath, *Zohar* the entire day" (*Ma'amarei Admor Ha-Zakein, Al Parshiyos Ha-Torah ve-ha-mo'adim,* vol. 2 (Brooklyn: Kehos, 1983), p. 831).

But the current work is a discourse on "unity and faith." It seeks to inform us of the facts about G-d's unity that we ought to believe. So here, *in this text,* "it is not our business to delve into hidden matters," but to state that we must *"believe with perfect faith that 'He and the attributes that He causes are one.'"*

דְּהַיְינוּ מִדּוֹתָיו שֶׁל הַקָּדוֹשׁ בָּרוּךְ הוּא וּרְצוֹנוֹ וְחָכְמָתוֹ וּבִינָתוֹ וְדַעְתּוֹ — **Meaning to say** that G-d's emotional **attributes, His will, and His** *chochmah, binah* and *da'as,* הַמְרוֹמָם לְבַדּוֹ — are one **with His actual self,** עִם מַהוּתוֹ וְעַצְמוּתוֹ — and His

---

form ("vessels"). There is a vast literature explaining this interaction, but the *Tanya* mentions it here for a specific reason, as we shall soon see.

(The following is essentially a restatement of the author's "note" to Chapter 2 of Part One of the *Tanya*. See *The Practical Tanya,* volume one, pp. 46-48.)

וְהִנֵּה אַחַר שֶׁנִּתְלַבֵּשׁ אוֹר אֵין סוֹף בִּבְחִינוֹת כֵּלִים דְּחָכְמָה בִּינָה וָדַעַת — **Now, after the light of the *Ohr Ein Sof* has "dressed" in the vessels of *chochmah, binah* and** *da'as,* אָז שַׁיָּיךְ לוֹמַר מַה שֶׁכָּתַב הָרַמְבַּ"ם הוּא הַיּוֹדֵעַ וְהוּא הַמַּדָע וְהוּא הַיָּדוּעַ — only **at that point** in the chain of emanation **is *Rambam's* statement applicable, that** G-d **is** simultaneously **the "knower," the "power to know," and the "known"** (*Laws of Foundations of the Torah* 2:10), וּבִידִיעַת עַצְמוֹ וְכוּ' — **and that through knowing Himself,** He knows everything that exists (ibid. 9).

In the chain of emanation, the "form" of intellect only emerges at the level of the "vessels" of the Divine intellectual powers (*chochmah, binah* and *da'as*). At that point, human intellect *is* a (partially) adequate tool to discover truth about the Divine. Above that point (from the "lights" of those attributes upwards) intellect is totally inadequate, and we must rely on received wisdom (Kabbalah).

Rambam, who was a philosopher, presented his arguments based on rational inquiry and not received wisdom. Therefore, the *Tanya* indicates here, they speak at the level of the "vessels" where intellect is still an adequate tool.

לבדו רוממות אין קץ מבחי' | דאצילות נעשים נשמה וחיות לבי"ע
חכמה ושכל והשגה ולכן | ולכל אשר בהם אבל בלי צמצום
גם יחודו שמתייחד עם | והלבשה הנ"ל לא שייך כלל לומר הוא
מדותיו שהאציל מאתו ית' | היודע והוא המדע וכו' כי אינו בבחי'
ג"כ אינו בבחי' השגה | וגדר דעת ומדע כלל ח"ו אלא למעלה
להשיג איך מתייחד בהן | מעלה עילוי רב עד אין קץ אפי' מבחי'
ולכן נקראו מדותיו של | וגדר חכמה עד שבחי' חכמה נחשבת
אצלו ית' כבחי' עשיה גשמית:

actual self is **"alone exalted"** (*Liturgy, Morning Prayers*), רוֹמְמוּת אֵין קֵץ מִבְּחִינַת
חָכְמָה וְשֵׂכֶל וְהַשָּׂגָה — infinitely transcending His qualities of *chochmah,* intellect and understanding.

This is what we must believe. The Kabbalah is an extended commentary, helping us to come closer to this truth through rich symbolism. But regardless of to what extent we have mastered that material, it is axiomatic to Judaism to believe that a.) G-d's attributes reflect Him and are one with Him; and yet, b.) He completely transcends them.

וְלָכֵן גַּם יְחוּדוֹ שֶׁמִּתְיַחֵד עִם מִדּוֹתָיו שֶׁהֶאֱצִיל מֵאִתּוֹ יִתְבָּרֵךְ — **Therefore this unity, how He is one with the attributes which He emanated from Himself,** גַּם כֵּן אֵינוֹ
לְהַשִּׂיג אֵיךְ מִתְיַחֵד בָּהֶן — **is also not possible to be understood,** בִּבְחִינַת הַשָּׂגָה — you can't **understand how He is one with them.**

As we learned above in Section Three.

לְפִי שֶׁבְּחִינוֹת כֵּלִים דַּאֲצִילוּת נַעֲשִׂים נְשָׁמָה וְחַיּוּת לִבְרִיאָה יְצִירָה וַעֲשִׂיָּה — **For it is the vessels of** *Atzilus* **that provide the "soul" and spiritual energy for the created worlds,** *Beriah, Yetzirah* **and** *Asiyah,* וּלְכָל אֲשֶׁר בָּהֶם — **and everything contained in them.**

All the forms in our universe emerge from the "vessels." Therefore intellect, which functions in the world of form, can only reach as high as the "vessels."

אֲבָל בְּלִי צִמְצוּם וְהַלְבָּשָׁה הַנִּזְכָּר לְעֵיל — **But without the diminishment of the** Divine light **and its "dressing" in vessels that we have mentioned,** לֹא שַׁיָּיךְ כְּלָל — **you couldn't conceivably say that** G-d is the לוֹמַר הוּא הַיּוֹדֵעַ וְהוּא הַמַּדְע וְכוּ' — "knower," the "power to know," and the "known," כִּי אֵינוֹ בִּבְחִינַת וְגֶדֶר דַּעַת וּמַדָּע — **because** at that level, **He is not, G-d forbid, in the realm of knowledge and intellect at all,** כְּלָל חַס וְשָׁלוֹם — **rather** אֶלָּא לְמַעֲלָה מַעֲלָה עִילּוּי רַב עַד אֵין קֵץ — **He utterly transcends it, infinitely so,** אֲפִילוּ מִבְּחִינַת וְגֶדֶר חָכְמָה — transcending **even** *chochmah* to this degree, עַד שֶׁבְּחִינַת חָכְמָה נֶחְשֶׁבֶת אֶצְלוֹ יִתְבָּרֵךְ כִּבְחִינַת עֲשִׂיָּה גַּשְׁמִית — **to the extent that, to Him,** *chochmah* **is considered like physical action,** as we have discussed at length in this chapter.

הקדוש ב"ה שהן הספירות בזה"ק רזא דמהימנותא שהיא האמונה שלמעלה מן השכל:

וְלָכֵן נִקְרְאוּ מִדּוֹתָיו שֶׁל הַקָּדוֹשׁ בָּרוּךְ הוּא שֶׁהֵן הַסְּפִירוֹת בַּזֹּהַר הַקָּדוֹשׁ רָזָא דִמְהֵימְנוּתָא — That is why in the holy *Zohar*, G-d's attributes, His *sefiros,* are called *"secret of faith"* (*Zohar* 2, 134b), שֶׁהִיא הָאֱמוּנָה שֶׁלְמַעְלָה מִן הַשֵּׂכֶל — since their unity with Him is a matter of supra-rational faith.

Ultimately, the belief in G-d's attributes is paradoxical, a complexity we need to simply embrace. That is why, when describing the attributes (also known as *sefiros*), the *Zohar* refers to them as *"secret of faith."*

Our discussion in Section Three, how G-d transcends His attributes, refers to the level of "lights" before they are "dressed in vessels." Our discussion in Section Four, how G-d is identified with his attributes, speaks at the level of vessels.

The symbolism of "lights" and "vessels," then, is helpful in enabling us to picture these two contradictory qualities of the Divine attributes.

פרק י אך   מכל מקום הואיל ודברה תורה כלשון
בני אדם לשכך את האזן מה שהיא
יכולה לשמוע לכך ניתן רשות לחכמי האמת לדבר

CHAPTER 10

G-D'S ATTRIBUTES: TWO ASPECTS

SECTION ONE: CAN A METAPHOR TEACH US ABOUT G-D?

1ST TAMMUZ REGULAR | 4TH TAMMUZ LEAP

From Chapter 8 onwards, the *Tanya* has addressed the complex and nuanced issue of *intra-Divine unity,* how the numerous Divine attributes, intellectual and emotional, are utterly unified with G-d and do not in any way compromise His absolute oneness.

At the end of Chapter 9, we concluded that, ultimately, this mystical secret is *"not possible to be understood... you can't understand how He is one."*

But that's not the end of our discussion. Just because something can't be fully understood doesn't mean we shouldn't try. While our intellect is limited, our imagination and intuition can get a glimpse of the infinite through the rich symbolism of the Kabbalah.

In this chapter, the *Tanya* will offer us a physical analogy which will enable us to gain some insight, at least, into the *"secret of faith"* (*Zohar* 2, 134b), how G-d is one with His attributes.

אַך — **However,** even though G-d's attributes cannot be properly grasped by the intellect (as we concluded at the end of the previous chapter), מִכָּל מָקוֹם הוֹאִיל וְדִבְּרָה תוֹרָה כִּלְשׁוֹן בְּנֵי אָדָם — **nevertheless, since *"the Torah speaks of G-d in human terms"*** (*Talmud, Brachos* 31b), לְשַׁכֵּך אֶת הָאֹזֶן מַה שֶׁהִיא יְכוֹלָה לִשְׁמוֹעַ — *"to calm the ear, with that which it is capable of hearing"* (*Mechilta* to *Exodus* 19:18), לְכָך נִיתַּן רְשׁוּת לְחַכְמֵי הָאֱמֶת לְדַבֵּר בַּסְּפִירוֹת בְּדֶרֶך מָשָׁל — **there-fore, the Kabbalists deemed it appropriate to speak of the** Divine attributes, **the *sefiros*, with** worldly **symbols.**

The Torah is not afraid to speak of G-d with human metaphors. We read con-stantly of G-d's "anger," "compassion," "regret," and even physical limbs, such as "G-d's hand" and "G-d's eyes."

The two main streams of Jewish theology, Philosophy (*chakirah*) and Kabbal-ah, differed in their approach to these human terms. The Philosophers deemed

בספירות בדרך משל וקראו אותן אורות כדי שעל ידי
המשל הזה יובן לנו קצת ענין היחוד של הקדוש ב"ה

them to bear *no reflection whatsoever* on the Divine reality. The Torah merely "speaks in human terms" so as to be relatable to humans, but that does not mean to say that there is anything resembling these qualities in G-d.

The Kabbalists, however, took "human language" more literally. While they still understood the physical descriptions of G-d metaphorically, they nevertheless saw them as being symbolic of *actual Divine attributes that exist.*

Unlike the philosophers who viewed "human terms" as a mere gesture to human inadequacy, the Kabbalists saw the terms as something more real. Therefore, they *"deemed it appropriate to speak of the Divine attributes, the sefiros, with worldly symbols."*

SECTION TWO: A METAPHOR FOR INTRA-DIVINE UNITY

וְקָרְאוּ אוֹתָן אוֹרוֹת — In their symbolism, the Kabbalists **referred to** the Divine attributes, the *sefiros,* as **"lights,"** כְּדֵי שֶׁעַל יְדֵי הַמָּשָׁל הַזֶּה יוּבַן לָנוּ קְצָת עִנְיַן הַיִּחוּד שֶׁל הַקָּדוֹשׁ בָּרוּךְ הוּא וּמִדּוֹתָיו — **in order that through this metaphor, we can understand a little of G-d's unity with His attributes.**

The symbol which the Kabbalists associated with the Divine attributes is "light." But, even with this Kabbalistically precise metaphor, we will still only gain "a little" insight into the nature of the attributes, since, as noted above, the attributes cannot be properly understood.

The *Tanya* now explains why the metaphor of attributes as "lights" helps us understand intra-Divine unity.

שֶׁהוּא בְּדֶרֶךְ מָשָׁל כְּעֵין יִחוּד אוֹר הַשֶּׁמֶשׁ שֶׁבְּתוֹךְ גּוּף כַּדּוּר הַשֶּׁמֶשׁ עִם גּוּף הַשֶּׁמֶשׁ — The symbol of "lights" is used since G-d's unity with His attributes **somewhat resembles the way in which sunlight is united with the sun's globe, while** still **inside the sun's globe** (Rabbi Meir Ibn Gabbai, *Avodas Ha-Kodesh* 1:12; *Pardes Rimonim* 6:6; *Perush Zulasi* to *Mareches Ha-Elokus,* beg., chapter 9).

It is somewhat confusing that here the *Tanya* uses the example of "sunlight inside the sun's globe," because this same illustration was used earlier, in Chapter 3, *in an entirely different context.*

To understand why this is the case we need to review briefly the overall structure of this second book of *Tanya, Sha'ar Ha-Yichud ve-ha-Emunah.* The book is essentially a commentary on the statement, "G-d is one," which, in its Chasidic interpretation, implies two different truths:

1.) *G-d is alone.* "G-d is (the) one (thing that exists),"

ומדותיו שהוא בדרך משל כעין יחוד אור השמש שבתוך

גוף כדור השמש עם גוף השמש שנקרא מאור כמ"ש

2.) G-d's powers are unified within Him. "G-d is one (with His attributes)."

To demonstrate truth '1', that G-d is alone, we need to show that there is no real (independent) existence outside G-d. The *Tanya* devoted Chapters 1-7 to this theme.

To demonstrate truth '2', that G-d is one with His attributes, the *Tanya* devotes the current chapters, 8-12.

The two truths follow opposite paths of reasoning.

Truth '1' is a narrative of *negation* and *exclusion*. We learn how the existence of everything outside G-d is "null and void."

Truth '2' is a narrative of *validation* and *inclusion*. We learn that, while G-d's attributes are infinitely lower than His actual self, they are nevertheless, absolutely one with His self.

Strangely, the *Tanya* appears to use the same metaphor to depict these two opposite phenomena! The illustration of "sunlight within the sun" is cited both here in Chapter Ten, to illustrate Truth '2,' and earlier in Chapter Three, to illustrate the reverse dynamic of Truth '1'!

These two opposite readings of the same metaphor are clear from a close scrutiny of the *Tanya's* words. Here, we read that inside the sun, *"sunlight is **united** with the sun's globe."* The term "united" implies validation and inclusion: the sunlight is *actually present* and it is united with its source.

In Chapter Three, by contrast, we read, *"light rays are also found inside the physical globe of the sun itself... only there... one ray is considered **completely 'null and void.'"*** The phrase "completely 'null and void'" implies negation and exclusion. The light within the sun is voided and excluded from being categorized as "existent."

How can the same analogy, of sunlight within the sun, be assigned two opposite meanings? Is light inside the sun *present* and *included,* or *voided* and thereby *excluded?* We cannot have it both ways (*Notes on Tanya*).

To clarify this matter, the *Tanya* continues:

שֶׁנִּקְרָא מָאוֹר —The sun **is called "luminous source"** (*ma'or*), כְּמוֹ שֶׁכָּתוּב אֶת הַמָּאוֹר הַגָּדוֹל וְגוֹ' — **as Scripture states** in reference to the sun, that it is *"the great ma'or, etc."* (*Genesis* 1:16).

The analogy of the sun here in Chapter 10 is meant *in an entirely different context* to Chapter 3. Here, the *Tanya* makes clear, we are speaking of the sun as a "luminous source" (*ma'or*). In Chapter 3, the term is not used.

את המאור הגדול וגו' והזיו והניצוץ המתפשט ומאיר ממנו

The *Tanya's* message is: If we look at the sun as a physical body, the light inside teaches us a lesson of negation and exclusion (it is "null and void"). But if we look at the sun in the specific, *Biblical role* of a "luminous source," then we can derive the opposite message, that the light inside it is validated and included (it is "united").

What is the difference between these two characterizations ("sun" or "luminous source") that result in such opposite messages? Aren't they just two ways of saying the same thing?

The distinction revolves around the question: Can we *define* the sun by its capacity to produce light?

The simple answer to that question is: No. If you close the shades in your window, preventing light from entering your room, the sun is unaffected. The sun does not "care" whether it shines in your house or not. (By contrast, if you turn off the tap in your house, or use some electricity, the water/electricity sources which supply your house *are* affected, at least in a minimal way.) Light just "happens" to come out of the sun, as a result of the sun's internal properties; but the light itself is "null and void" to the sun, since the sun invests *no intentionality in producing it.*

It is in *this* context that Chapter 3 cites the analogy of the sun and its light.

But there is another way of looking at the relationship between the sun and its light, not based on its physical properties, but its *Biblical definition.* The Torah calls the sun a "luminous source," which implies that the sun's role *is* to produce light. That is why G-d made it!

This is the context of the sun analogy here in Chapter 10, as made clear from the *Tanya's* citation of *Genesis* 1:16. Unlike the physical sun, whose light is "irrelevant" to it, the "Biblical" sun was created to produce light. This intentionality confers the light with *validation;* and, as a result, its relationship with the sun is one of *inclusion.*

In conclusion: The *Tanya's* reference to "sunlight within the sun" here and in Chapter 3 are two radically different analogies. Chapter 3 speaks of the *physical sun,* whose light emerges incidentally and "unintentionally." This signifies a relationship between the world (light) and G-d (sun) as one of negation and exclusion; the world is "null and void." Chapter 10 speaks of the *Biblical sun,* whose light is significant to the sun and "intentional." This signifies the relationship between G-d's attributes (light) and Himself (sun) as one of validation and inclusion; the attributes are "united" with Him (*Notes on Tanya*).

וְהַזִּיו וְהַנִּיצוֹץ הַמִּתְפַּשֵּׁט וּמֵאִיר מִמֶּנּוּ נִקְרָא אוֹר — But only the ray/spark emerging and shining *from* the *ma'or* is called *ohr* (light).

נקרא אור כמ"ש ויקרא אלהים לאור יום וכשהאור הוא
במקורו בגוף השמש הוא מיוחד עמו בתכלית היחוד כי
אין שם רק עצם אחד שהוא גוף המאור המאיר כי הזיו

87B

Here the *Tanya* clarifies a further detail of the analogy, by answering a subtle (unstated) question. If the light within the (Biblical) sun is not "null and void" in its source, then we would imagine the light to be *distinctly present* within the sun's globe. Are we then to conclude that the light within the sun "is called light"?

The *Tanya* answers, no! Only the light "*emerging* and *shining from*" the sun's globe is "called light." Inside the globe, it is not.

But this requires some clarification:

1.) What is the *Tanya's* proof for this?

2.) If the light within the (Biblical) sun's globe is not called "light," what *is* it called?

3.) If the light in the Biblical sun's globe is indeed present and its existence validated, why can't we call it "light"?

The *Tanya* now answers these three questions (*Notes on Tanya*).

In response to question '1'—What is the proof that, in the Biblical model of the sun, the term "light" only refers to emergent light, and not the light within the sun's globe?—the *Tanya* answers:

כְּמוֹ שֶׁכָּתוּב וַיִּקְרָא אֱלֹהִים לָאוֹר יוֹם — **As the verse states, "*G-d called the light, 'day'*"** (ibid. 5).

"Day" refers to the phenomenon of *observable* light. This must have already emerged from the globe of the sun and be visible to us on earth.

In response to question '2'— If the light within the (Biblical) sun's globe is not called "light," what is it called?—the *Tanya* answers:

וּכְשֶׁהָאוֹר הוּא בִּמְקוֹרוֹ בְּגוּף הַשֶּׁמֶשׁ — **When the light is in its source, in the sun's globe,** הוּא מְיוּחָד עִמּוֹ בְּתַכְלִית הַיִּחוּד — the light **is absolutely unified with** the source, כִּי אֵין שָׁם רַק עֶצֶם אֶחָד שֶׁהוּא גוּף הַמָּאוֹר הַמֵּאִיר — **to the extent that there is only one entity present, a luminous body (ma'or) which shines.**

Inside the sun's globe, the luminous body (*ma'or*) and the light (*ohr*) are so deeply integrated that you cannot draw any distinction between them. We do not have two separate entities: *ma'or* and *ohr*; rather, just one thing: "*a luminous body (ma'or) which shines.*"

In response to question '3'— If the light in the Biblical sun's globe is indeed present and its existence validated, why can't we call it "light"?—the *Tanya* answers:

והאור שם עצם אחד ממש עם גוף המאור המאיר ואין לו
שום מציאות כלל בפני עצמו וכדברים האלה ממש ויותר
מזה הן מדותיו של הקב"ה ורצונו וחכמתו בעולם
האצילות עם מהותו ועצמותו כביכול המתלבש בתוכם
ומתייחד עמהם בתכלית היחוד מאחר שנמשכו ונאצלו
מאתו ית' ע"ד משל כדרך התפשטות האור מהשמש
אך לא ממש בדרך זה רק בדרך רחוקה ונפלאה

Since the light ray is — כִּי הַזִּיו וְהָאוֹר שָׁם עֶצֶם אֶחָד מַמָּשׁ עִם גוּף הַמָּאוֹר הַמֵּאִיר
literally one entity with the luminous body which shines, וְאֵין לוֹ שׁוּם מְצִיאוּת
כְּלָל בִּפְנֵי עַצְמוֹ — so the light has *no separate identity* whatsoever.

Since the light "has no separate identity" it cannot be given its own name.

The "Biblical sun," therefore, gives us a good (though imperfect) analogy for
the unity of G-d's attributes with Himself. Just as the light within the Biblical sun
is so unified with its source that it cannot be identified as "light," similarly, G-d's
attributes are absolutely unified with His actual self.

And *"things of this sort,"* (Genesis 39:17), lit- — וְכַדְּבָרִים הָאֵלֶּה מַמָּשׁ וְיוֹתֵר מִזֶּה
erally, and even more so, הֵן מִדּוֹתָיו שֶׁל הַקָּדוֹשׁ בָּרוּךְ הוּא וּרְצוֹנוֹ וְחָכְמָתוֹ בָּעוֹלָם
הָאֲצִילוּת עִם מַהוּתוֹ וְעַצְמוּתוֹ כִּבְיָכוֹל הַמִּתְלַבֵּשׁ בְּתוֹכָם וּמִתְיַחֵד עִמָּהֶם בְּתַכְלִית
הַיִּחוּד — are G-d's attributes/will/wisdom in the World of *Atzilus* totally united
with His actual essence, which "dresses" in them, so to speak, מֵאַחַר שֶׁנִּמְשְׁכוּ
וְנֶאֶצְלוּ מֵאִתּוֹ יִתְבָּרֵךְ עַל דֶּרֶךְ מָשָׁל כְּדֶרֶךְ הִתְפַּשְׁטוּת הָאוֹר מֵהַשֶּׁמֶשׁ — since the attributes **are, figuratively speaking, emanated from Him like light emanates from
its luminous source, the sun.**

In the realm of the Divine attributes (called the World of *Atzilus* or "Emanation"), G-d's attributes are "totally united" with G-d's essence, like *"light in its
source, in the sun's globe, is absolutely unified with its source to the extent that
there is just one entity,"* as stated above.

SECTION THREE: LIMITATIONS OF THE METAPHOR

While the above metaphor is extremely helpful, we must also acknowledge its
limitations.

But the comparison is imprecise, — אַךְ לֹא מַמָּשׁ בְּדֶרֶךְ זֶה — רַק בְּדֶרֶךְ רְחוֹקָה וְנִפְלָאָה
מֵהַשָּׂגָתֵינוּ — rather, G-d's emanation of His attributes **is something elusive and
distant from our intellect,** כִּי גָבְהוּ דְרָכָיו מִדְּרָכֵינוּ — since *"His ways are higher
than our ways"* (see Isaiah 55:9).

מהשגתינו כי גבהו דרכיו מדרכינו ומ"מ לשכך האזן
נשמע ונתבונן ממשל אור השמש המיוחד ובטל במקורו
ואינו עולה בשם כלל בפ"ע רק שם המקור לבדו כך כל
מדותיו של הקדוש ב"ה ורצונו וחכמתו אינן עולות

5TH TAMMUZ LEAP

What, exactly, is the metaphor's drawback to which the *Tanya* refers?

In our model of the "Biblical sun," the purpose of the sun is to give light. Obviously, this is not true of G-d: G-d does not exist merely in order to emanate His attributes! In fact, as we learned in the previous chapter, G-d "*infinitely* transcends" His attributes.

So the "Biblical sun" metaphor is *not accurate at all* as a description of G-d Himself.

But that doesn't mean the metaphor is useless. As the *Tanya* now clarifies, we must be selective in what we learn from the metaphor, and what we reject (*Notes on Tanya*).

PRACTICAL LESSONS

A good example we have to illustrate G-d's attributes is *sunlight*.

But to compare G-d to a "luminous body" is a useful comparison in one respect only, to help us contemplate how G-d is one with His attributes.

וּמִכָּל מָקוֹם לְשַׁכֵּךְ הָאֹזֶן — While it is utterly inappropriate to refer to G-d as a luminous source, which implies that He only exists to give light, **nevertheless to "calm the ear,"** נִשְׁמַע וְנִתְבּוֹנֵן מִמְּשַׁל אוֹר הַשֶּׁמֶשׁ הַמְיוּחָד וּבָטֵל בִּמְקוֹרוֹ — it is still useful to "hear" and contemplate the above **metaphor of sunlight that is unified in its source and voided** of its separate identity, וְאֵינוֹ עוֹלֶה בְּשֵׁם כְּלָל בִּפְנֵי עַצְמוֹ — "voided" in this case meaning, not that its existence is negated, but that the light is so unified with its source **that it cannot be given its own name,** רַק שֵׁם הַמָּקוֹר לְבַדּוֹ — **and is** simply **named along with its source,** as *"a luminous body (ma'or) which shines."*

The metaphor of Section Two *is* useful to describe *the relationship* between G-d's attributes (the light) and Himself (the luminous body), that *"the light ray is **literally one entity** with the luminous body."*

In summary: The *Tanya* tells us here that to compare G-d to a "luminous body" is a useful comparison *in one respect only,* to help us contemplate how G-d is one with His attributes.

We must be careful to apply the metaphor where it works, and reject it where it doesn't (*Notes on Tanya*).

ונקראות בשמות אלו כלל אלא לגבי הנבראים עליונים
ותחתונים שהוויתם וחיותם והנהגתם שהקב"ה מהוה
ומחיה אותם ומנהיגם הוא ברצונו וחכמתו ובינתו ודעתו
המתלבשות במדותיו הקדושות כדאיתא במדרש בעשרה
דברים נברא העולם בחכמה בתבונה ובדעת וכו' דכתיב

SECTION FOUR: WHY DO THE ATTRIBUTES HAVE NAMES?

In the previous sections we learned that each of the Divine attributes is comparable to light in the sun, so unified with its luminous source that it *"cannot be
given its own name"* of "light." If this is the case, why do we find that the Divine
attributes *are* given their own names, like *chochmah* and *chesed*?

The *Tanya* answers:

כָּךְ כָּל מִדּוֹתָיו שֶׁל הַקָּדוֹשׁ בָּרוּךְ הוּא וּרְצוֹנוֹ וְחָכְמָתוֹ אֵינָן עוֹלוֹת וְנִקְרָאוֹת בְּשֵׁמוֹת אֵלּוּ
Thus, it is only from the perspec- — כְּלָל אֶלָּא לְגַבֵּי הַנִּבְרָאִים עֶלְיוֹנִים וְתַחְתּוֹנִים
**tive of the creations (celestial or terrestrial), that G-d's attributes/will/wisdom
are designated by the specific names** which we use.

If we had a real perception of how G-d's attributes were one with His self, we
wouldn't call them by names. Only, "from the perspective of the creations," we
see the attributes as causing different activities, so we ascribe them different
names. (The same is true for the perception of "celestial" beings, such as the
angels.)

שֶׁהֲוָיָיתָם וְחִיּוּתָם וְהַנְהָגָתָם שֶׁהַקָּדוֹשׁ בָּרוּךְ הוּא מְהַוֶּה וּמְחַיֶּה אוֹתָם וּמַנְהִיגָם **Since**
from the creations' perspective, **our existence/energy/conduct by which G-d
creates/energizes/conducts us,** הוּא בִּרְצוֹנוֹ וְחָכְמָתוֹ וּבִינָתוֹ וְדַעְתּוֹ הַמִּתְלַבְּשׁוֹת
בְּמִדּוֹתָיו הַקְּדוֹשׁוֹת — **is** a result of **G-d's will/*chochmah/binah/da'as* "dressing"
in His** seven **holy** emotional **attributes.**

G-d conducts the world through His intellectual/emotional attributes, and
that is the filter through which all creations perceive Him. The Torah uses different names for G-d, to indicate that a particular intellectual or emotional attribute
is dominant in a particular worldly activity. These names do not accurately describe any attribute *within G-d*, which, like light within the sun, *"cannot be given
its own name."*

The *Tanya* cites sources from Scripture, *Midrash* and *Zohar* that indicate the
role of the attributes in the creation process.

כְּדְאִיתָא בַּמִּדְרָשׁ בַּעֲשָׂרָה דְּבָרִים נִבְרָא הָעוֹלָם בְּחָכְמָה בִּתְבוּנָה וּבְדַעַת וְכוּ' — **As the
Midrash states, "The world was created through ten statements, *chochmah,
tevunah* and *da'as* etc.,"** (*Talmud, Chagigah* 12a).

ה' בחכמה יסד ארץ כונן שמים בתבונה בדעתו תהומות
נבקעו וגו' וכמאמר אליהו דאפיקת עשר תיקונין וקרינן
להון עשר ספירן לאנהגא בהון עלמין סתימין דלא
אתגליין ועלמין דאתגליין ובהון אתכסיאת כו' עד"מ ביום

G-d created the world by "dressing" His attributes of *"chochmah, tevunah (binah) and da'as"* in His emotional attributes, represented by the "ten state-ments" of the Genesis narrative.

As the — דִּכְתִיב ה' בְּחָכְמָה יָסַד אֶרֶץ כּוֹנֵן שָׁמַיִם בִּתְבוּנָה בְּדַעְתּוֹ תְּהוֹמוֹת נִבְקָעוּ וְגוֹ' **verse states,** *"G-d through wisdom (chochmah) founded earth, set heav-ens firm through discernment (tevunah); through His knowledge (da'as) the depths burst open, etc."* (*Proverbs* 3:19-20).

The creative role of the Divine attributes (*sefiros*) is more explicit in the *Tiku-nei Zohar.*

And as in the saying of Elijah, — וּכְמַאֲמַר אֵלִיָהוּ דְּאַפִּיקַת עֲשַׂר תִּקוּנִין וְקָרִינָן לְהוֹן עֲשַׂר סְפִירָן לְאַנְהָגָא בְּהוֹן עָלְמִין — *"It is You who produced ten 'adornments,' we call them the ten sefiros, to conduct worlds"* (*Tikunei Zohar* 17a).

The *sefiros* **create both** *"hidden* **worlds** — סְתִימִין דְּלָא אִתְגַלְיָין וְעָלְמִין דְּאִתְגַלְיָין *that are not revealed, as well as revealed worlds"* (*ibid.*).

The *sefiros* are responsible for the creation of both "hidden" celestial worlds and the "revealed" terrestrial world.

All this is *"from the perspective of creations,"* where we perceive each at-tribute as having a separate creative power. But from G-d's perspective, each of the attributes is "unified in its source" to the extent that it *"has no separate identity whatsoever."* Therefore,

"in the sefiros **You conceal Yourself etc."** — וּבְהוֹן אִתְכְּסִיאַת כו' (*ibid.*).

From our perspective, the separate creative contributions of each of the at-tributes *veils* their true identity. In reality, they are one and unified; but we per-

---

A CHASIDIC THOUGHT

"All G-d's attributes are one, and each one of them is included in the other. He acts in all of them as one; or He acts in one and includes all of them within it."

Rabbi Asher ben David (13th Century), Sefer Ha-Yichud, p. 62.

רִאשׁוֹן מִשֵּׁשֶׁת יְמֵי בְרֵאשִׁית נִגְלֵית מִדַּת הַחֶסֶד כְּלוּלָה
מִכָּל מִדּוֹתָיו הַקְּדוֹשׁוֹת וּרְצוֹנוֹ וְחָכְמָתוֹ וּבִינָתוֹ וְדַעְתּוֹ
מְלוּבָּשִׁין בָּהּ וּבָרָא בָּהּ אֶת הָאוֹר בְּמַאֲמַר יְהִי אוֹר שֶׁהִיא
בְּחִי' הַתְפַּשְּׁטוּת וְהַמְשָׁכַת הָאוֹר לָעוֹלָם מִלְמַעְלָה
וְהִתְפַּשְּׁטוּתוֹ בָּעוֹלָם מִסּוֹף הָעוֹלָם עַד סוֹפוֹ שֶׁהִיא בְּחִי'

ceive them as different. On a superficial level they reveal G-d to us, but on a deeper level, they also hide the inner unity He has with His attributes.

SECTION FIVE: TWO ASPECTS OF THE "SEFIROS" COME TO LIGHT

2ND TAMMUZ REGULAR | 6TH TAMMUZ LEAP

In the previous section we discussed the contrast between the *creative role* of the various attributes/*sefiros* (our perspective) and *their true nature* as unified expressions of G-d's infinite essence (G-d's perspective). While G-d's perspective is largely hidden to us, the *Tanya* will now demonstrate how both aspects of the *sefiros* actually came to light in the creation process. Their overt activity will be as separate powers, but we will also be able to discern their unified nature.

עַל דֶּרֶךְ מָשָׁל בְּיוֹם רִאשׁוֹן מִשֵּׁשֶׁת יְמֵי בְרֵאשִׁית נִגְלֵית מִדַּת הַחֶסֶד — **So, for example, on the first of the six creation days,** G-d's **attribute of** *chesed* **(benevolence) was overtly disclosed.**

In a revealed way, *chesed* acted as a separate power on the first creation day.

כְּלוּלָה מִכָּל מִדּוֹתָיו הַקְּדוֹשׁוֹת וּרְצוֹנוֹ וְחָכְמָתוֹ וּבִינָתוֹ וְדַעְתּוֹ מְלוּבָּשִׁין בָּהּ — But *chesed* also **contained all His** other **holy attributes, and His will/chochmah/binah/da'as** "dressed" within it.

In a concealed way, *chesed* acted as a power unified with the other attributes.

וּבָרָא בָּהּ אֶת הָאוֹר בְּמַאֲמַר יְהִי אוֹר — **And with** *chesed,* including both its revealed and hidden aspects, G-d **created light, with the statement, "Let there be light"** (Genesis 1:3).

First the *Tanya* explains how the creation of light was an expression of G-d's *chesed* (benevolence) as a revealed, specific power.

שֶׁהִיא בְּחִינַת הַתְפַּשְּׁטוּת וְהַמְשָׁכַת הָאוֹר לָעוֹלָם מִלְמַעְלָה — Through a disclosure of *chesed,* **G-d extended and drew light from above into the world,** וְהִתְפַּשְּׁטוּתוֹ בָּעוֹלָם מִסּוֹף הָעוֹלָם עַד סוֹפוֹ — **extending to the world, from one end of the universe to the other,** שֶׁהִיא בְּחִינַת מִדַּת חֶסֶד — **for that is** G-d's **attribute of** *chesed* **(benevolence).**

88A מדת חסד רק מפני שכלולה גם ממדת גבורה לכן לא
היה רוחני כאור של מעלה ממש וגם נתלבש בע"הז
שהוא בבחי' גבול ותכלית שהוא מהלך ת"ק שנה מהארץ
לרקיע וממזרח למערב וכן ביום שני נגלית מדת גבורה

Benevolence implies *expansion* and *extension* to another. G-d's specific quality of *chesed* was expressed through the expansion and extension of light throughout the universe.

Now the *Tanya* addresses the "hidden" expression of the inner aspect of *chesed* (how it is unified with all the other *sefiros*) in the creation process.

רַק מִפְּנֵי שֶׁכְּלוּלָה גַּם מִמִּדַּת גְּבוּרָה — **Only, since** G-d's *chesed* **also contained** all His other attributes, including the **attribute of *gevurah*,** לְכֵן לֹא הָיָה רוּחָנִי כְּאוֹר שֶׁל מַעְלָה מַמָּשׁ — **therefore** the light created on the first day **was not spiritual, like the** original **light found above,** from which it emerged.

Overtly, *chesed* expressed G-d's benevolence and expansiveness: light was spread across the universe. But, more subtly, it also expressed His *gevurah* (power of diminishment/withholding). We see this from the fact that the physical light created was *downgraded* from the spiritual light from which it originated.

וְגַם נִתְלַבֵּשׁ בָּעוֹלָם הַזֶּה שֶׁהוּא בִּבְחִינַת גְּבוּל וְתַכְלִית — **And** the light **was also** significantly downgraded from its *infinite* source in G-d so as to **be "dressed" in this completely *finite* world,** שֶׁהוּא מַהֲלַךְ ת"ק שָׁנָה מֵהָאָרֶץ לָרָקִיעַ — and see that the world is finite **since "a journey from the earth to the firmament takes five hundred years"** (*Talmud, Chagigah* 13a), וּמִמִּזְרָח לְמַעֲרָב — which is *"also the distance from east to west"* (*ibid., Tamid* 32a).

The transition from spiritual/infinite light to physical/finite light is a formidable downgrade. This was the influence of *gevurah*-included-in-*chesed*.

From this example we see that the inner, unified dimension of the *sefiros* is not something only perceptible to G-d, it can also be discerned by us.

The *Tanya* now offers us a similar illustration from the second day of creation.

וְכֵן בְּיוֹם שֵׁנִי נִגְלֵית מִדַּת גְּבוּרָה — **And likewise on the second day,** overtly it was

A CHASIDIC THOUGHT

"Each one of the *sefiros* (Divine attributes) contains all the others. They are always united with their emanating source in absolute unity."

Rabbi Menachem Azaria De-Fano (16th Century), Ma'amar Me'ah Kesitah, sec. 62.

כלולה משאר מדות ורצונו כו' ובר בה הרקיע במאמר
יהי רקיע בתוך המים ויהי מבדיל בין מים למים שהיא
בחי' צמצום וגבורות להעלים מים העליונים הרוחניים
ממים התחתונים ועל ידי זה נתגשמו התחתונים בהבדלם
מהעליונים ומדת חסד כלולה בה כי עולם חסד יבנה
שהכל כדי שתראה היבשה ואדם עליה לעבוד ה' וכן

כְּלוּלָה מִשְׁאָר מִדּוֹת וּרְצוֹנוֹ כוּ' — G-d's **attribute of** *gevurah* **that was disclosed,**
but that *gevurah* also **contained the other attributes and His will** *etc.*

First the *Tanya* explains how G-d's *gevurah* was expressed in a revealed, specific power.

וּבָרָא בָּהּ הָרָקִיעַ בְּמַאֲמַר יְהִי רָקִיעַ — **With** *gevurah,* **He created the "firmament,"**
through the statement, *"Let there be a firmament within the water, and let it divide water from water"* (Genesis 1:6), — בְּתוֹךְ הַמַּיִם וִיהִי מַבְדִּיל בֵּין מַיִם לָמָיִם
שֶׁהִיא בְּחִינַת צְמְצוּם וּגְבוּרוֹת — **which,** overtly, **is an expression of diminishment and** *gevurah* **powers,**
— לְהַעֲלִים מַיִם הָעֶלְיוֹנִים הָרוּחָנִיִּים מִמַּיִם הַתַּחְתּוֹנִים
since the "firmament" served **to conceal the upper, spiritual waters from the lower waters,** וְעַל יְדֵי זֶה
— נִתְגַּשְׁמוּ הַתַּחְתּוֹנִים בְּהַבְדָּלָם מֵהָעֶלְיוֹנִים — resulting in
the lower waters **becoming physical, through their separation from the upper** waters.

PRACTICAL LESSONS

True unity means that each of G-d's attributes contains all the others. When one attribute is at work you can always discern the others in the background too—if you know how to look!

Nevertheless, in a more subtle way, *gevurah* acted as a power unified with the other attributes, including its opposite, *chesed.*

וּמִדַּת חֶסֶד כְּלוּלָה בָּהּ — **But the attribute of** *chesed* **was also included in** the creative work of *gevurah,* on the second day, כִּי עוֹלָם חֶסֶד יִבָּנֶה — **for** *"the world was built on chesed"* (Psalms 89:3), so all creative activity is, in a sense, a form of *chesed,* שֶׁהַכֹּל כְּדֵי
שֶׁתֵּרָאֶה הַיַּבָּשָׁה וְאָדָם עָלֶיהָ לַעֲבוֹד ה' — as we see on
the second day, **that** the creation of the "firmament"
was all in order that *"dry land shall appear"* (Genesis 1:9), **so that humans could worship G-d upon it.**

The *gevurah* activity of *"dividing water from water"* was, indirectly, an act of *chesed,* since it created dry land, our home.

וְכֵן כּוּלָּן — **And the same follows with all** the other attributes on the remaining creation days.

כּוּלַן וז"ש אליהו בתיקונים שם לאחזאה איך אתנהיג
עלמא בצדק ומשפט כו' צדק איהו דין משפט איהו
רחמי כו' כולא לאחזאה איך אתנהיג עלמא אבל לאו
דאית לך צדק ידיעא דאיהו דין ולא משפט ידיעא דאיהו
רחמי ולאו מכל אינון מדות כלל:

Having explained that even the opposite traits of *chesed* and *gevurah* managed to express each other, we can be assured that the same is true of all the other attributes on the other creation days. While each day overtly expresses just one attribute, the power of the other attributes included in the dominant attribute can always be subtly discerned.

וְזֶהוּ שֶׁאָמַר אֵלִיָּהוּ בַּתִּיקוּנִים שָׁם — **And this** notion of two aspects of the *sefiros* **is** the message of **Elijah's statement in** *Tikunei Zohar ibid.,* לְאַחֲזָאָה אֵיךְ אִתְנַהִיג עָלְמָא בְּצֶדֶק וּמִשְׁפָּט כוּ' — *"to show them how the world is conducted... by justice and lawfulness,"* צֶדֶק אִיהוּ דִין מִשְׁפָּט אִיהוּ רַחֲמֵי כוּ' — *"'justice'... is the* attribute of *judgment... 'lawfulness'... is the* attribute of *compassion."*

I.e., from the world's perspective (*"how the world is conducted"*), the *sefiros* have very defined, distinct properties.

כּוּלָא לְאַחֲזָאָה אֵיךְ אִתְנַהֲגָ עָלְמָא — *"All this is to show how the world functions,"* אֲבָל לָאו דְּאִית לָךְ צֶדֶק יְדִיעָא דְּאִיהוּ דִין — *"but not that You have any known exacting justice (which is judgment),"* וְלָא מִשְׁפָּט יְדִיעָא דְּאִיהוּ רַחֲמֵי — *"nor any known lawfulness (which is compassion),"* וְלָאו מִכָּל אִינוּן מִדוֹת כְּלָל — *"You do not have any of these attributes at all!"*

The separate qualities of the attributes are only from the perspective of "how the world functions." But from G-d's perspective, *"You do not have any of these attributes at all,"* since each of the attributes is totally unified with G-d in its source and *"cannot be given its own name."*

פרק יא וְהִנֵּה גם עשרה מאמרות ג"כ נקראו בשם
מאמרו' לגבי הנבראי' בלבד כי כמו

CHAPTER 11

G-D'S SPEECH & HIS ATTRIBUTES

SECTION ONE: THE TEN "STATEMENTS" ARE DIVINE

3RD TAMMUZ REGULAR | 7TH TAMMUZ LEAP

In the previous chapters we learned that the *sefiros* (Divine attributes) can be viewed from two perspectives:

From the world's perspective, each of the *sefiros* has a completely different function and creative role; but from G-d's perspective, all the *sefiros* are absorbed in His oneness and have no separate identity.

In this chapter we will learn that the same is true of G-d's "ten statements" (verbal utterances in the Genesis narrative), which can also be viewed from two different perspectives.

וְהִנֵּה גַּם עֲשָׂרָה מַאֲמָרוֹת — **Now even the "ten statements"** through which the world was created, גַּם כֵּן נִקְרְאוּ בְּשֵׁם מַאֲמָרוֹת לְגַבֵּי הַנִּבְרָאִים בִּלְבָד — **are,** like the *sefiros,* **also only called** separate **"statements" from the perspective of** us **creations.**

The *sefiros* do not create the world directly. They do so through the vehicle of Divine speech (the "ten statements"), as we learned in Chapter One. The *Tanya* teaches us here that the "statements" have an identity similar to the *sefiros:* they are Divine powers which, to some extent, have "departed" from G-d's actual self, and project His energy towards the universe; but, from a deeper perspective, they have not departed at all, and remain one with Him.

Since the "statements" are looked upon as *outward projections* to the actual creations, the notion of "statements" being one with G-d is more remarkable than the notion of *sefiros* being one with Him. Even G-d's outward projections remain within Him!

In this chapter, the *Tanya* will clarify both perspectives separately:

In the following section we will explore the identity of the "statements" as *separate energies* that each have a distinct creative role.

Later, in Section Four, the *Tanya* will look at the "statements" as *unified energies* within G-d.

שהמדות שבנשמת האדם כשבאות להתגלו' במעשה
הן באות מלובשות באותיות המחשבה כגון מדת חסד
ורחמים שבנשמה א"א לבא לידי התגלות בפועל ממש
כ"א ע"י שמחשב בדעתו ומהרהר מעשה הצדקה וחסד
לעשותה בפ"מ כי א"א לעשות בלי מחשבה ואם מצוה
לאחרים לעשות כמו המלך אזי מתלבשת מדת החסד
וגם אותיות המחשבה באותיות הדבור [וכן כשמדבר

SECTION TWO: THE "STATEMENTS" AS SEPARATE POWERS

In order to explain the role of Divine "statements," the *Tanya* offers us an illustration: the emergence of human speech from the soul.

כִּי כְּמוֹ שֶׁהַמִּדּוֹת שֶׁבְּנִשְׁמַת הָאָדָם — For just as the prelingual **powers of your soul,** כְּשֶׁבָּאוֹת לְהִתְגַּלּוֹת בְּמַעֲשֶׂה — when they emerge to be expressed in action, הֵן בָּאוֹת מְלוּבָּשׁוֹת בְּאוֹתִיּוֹת הַמַּחֲשָׁבָה — must first be "dressed" into letters within your thought, before they can power action, the same is true of G-d's powers, which must also first be "dressed" in Divine letters ("statements") before they can be expressed in action.

כְּגוֹן מִדַּת חֶסֶד וְרַחֲמִים שֶׁבַּנִּשְׁמָה — For example, your prelingual soul-**powers of** *chesed* (benevolence) **and** *rachamim* (compassion), אִי אֶפְשָׁר לָבֹא לִידֵי הִתְגַּלּוּת — cannot actually be expressed in action, כִּי אִם עַל יְדֵי שֶׁמְּחַשֵּׁב בְּפוֹעַל מַמָּשׁ — unless you first contemplate in your mind, וּמְהַרְהֵר מַעֲשֵׂה הַצְּדָקָה בְּדַעְתּוֹ — thinking of actually doing the act of charity or kindness, וָחֶסֶד לַעֲשׂוֹתָהּ בְּפוֹעַל מַמָּשׁ — since intentional action can't happen without prior contemplation. כִּי אִי אֶפְשָׁר לַעֲשׂוֹת בְּלִי מַחֲשָׁבָה

Language is the vehicle of expression of the soul. This begins internally, in thought.

In the transition from a (prelingual) whim of the soul to tangible action, the intermediate phase is a (lingual) thought.

וְאִם מְצַוֶּה לַאֲחֵרִים לַעֲשׂוֹת — And if one person instructs another to perform the action, כְּמוֹ הַמֶּלֶךְ — such as a king commanding his officers, אֲזַי מִתְלַבֶּשֶׁת מִדַּת הַחֶסֶד וְגַם אוֹתִיּוֹת הַמַּחֲשָׁבָה בְּאוֹתִיּוֹת הַדִּבּוּר — then the commanding **person's** prelingual **power of** *chesed* and also his letters of thought, become "dressed" in speech before action occurs.

The transition between a (prelingual) whim of the soul to a tangible action may also involve speech (between thought and action). But the speech merely discloses the "letters" which were already present in thought. (This will become significant later, when we draw a distinction between Divine thought and speech.)

דברי חסד ורחמים לרעהו] כך עד"מ מדותיו של הקב"ה
כשבאות לבחי' התגלות פעולתן בתחתוני' נקרא גילוי זה
והמשכת פעולה זו בשם מאמר וצירוף אותיו' שהרי א"א
שתהיה שום פעולה נמשכת ממדותיו הקדושות בלי
צירופים הנקראי' בשם אותיות כגון לבריאת האור ממדת
החסד נמשך ממנה המשכת פעולה וכח לפעול ולברוא
בו את האור והמשכת כח זה וחיות זו נקראת בשם

88B

[וְכֵן כְּשֶׁמְּדַבֵּר דִּבְרֵי חֶסֶד וְרַחֲמִים לְרֵעֵהוּ] — **And, so too, when you speak words of kindness and compassion to your friend,** even when no action is involved, your speech is merely a disclosure of whatever already exists in your thought.

The *Tanya* now compares the emergence of human, lingual thought to the process by which the creative "statements" appear from G-d's powers.

כָּךְ עַל דֶּרֶךְ מָשָׁל מִדּוֹתָיו שֶׁל הַקָּדוֹשׁ בָּרוּךְ הוּא — **The same is true, metaphorically speaking, with the Divine powers** of *chesed, rachamim etc.,* כְּשֶׁבָּאוֹת לִבְחִינַת

הִתְגַּלוּת פְּעוּלָתָן בַּתַּחְתּוֹנִים — **when they come to be disclosed and active** here in the lower worlds, נִקְרָא גִּילוּי זֶה וְהַמְשָׁכַת פְּעוּלָה זוֹ בְּשֵׁם מַאֲמָר — this disclosure and energetic **flow** from a Divine power, leading to an **action, is called a** Divine **"statement,"** וְצֵירוּף אוֹתִיוֹת — meaning a **string of letters.**

PRACTICAL LESSONS

The "ten statements" through which G-d created the world are something of a paradox. They are *outward* projections of Divine energy; but they are still *one with G-d.*

שֶׁהֲרֵי אִי אֶפְשָׁר שֶׁתִּהְיֶה שׁוּם פְּעוּלָה נִמְשֶׁכֶת מִמִּדּוֹתָיו הַקְּדוֹשׁוֹת — **For,** as in our illustration from the human soul, **action will not flow from the holy** Divine **powers,** בְּלִי צֵירוּפִים הַנִּקְרָאִים בְּשֵׁם אוֹתִיוֹת — **without the** prior **stringing together** of energies **called "letters."**

The ten creative "statements" in Genesis are not purely symbolic. The constituent letters of these statements represent precise "packets" of energetic flow which have emerged from the Divine attributes, in order to power the creative process. G-d really did "speak," in the sense that energies emerged from Him like letters of thought/speech emerge from your soul.

The *Tanya* offers us a more detailed example.

כְּגוֹן לִבְרִיאַת הָאוֹר מִמִּדַּת הַחֶסֶד — **For example, in order to create** physical **light from the** Divine **power of** *chesed,* נִמְשָׁךְ מִמֶּנָּה הַמְשָׁכַת פְּעוּלָה — *chesed* must first **produce an energetic flow** to cause **that action,** וְכֹחַ לִפְעוֹל וְלִבְרוֹא בּוֹ אֶת הָאוֹר — namely, **the power to cause and create the** physical **light,** וְהַמְשָׁכַת כֹּחַ זֶה וְחִיּוּת זוֹ נִקְרֵאת בְּשֵׁם מַאֲמָר וְאוֹתִיּוֹת יְהִי אוֹר — **and this flow of power/energy**

מאמר ואותיות יהי אור כי אף שאינן כאותיות מחשבה
שלנו ח"ו מ"מ הם ענין המורה על התהוו' האור מאין
ליש שלכן נברא האור מהמשכת כח זה ולא נבראו
ממנו דברים אחרים שנבראו ג"כ ממדת חסד כמו מים
וכיוצא בהם מפני שנתלבשו בהם כחות בבחי' צירופים

is called a "statement" consisting **of the letters** of the phrase, *"Let there be light!"* (*Genesis* 1:3).

Of course the comparison between human language and Divine language is a distant one, as the *Tanya* is quick to make clear.

כִּי אַף שֶׁאֵינָן כְּאוֹתִיּוֹת מַחֲשָׁבָה שֶׁלָנוּ חַס וְשָׁלוֹם — **For while** the Divine "letters" **are not, G-d forbid, like the letters of our thought,** G-d's "letters" nevertheless do exist.

G-d's "letters," are, of course, not comparable to human letters, but that does not mean that they are purely metaphorical. The letters of G-d's speech are *real* "packets" of Divine energy, with a specific creative function.

מִכָּל מָקוֹם — **Nevertheless,** while we cannot accurately compare Divine speech to human speech, הֵם עִנְיָן הַמּוֹרֶה עַל הִתְהַוּוּת הָאוֹר מֵאַיִן לְיֵשׁ — we can affirm that the letters of G-d's statement, *"let there be light,"* **are something associated** in particular **with the creation of light, something-from-nothing.**

The letters of G-d's speech are not generic packets of energy; they have a particular creative power. Therefore, not all the letters produced by the Divine attribute of *chesed* will create the same things.

שֶׁלָכֵן נִבְרָא הָאוֹר מֵהַמְשָׁכַת כֹּחַ זֶה וְלֹא נִבְרָאוּ מִמֶּנּוּ דְּבָרִים אֲחֵרִים — **And that is why** **light, and not something else, was created from the flow of this** Divine **energy,** expressed through the words, *"Let there be light,"* שֶׁנִּבְרְאוּ גַּם כֵּן מִמִּדַּת חֶסֶד — even though other things **too were created from the Divine power of *chesed*,** כְּמוֹ מַיִם וְכַיוֹצֵא בָּהֶם — **such as water, *etc.***

A CHASIDIC THOUGHT

"All twenty-two letters exist in thought, which is the root of all letters. That's why you can't speak anything aloud without thinking of it first. (If you do utter a word without any thought, it will lack understanding, wisdom and intelligence.) So thought is the root of all the worlds, which were revealed through speech."

The Maggid of Mezritch, Likutim Yekarim, sec. 264.

אחרים המורים על התהוות המים וכיוצא ונמצא כי כל
חיות וכחות הנמשכות ממדותיו הקדושות לתחתונים
לבראם מאין ליש ולהחיות' ולקיימם נקראו' בשם אותיו'
הקדושות שהן בחי' המשכת החיות מרצונו וחכמתו
ומדותיו להתהוות עולמות ולהחיותם והם שני מיני

Both light and water were created through *chesed,* but when the words "let there be light" emerged from *chesed,* only light appeared. That is because the energetic content of this particular string of letters matched the properties of light. How, then, was water created from *chesed?* The *Tanya* reminds us of its earlier teaching that things not mentioned explicitly in the Genesis narrative were created by taking letters from the statements and re-shuffling them.

PRACTICAL LESSONS

A string of Divine "letters" is an individualized "package" of Divine energy which is tailor-made to "dress" in a specific creation.

מִפְּנֵי שֶׁנִּתְלַבְּשׁוּ בָּהֶם כֹּחוֹת בִּבְחִינוֹת צֵירוּפִים אֲחֵרִים — **For in those** things not mentioned explicitly, **other** Divine **energies and** letter **combinations** from *chesed* were "dressed," הַמּוֹרִים עַל הִתְהַוּוֹת הַמַּיִם וְכַיּוֹצֵא — **which were associated with the creation of water or** whatever was being created by *chesed.*

The *Tanya* sums up its argument.

וְנִמְצָא כִּי כָּל חַיּוּת וְכֹחוֹת הַנִּמְשָׁכוֹת מִמִּדּוֹתָיו הַקְּדוֹשׁוֹת לַתַּחְתּוֹנִים לְבָרְאָם מֵאַיִן לְיֵשׁ וּלְהַחֲיוֹתָם וּלְקַיְּמָם נִקְרָאוֹת

בְּשֵׁם אוֹתִיּוֹת הַקְּדוֹשׁוֹת — **In summation: All forms of energy and power which** flow from the Divine attributes to the lower worlds (to create them something-from-nothing, to energize them and sustain them), are called "sacred, Divine **letters,"** שֶׁהֵן בְּחִינַת הַמְשָׁכַת הַחַיּוּת מֵרְצוֹנוּ וְחָכְמָתוֹ וּמִדּוֹתָיו לְהִתְהַוּוֹת עוֹלָמוֹת וּלְהַחֲיוֹתָם — "sacred letters" **are the channels of energy which flow from G-d's will/intellect/emotions to create the worlds and energize them.**

SECTION THREE: TWO TYPES OF SACRED LETTERS

As discussed in Section One, human language exists both in thought and speech. For an action to occur, a whim of the soul is first articulated in lingual thought, and then it may be spoken, before it is finally acted upon.

In the case of humans, thought is a *personal experience* which has no external manifestation. However, as we shall now see, the same is not true of G-d, whose thought has *outward creative power,* like His speech.

עולמות עלמין סתימין דלא אתגליין הם המתהוים וחיים
וקייימים מכחות והמשכות נעלמות כמו אותיו' המחשבה
שבנשמת האדם עד"מ ועלמין דאתגליין נבראו וחיים
מהתגלות שנתגלו כחות והמשכות הנעלמות הנקראות
בשם אותיו' המחשב' וכשהן בבחי' התגלות להחיו' עלמין
דאתגליין נקראות בשם מאמרות ודבר ה' ורוח פיו כמו
אותיות הדבור באדם עד"מ שהן מגלות לשומעים מה

וְהֵם שְׁנֵי מִינֵי עוֹלָמוֹת — **There are two types of worlds** formed from G-d's sacred letters, עָלְמִין סְתִימִין דְּלָא אִתְגַּלְיָין — the first is, *"hidden worlds that are not revealed"* (*Tikunei Zohar* ibid.), הֵם הַמִּתְהַוִּים וְחַיִּים וְקַיָּימִים מִכֹּחוֹת וְהַמְשָׁכוֹת נֶעְלָמוֹת — which are created/energized/sustained through hidden forms of Divine energy/flow, כְּמוֹ אוֹתִיּוֹת הַמַּחֲשָׁבָה שֶׁבְּנִשְׁמַת הָאָדָם עַל דֶּרֶךְ מָשָׁל — "hidden" being comparable to the letters of thought in a human soul.

The key distinction between G-d's thought and His speech is that His more hidden thought creates "hidden worlds," whereas, as we shall now see, His more overt speech creates "revealed worlds."

וְעָלְמִין דְּאִתְגַּלְיָין — **And** the second type is, *"revealed worlds"* (ibid.), נִבְרְאוּ וְחַיִּים מֵהִתְגַּלּוּת — which are created/energized by Divine disclosure, שֶׁנִּתְגַּלּוּ כֹּחוֹת וְהַמְשָׁכוֹת הַנֶּעְלָמוֹת הַנִּקְרָאוֹת בְּשֵׁם אוֹתִיּוֹת הַמַּחֲשָׁבָה — namely that the hidden forms of Divine energy/flow (called "letters of thought") are disclosed, וּכְשֶׁהֵן בִּבְחִינַת הִתְגַּלּוּת — and לְהַחֲיוֹת עָלְמִין דְּאִתְגַּלְיָין נִקְרָאוֹת בְּשֵׁם מַאֲמָרוֹת — when the "letters of thought" are in a state of disclosure, to energize the "revealed worlds," the "letters of thought" **are called** verbal **"statements,"** וּדְבַר ה' וְרוּחַ פִּיו — **"G-d's word"** and **"the breath of His mouth,"** כְּמוֹ אוֹתִיּוֹת הַדִּבּוּר בָּאָדָם עַל דֶּרֶךְ מָשָׁל — comparable to the letters of human speech, שֶׁהֵן מְגַלּוֹת לַשּׁוֹמְעִים מַה שֶׁהָיָה צָפוּן וְסָתוּם בְּלִבּוֹ — which disclose to listeners what was previously hidden and concealed in the speaker's heart.

PRACTICAL LESSONS

Even G-d's "thought" has creative power. It creates "hidden worlds."

G-d's more hidden letters of thought create "hidden worlds," reflecting their concealed source; whereas the more revealed letters of Divine speech create "revealed worlds."

So G-d's "sacred letters," whether in His thought or speech, are *always* channels of creative energy flowing outwards to the worlds. This differs from the "letters" of humans, who only project their speech outwards, but keep their thoughts to themselves.

שהיה צפון וסתום בלבו אבל באמת בחי' אותיות הדבור
של מעלה היא למעלה ממדרגת ומהות חכמה
ושכל הנבראי' שהרי במאמר ואותיו' נעשה אדם בצלמינו
וגו' נברא האדם בעל חכמה ושכל או אפי' בהבל העליון

SECTION FOUR: DIVINE SPEECH TRANSCENDS HUMAN SPEECH

The Divine letters are energies which have flowed outwards from G-d, to power the creative process. The symbolism of "letters" suggests that these energies have acquired an identity of their own, like a "quote" which becomes independent of its author.

So you might think that the Divine letters are "packets" of energy which have departed from their source in G-d, and are just one step away from the multiplicity of the creations which they bring about.

However, as we have already learned at the beginning of this chapter, *"the 'ten statements'... are only called 'statements' from the perspective of us creations."* The separateness of the letters is only real *from our vantage point.*

בְּחִינַת אוֹתִיּוֹת הַדִּבּוּר שֶׁל מַעֲלָה — G-d's spoken letters can't be compared to the speech of us creations, which actually depart from the speaker. אֲבָל בֶּאֱמֶת — But in truth,

הִיא לְמַעֲלָה מַעֲלָה מִמַּדְרֵגַת וּמַהוּת חָכְמָה וְשֵׂכֶל הַנִּבְרָאִים — In fact, Divine speech vastly transcends the level/quality of *chochmah* and intellect possessed by creations.

Human *chochmah* is the pinnacle of creation and the closest thing in our universe to G-d; but it is nevertheless a creation and therefore, by definition, it must be separate from G-d. Divine speech, on the other hand, has really not departed from the Divine realm, and remains one with G-d. Therefore, Divine speech *"vastly transcends"* our *chochmah* and cannot be compared to it.

The *Tanya* brings a proof of this point.

שֶׁהֲרֵי בְּמַאֲמַר וְאוֹתִיּוֹת נַעֲשֶׂה אָדָם בְּצַלְמֵנוּ וְגוֹ' נִבְרָא הָאָדָם בַּעַל חָכְמָה וְשֵׂכֶל — We see this since it was through the letters of the Divine statement, *"Let us make man, etc."* (Genesis 1:26), that a human possessing *chochmah* and intellect was created.

Divine speech must "vastly transcend" human *chochmah,* since human beings (including their *chochmah*) were created by Divine speech!

אוֹ אֲפִילוּ בַּהֶבֶל הָעֶלְיוֹן לְבָד — In fact, even the Divine "breath" alone, which leads to speech, has its own creative power, כְּדִכְתִיב וַיִּפַּח בְּאַפָּיו נִשְׁמַת חַיִּים — as the verse states, *"And He blew into his nostrils the breath of life"* (ibid. 2:7).

לבד כדכתי' ויפח באפיו נשמת חיים וא"כ הדבור והבל **89A**
העליון הוא מקור החכמה והשכל שבנשמת אדם
הראשון הכוללת כל נשמות הצדיקים שהם גדולים
ממלאכי השרת והיינו לפי שאותיות דיבורו ית' הן בחי'
המשכות כחות וחיות ממדותיו ית' המיוחדות במהותו
ועצמותו בתכלית היחוד שהוא למעלה מעלה לאין קץ

The *Tanya* continues its argument.

If — וְאִם כֵּן הַדִּבּוּר וְהַהֶבֶל הָעֶלְיוֹן הוּא מְקוֹר הַחָכְמָה וְהַשֵּׂכֶל שֶׁבְּנִשְׁמַת אָדָם הָרִאשׁוֹן
so, we see that **Divine "speech" and "breath" is the** creative **source of the**
chochmah **and intellect found in the soul of Adam, the first man,** הַכּוֹלֶלֶת כָּל
נִשְׁמוֹת הַצַּדִּיקִים — a super-soul **which contained the souls of all** future *tzadi-*
kim (*Shemos Rabah* 40:3; *Sha'ar Ha-Gilgulim* chapter 6), שֶׁהֵם גְּדוֹלִים מִמַּלְאֲכֵי
הַשָּׁרֵת — **who are greater than the ministering angels** (*Sanhedrin* 93a).

G-d's breath and speech was the creative source of the first man, whose
chochmah was the highest to be found in the universe.

Clearly, then, we have proven that Divine speech
"vastly transcends the level/quality of chochmah and
intellect possessed by creations."

וְהַיְינוּ לְפִי שֶׁאוֹתִיוֹת דִּיבּוּרוֹ יִתְבָּרֵךְ הֵן בְּחִינוֹת הַמְשָׁכוֹת
כֹּחוֹת וְחַיּוּת מִמִּדוֹתָיו יִתְבָּרֵךְ — **And** the ability of G-d's
speech to create such a lofty thing as *chochmah* **is**
because the letters of G-d's speech are channels
of flow/energy from the Divine attributes, הַמְיוּחֲדוֹת
בְּמַהוּתוֹ וְעַצְמוּתוֹ בְּתַכְלִית הַיִּחוּד — attributes **which**
are unified with G-d's essence and being in total
unity, שֶׁהוּא לְמַעְלָה מַעְלָה לְאֵין קֵץ מִמַּדְרֵגַת חָכְמָה
שֶׁבַּנִּבְרָאִים — and G-d's essence **vastly and infinitely**
transcends the level of *chochmah* **found in created**
beings.

PRACTICAL LESSONS

G-d's speech conveys
and channels His
attributes which are
one with His actual
self. So, at least from
His perspective, His
speech is totally
one with Him.

G-d's speech conveys and "channels" His attri-
butes; and, as we have learned, those attributes are one with His actual self.
Obviously, G-d's actual self "vastly and infinitely transcends the level of *choch-*
mah found in created beings," and that superiority is carried along into His
attributes and speech, all of which are united with Him. That is why His speech,
which appears to be something relatively low in the Divine sphere, can create
chochmah: because the speech is, in fact, conveying a much higher power.

Why then do we even use the term "speech," which implies separateness
from source, if the energies channeled by the speech are one with Him?

ממדרגת חכמה שבנבראים ולא נקראו בשם אותיות
לגבי הנבראים אלא לגבי מדותיו ית' בכבודן ובעצמן
והנה הן כ"ב מיני המשכות חיות וכחות שונים זה מזה
שבהן נבראו כל העולמות עליונים ותחתונים וכל
הברואים שבתוכם שכך עלה ברצונו וחכמתו ית' לברוא
העולם בכ"ב מיני המשכות שונות דוקא לא פחות ולא

וְלֹא נִקְרְאוּ בְּשֵׁם אוֹתִיּוֹת לְגַבֵּי הַנִּבְרָאִים — And Divine speech **is not referred to as "letters"** (implying separateness) **to depict the way creations view them,** since from the creations' point of view the "letters" are one with G-d, and not separate from Him, אֶלָּא לְגַבֵּי מִדּוֹתָיו יִתְבָּרֵךְ בִּכְבוֹדָן וּבְעַצְמָן — **rather** the term "letters" is used **to depict the way the honorable and glorious Divine attributes view** the "letters," as something more separate from G-d than the attributes themselves.

Compared to the Divine attributes, which are completely and utterly one with G-d, the "letters" of G-d's speech are indeed more separate. But "separate" is a relative term. *From our point of view,* the energy of these "letters" is Divine and totally one with G-d.

So, ultimately, the term "letters," which implies a certain separateness, is more appropriate for the perspective of the attributes than our perspective.

SECTION FIVE: THE EMERGENCE OF HUMAN SPEECH

Having stressed how Divine speech is *not* like human speech, the *Tanya* will suggest now that there is perhaps more similarity than we have previously imagined.

וְהִנֵּה הֵן כ"ב מִינֵי הַמְשָׁכוֹת חַיּוּת וְכֹחוֹת שׁוֹנִים זֶה מִזֶּה — **Now the** Divine letters **are twenty-two different channels of energy flow, powers that differ from one another,** שֶׁבָּהֶן נִבְרְאוּ כָּל הָעוֹלָמוֹת עֶלְיוֹנִים וְתַחְתּוֹנִים — **and through them all the worlds were created, upper and lower,** וְכָל הַבְּרוּאִים שֶׁבְּתוֹכָם — **as well as all the creatures within them,** שֶׁכָּךְ עָלָה בִּרְצוֹנוֹ וְחָכְמָתוֹ יִתְבָּרֵךְ לִבְרוֹא הָעוֹלָם בְּכ"ב — **for it arose in G-d's will and wisdom to create the world with exactly twenty-two types of energetic flow,** מִינֵי הַמְשָׁכוֹת שׁוֹנוֹת דַּוְקָא — no לֹא פָּחוֹת וְלֹא יוֹתֵר — no more, and no less.

As the *Ba'al Shem Tov* taught: *"Just as there are twenty-two letters in the words of Torah and prayer, so too, all material, physical things in the world have twenty-two letters, through which the world and all its contents were created"* (*Toldos Ya'akov Yosef* page 8c).

How are these "letters" of energetic flow, which *are an expression of their*

יוֹתֵר וְהֵן הֵן כ״ב אוֹתִיּוֹת הַקְּבוּעוֹת בְּפֶה וְלָשׁוֹן כְּדִתְנָן
בְּס׳ יְצִירָה [וְתָמוּנָתָן בְּכְתָב הִיא מוֹרָה עַל צִיּוּר הַהַמְשָׁכָה
כְּמ״ש לְקַמָּן] שֶׁגַּם אוֹתִיּוֹת הַדִּבּוּר וְהַמַּחֲשָׁבָה שֶׁבַּנֶּפֶשׁ
הָאָדָם הֵן הַמְשָׁכוֹת מֵהַשֵּׂכֶל וְהַמִּדּוֹת שֶׁבַּנֶּפֶשׁ מִמַּהוּתָן
וְעַצְמוּתָן כְּמ״ש בְּמ״א:

source, comparable in any way to human speech, which takes form only from the lips outwards, and is *not* found in its source, the soul itself?

וְהֵן הֵן כ״ב אוֹתִיּוֹת הַקְּבוּעוֹת בְּפֶה וְלָשׁוֹן — **And these are, in fact, the very same twenty-two letters which assume a precise form in the** human **mouth and tongue,** כְּדִתְנָן בְּסֵפֶר יְצִירָה — **as stated in** *Sefer Yetzirah* (1:2).

The *Tanya* answers that letters only "assume a precise form" in the mouth, implying that they *did* exist previously in the soul, as a more fluid energy.

The emergence of letters, then, does not *begin* in the "mouth and tongue"; subtle precursors of the letters are to be found in the soul itself.

So we see that even human letters have a certain unity with their source, like the Divine letters (*Notes on Tanya*).

[וְתָמוּנָתָן בִּכְתָב הִיא מוֹרָה עַל צִיּוּר הַהַמְשָׁכָה כְּמוֹ שֶׁיִּתְבָּאֵר לְקַמָּן] — **And the graphic shape of the written letters indicates the form of the** energy **which they channel** from the soul, **as will be explained below** in chapter 12, in the author's note.

שֶׁגַּם אוֹתִיּוֹת הַדִּבּוּר וְהַמַּחֲשָׁבָה שֶׁבַּנֶּפֶשׁ הָאָדָם הֵן הַמְשָׁכוֹת מֵהַשֵּׂכֶל וְהַמִּדּוֹת שֶׁבַּנֶּפֶשׁ מִמַּהוּתָן וְעַצְמוּתָן — **For even in the human soul, letters of speech and thought are** *channels of flow* **from the soul's core intellectual and emotional powers,** and in this sense they resemble the Divine letters which are likewise channels of flow.

כְּמוֹ שֶׁנִּתְבָּאֵר בְּמָקוֹם אַחֵר — **As was explained elsewhere** (*Tanya, Igeres Ha-Kodesh* sec. 5).

PRACTICAL LESSONS

While they are worlds apart, there is one similarity between Divine and human language: both are *channels of flow*.

פרק יב רק שהברואים מתחלקים למיניהם בכללות
ובפרטות ע"י שינויי הצירופים וחילופים

CHAPTER 12

UNITY THROUGH LETTERS
SECTION ONE: EVERTHING EMERGES FROM JUST 22 LETTERS

5TH TAMMUZ REGULAR | 9TH TAMMUZ LEAP

In the previous chapter, we described the flow of creative energy from G-d into the ten verbal "statements" through which the world was created. In this chapter we will discuss how the energy of these ten core "statements" is subsequently split and downgraded to produce millions of different creations.

Although there are just twenty-two different letters, representing a relatively small, fixed number of core energies, we learned at the end of the previous chapter that the Divine letters *"are twenty-two different channels of energy flow... and through them all the worlds were created, upper and lower, as well as all the creatures within them."* How are millions of different creations formed from just twenty-two types of energy?

רַק שֶׁהַבְּרוּאִים מִתְחַלְּקִים לְמִינֵיהֶם בִּכְלָלוּת וּבִפְרָטוּת — **Only** from twenty-two different letters, all **creations** were made, **divided into** millions of **different categories, general and particular.**

While other works, such as *Sefer Yetzirah,* offer a detailed analysis of how different energies emerge from the twenty-two letters, the *Tanya's* intention here is to stress the *overall unity* which the letters bring to the universe (since this Second Book of *Tanya* is a treatise on unity). *While there are millions of different creations, they are all powered by just twenty-two letters.* In the following lines, as the *Tanya* describes this process, we get a sense of how everything in the universe is just one or two steps away from a single energetic source (*Notes on Tanya*).

עַל יְדֵי שִׁינּוּיֵי הַצֵּירוּפִים וְחִילוּפִים וּתְמוּרוֹת — And this was achieved **through** letter **rearrangements,** via **switching and exchanging** the letters, כַּנִּזְכָּר לְעֵיל — **as mentioned above,** in Chapters One and seven.

ותמורות כנ"ל כי כל אות היא המשכת חיות וכח מיוחד
פרטי וכשנצטרפו אותיות הרבה להיות תיבה אזי מלבד
ריבוי מיני כחות וחיות הנמשכים כפי מספר האותיות
שבתיבה עוד זאת העולה על כולנה המשכת כח עליון
וחיות כללית הכולל' ושקולה כנגד כל מיני הכחו' והחיות
פרטיות של האותיות ועולה על גביהן והיא מחברתן
ומצרפתן יחד להשפיע כח וחיות לעולם הנברא

As we have learned, "switching" is a process of taking the same letters and changing their order, like an anagram. When letters are "exchanged" they are swapped for different letters which are then arranged into the desired word. Exchanging the letters is a very different process because it *diminishes* their energy significantly more than switching. This makes possible the creation of lower forms.

How does rearranging the letters *of the same word* change its energetic content? If each letter delivers a particular "packet" of energy, why does the order of the letters make any difference?

The *Tanya* explains:

כִּי כָּל אות הִיא הַמְשָׁכַת חַיּוּת — For every letter is an energetic flow, וְכֹחַ מְיוּחָד פְּרָטִי — a particular, specific power, וּכְשֶׁנִּצְטָרְפוּ אוֹתִיּוֹת הַרְבֵּה לִהְיוֹת תֵּיבָה — and when many letters are strung together to form a word, אֲזֵי מִלְּבַד רִיבּוּי מִינֵי כֹחוֹת וְחַיּוּת הַנִּמְשָׁכִים כְּפִי מִסְפַּר הָאוֹתִיּוֹת שֶׁבַּתֵּיבָה — then, besides the multiple individual flows of energetic power, indicated by the number of letters in the word, עוֹד זֹאת הָעוֹלָה עַל כּוּלָנָה הַמְשָׁכַת כֹּחַ עֶלְיוֹן וְחַיּוּת כְּלָלִית — in addition, there is a *collective* energetic flow, a superior power which surpasses all the individual flows, הַכּוֹלֶלֶת וּשְׁקוּלָה כְּנֶגֶד כָּל מִינֵי הַכֹּחוֹת וְהַחַיּוּת פְּרָטִיּוֹת שֶׁל הָאוֹתִיּוֹת וְעוֹלָה עַל גַּבֵּיהֶן — since it encompasses every individual energetic flow from each of the letters, equaling and even surpassing them, וְהִיא מְחַבַּרְתָּן וּמְצָרַפְתָּן יַחַד — and this collective flow binds and joins the individual flows together, לְהַשְׁפִּיעַ כֹּחַ וְחַיּוּת לְעוֹלָם הַנִּבְרָא בְּתֵיבָה זוֹ — delivering power and energy to the world, which was created through this word, לִכְלָלוֹ וְלִפְרָטָיו — to both general and particular categories of creation.*

A word is more than the sum of the energy of its constituent letters. The precise order of the letters also draws upon them a "collective" energy, unique to that particular sequence of letters. And the collective energy is: a.) More pow-

בתיבה זו לכללו ולפרטיו*
כגון ד"מ בתיבו' שבמאמר
יהי רקיע וגו' שנבראו בהן
ז' רקיעים וכל צבא השמים
אשר בהם כמאמר רז"ל

הגה"ה

(ולפי שכל אות ואות מכ"ב אותיות
התורה היא המשכת חיות וכח מיוחד
פרטי שאינו נמשך באות אחרת לכך
גם תמונתן בכתב כל אות היא בתמונה
מיוחדת פרטית המורה על ציור

erful than the individual powers of the letters themselves; and b.) It unites and binds the individual energies together.

SECTION TWO: AN ILLUSTRATION

כְּגוֹן דֶּרֶךְ מָשָׁל — Let's consider the following example.

בְּתֵיבוֹת שֶׁבְּמַאֲמַר יְהִי רָקִיעַ וְגוֹ' — Through the words in the statement, "*Let there be a firmament, etc.*" (*Genesis* 1:6), שֶׁנִּבְרְאוּ בָּהֶן ז' רְקִיעִים וְכָל צְבָא הַשָּׁמַיִם אֲשֶׁר בָּהֶם — the "seven firmaments" and all their celestial contents were created.

The "seven firmaments" represent a huge expanse and, as we shall soon see, they have a staggering amount of different content. Yet all of this emerged from just one short string of letters, *"Let there be a firmament."*

From this illustration, the theme of our chapter will be brought home, that a great variety of creations emerge from a very small cluster of energies. The extreme multiplicity of the universe is closely bound with a unified source (*Notes on Tanya*).

כְּמַאֲמַר רַבּוֹתֵינוּ זִכְרוֹנָם לִבְרָכָה — As in the following **teaching of our Sages of blessed memory,** which describes the various firmaments and their own specific contents (*Chagigah* 12b; *Zohar* 2, 10b).

The seven firmaments are:

a.) *Vilon* ("Curtain"), which is "rolled up and down."

b.) *Rakia* ("Sky"), where the sun, moon, and stars are found.

הַגָּהָה — *NOTE*

In this note we learn that the unique energetic flow of each letter is reflected by its graphic shape.

וּלְפִי שֶׁכָּל אוֹת וָאוֹת מִכ"ב אוֹתִיּוֹת הַתּוֹרָה — And since each letter of the twenty-two letters of the Torah, הִיא הַמְשָׁכַת חַיּוּת וְכֹחַ מְיוּחָד פְּרָטִי — is a separate, particular flow of energy/power, שֶׁאֵינוֹ נִמְשָׁךְ בְּאוֹת אַחֶרֶת — which cannot flow through any other letter, לְכָךְ גַּם תְּמוּנָתָן בִּכְתָב כָּל אוֹת הִיא בִּתְמוּנָה מְיוּחֶדֶת

שְׁחָקִים שֶׁבּוֹ רֵחַיִים
עוֹמְדוֹת וְטוֹחֲנוֹת מָן
לַצַּדִּיקִים וְכוּ' זְבוּל שֶׁבּוֹ
יְרוּשָׁלַיִם וּבֵה"מִק וּמִזְבֵּחַ
וְכוּ' מָכוֹן שֶׁבּוֹ אוֹצָרוֹת שֶׁלֶג וְאוֹצָרוֹת בָּרָד וְכוּ' שְׁכָלְלוֹת

הַהַמְשָׁכָה וְהִתְגַּלּוּת הָאוֹר וְהַחִיּוּ' וְהַכֹּחַ
הַנִּגְלֶה וְנִמְשָׁךְ בְּאוֹת זוֹ אֵיךְ הוּא נִמְשָׁךְ
וְנִתְגַּלֶּה מִמִּדּוֹתָיו שֶׁל הַקָּבָּ"ה וּרְצוֹנוֹ
וְחָכְמָתוֹ וְכוּ'):

שְׁחָקִים שֶׁבּוֹ רֵחַיִים עוֹמְדוֹת וְטוֹחֲנוֹת מָן לַצַּדִּיקִים וְכוּ' — c.) **"Shechakim ('Heights'), which contains millstones that grind manna for the righteous, etc.,"**

זְבוּל שֶׁבּוֹ יְרוּשָׁלַיִם וּבֵית הַמִּקְדָּשׁ וּמִזְבֵּחַ וְכוּ' — d.) **"Zevul ('Abode'), which contains** (the heavenly) **Jerusalem, Temple and Altar etc.,"**

e.) Ma'on ("habitation"), where groups of angels recite song at night.

מָכוֹן שֶׁבּוֹ אוֹצָרוֹת שֶׁלֶג וְאוֹצָרוֹת בָּרָד וְכוּ' — f.) **"Machon ('Dwelling'), which contains storehouses of** (punishing) **snow and vaults of hail, etc.,"**

g.) Aravos ("Skies"), which contains righteousness; justice; charity; the treasuries of life; the treasuries of peace; the treasuries of blessing; the souls of the righteous; the spirits and souls that are to be created; and the dew that the Blessed Holy One will use to revive the dead (Chagigah ibid).

(For an explanation why the Tanya mentions here explicitly just three of the seven firmaments, see Notes on Tanya.)

How is it possible for the single phrase "Let there be a firmament" to power the creation of so many different things?

The Tanya explains:

פְּרָטִית — therefore the shape of each letter, as it is written scribally, has its own unique form, הַמּוֹרָה עַל צִיּוּר הַהַמְשָׁכָה וְהִתְגַּלּוּת הָאוֹר וְהַחַיּוּת וְהַכֹּחַ הַנִּגְלֶה which indicates the form of the flow/disclosure of the light/energy/power which is disclosed and flows through this letter, וְנִמְשָׁךְ בְּאוֹת זוֹ אֵיךְ הוּא נִמְשָׁךְ how it flows and is וְנִתְגַּלֶּה מִמִּדּוֹתָיו שֶׁל הַקָּדוֹשׁ בָּרוּךְ הוּא וּרְצוֹנוֹ וְחָכְמָתוֹ וְכוּ' disclosed from G-d's attributes/will/wisdom etc.

The mystic significance of the letter shapes is first described in detail in Sefer Ha-Temunah (Koretz, 1784; an early work of Kabbalah which has been attributed to the Tannaic sage Rabbi Nechunya ben Ha-Kanah), and it is a theme echoed in later Kabbalistic writings.

"The Ba'al Shem Tov revealed the meaning of the shapes of the letters. So I heard from my master, Rabbi Dov Ber, that there are reasons for the shape of the letters, which are supernal lights" (Rabbi Levi Yitzchak of Berdichev, Kedushas Levi (New York, Monsey: 1995), pp. 517-518).

הרקיעים נבראו וחיים וקיימים בכללות תיבות אלו
שבמאמר יהי רקיע וכו' ופרטי הברואים שבז' רקיעים
נברא כל פרט מהם וחי וקיים מאיזה צירוף אותיות
מתיבות אלו או חילופיהן ותמורותיהן שהן כפי בחי'
חיות הנברא הפרטי ההוא כי כל שינוי צירוף הוא
הרכבת ואריגת הכחו' והחיות בשינוי שכל אות
הקודמת בצירוף היא הגוברת והיא העיקר בבריאה
זו והשאר טפילות אליה ונכללות באורה ועי"ז נבראת

— שֶׁכְּלָלוּת הָרְקִיעִים נִבְרְאוּ וְחַיִּים וְקַיָּימִים בִּכְלָלוּת תֵּיבוֹת אֵלּוּ שֶׁבְּמַאֲמָר יְהִי רָקִיעַ וְכוּ'
The *firmaments themselves* are created/energized/sustained from the *words*
of the statement, *"Let there be a firmament,"* וּפְרָטֵי הַבְּרוּאִים שֶׁבְּז' רְקִיעִים נִבְרָא
— whereas each of the כָּל פְּרָט מֵהֶם וְחַי וְקַיָּים מֵאֵיזֶה צֵירוּף אוֹתִיּוֹת מִתֵּיבוֹת אֵלּוּ
particular contents of these "seven firmaments" are individually created/en-
ergized/sustained through a specific *letter rearrangement* from these words,
"Let there be a firmament," אוֹ חִילוּפֵיהֶן וּתְמוּרוֹתֵיהֶן — or through the switching
or exchanging of its letters, שֶׁהֵן כְּפִי בְחִינַת חַיּוּת הַנִּבְרָא הַפְּרָטִי הַהוּא — reflecting the specific energetic properties of the thing being created.

PRACTICAL LESSONS

Through letter
re-arrangements,
switching and
exchanging, millions
of different entities
can be created
from just twenty-
two fundamental
building blocks.

The firmaments themselves are created from the
phrase, *"Let there be a firmament."* The millions of
things found in the heavens are created through letter
rearrangements, switching and exchanging.

The *Tanya* reflects further on the effects of letter re-
arrangements.

כִּי כָּל שִׁינּוּי צֵירוּף הוּא הַרְכָּבַת וַאֲרִיגַת הַכֹּחוֹת וְהַחַיּוּת
בְּשִׁינּוּי — For each letter rearrangement causes a
new grafting and weaving of the letters' powers/en-
ergy, שֶׁכָּל אוֹת הַקּוֹדֶמֶת בְּצֵירוּף הִיא הַגּוֹבֶרֶת — since, in
any string of letters, the energetic formulation is dominated by the first letter, וְהִיא הָעִיקָר בִּבְרִיאָה זוֹ — the
first letter provides the main creative energy for this
thing, וְהַשְּׁאָר טְפֵילוֹת אֵלֶיהָ וְנִכְלָלוֹת בְּאוֹרָהּ — and the
remaining letters are subordinate to it, and subsumed
in its light, וְעַל יְדֵי זֶה נִבְרֵאת בְּרִיָּה חֲדָשָׁה — and with
this unique letter combination a new creation is formed.

We have now learned three factors that determine the energetic properties
of a letter rearrangement: 1.) The individual constituent letters. 2.) The overall
energy of the collective letters. 3.) The first letter, whose energy dominates.

בריה חדשה וכן בחילופי אותיות או תמורותיהן
נבראות בריאות חדשו' פחותי המעלה בערך הנבראים
מהאותיות עצמן כי הן ד"מ דוגמת אור המאיר בלילה
בארץ מן הירח ואור הירח הוא מהשמש ונמצא אור
שעל הארץ הוא אור האור של השמש וככה ממש
ד"מ האותיות שבמאמרות הן כללות המשכת החיות
והאור והכח ממדותיו של הקב"ה לברוא העולמו'
מאין ליש ולהחיותן ולקיימן כ"ז משך רצונו ית'
ומכללות המשכה והארה גדולה הזו האיר ה' והמשיך
ממנה תולדותיה כיוצא בה וענפיה שהן תולדות

90A

פְּחוּתֵי הַמַּעֲלָה בְּעֵרֶךְ — וְכֵן בְּחִילּוּפֵי אוֹתִיּוֹת אוֹ תְּמוּרוֹתֵיהֶן — So through switching or exchanging letters, נִבְרָאוֹת בְּרִיאוֹת חֲדָשׁוֹת — new creations are formed, פְּחוּתֵי הַמַּעֲלָה בְּעֵרֶךְ — of a lower order when compared with the creations which come from the unmodified letters themselves. הַנִּבְרָאִים מֵהָאוֹתִיּוֹת עַצְמָן

As we learned previously, switching and exchanging letters diminishes their energetic content, like a code which veils and confuses the meaning of a word.

6TH TAMMUZ REGULAR | 10TH TAMMUZ LEAP

The *Tanya* offers an illustration of this point.

כִּי הֵן דֶּרֶךְ מָשָׁל דּוּגְמַת אוֹר הַמֵּאִיר בַּלַּיְלָה בָּאָרֶץ מִן הַיָּרֵחַ — These lesser creations formed through switching and exchanging could be compared to the moonlight shining at night, on the earth, וְאוֹר הַיָּרֵחַ הוּא מֵהַשֶּׁמֶשׁ — for since moonlight is actually reflected sunlight, וְנִמְצָא אוֹר שֶׁעַל הָאָרֶץ הוּא אוֹר הָאוֹר שֶׁל הַשֶּׁמֶשׁ — it follows that the light shining on the earth at night from the moon is actually modified sunlight.

Sunlight here represents an unmodified word from the ten "statements." Once the letters are switched or exchanged, the resulting energy is a mere glimmer of the original word's energy, comparable to the weaker light of the moon which merely reflects the sun.

וְכָכָה מַמָּשׁ דֶּרֶךְ מָשָׁל הָאוֹתִיּוֹת שֶׁבַּמַּאֲמָרוֹת — This is a precise analogy for how the letters of the original unmodified statements, הֵן כְּלָלוּת הַמְשָׁכַת הַחַיּוּת וְהָאוֹר — are the general source of flow/energy/light/power from the Divine attributes, וְהַכֹּחַ מִמִּדּוֹתָיו שֶׁל הַקָּדוֹשׁ בָּרוּךְ הוּא — to create the worlds, something-from-nothing, לִבְרוֹא הָעוֹלָמוֹת מֵאַיִן לְיֵשׁ — and to energize and sustain the worlds, so long as G-d wills it. וּלְהַחֲיוֹתָן וּלְקַיְּימָן כָּל זְמַן מֶשֶׁךְ רְצוֹנוֹ יִתְבָּרֵךְ

וּמִכְּלָלוּת הַמְשָׁכָה וְהֶאָרָה גְּדוֹלָה הַזּוֹ — And from this great, encompassing source of flow/light, הֵאִיר ה' וְהִמְשִׁיךְ מִמֶּנָּה תּוֹלְדוֹתֶיהָ כַּיּוֹצֵא בָּהּ וַעֲנָפֶיהָ — G-d

וְהַמְשָׁכַת הָאוֹר מֵהָאוֹתִיּוֹת וְהֵן הֵן חִילוּפֵי אוֹתִיּוֹת
וּתְמוּרוֹתֵיהֶן וּבָרָא בָּהֶן בְּרוּאִים פְּרָטִים שֶׁבְּכָל עוֹלָם
וְכֵן הֵאִיר ה' עוֹד וְהִמְשִׁיךְ וְהוֹרִיד הֶאָרָה דְּהֶאָרָה
מֵהֶאָרוֹת הָאוֹתִיּוֹ' וְכֵן הִמְשִׁיךְ עוֹד וְהוֹרִיד עַד לְמַטָּה
מַטָּה בִּבְחִי' הִשְׁתַּלְשְׁלוּת עַד שֶׁנִּבְרָא הַדּוֹמֵם מַמָּשׁ
כָּאֲבָנִים וְעָפָר וּשְׁמוֹתֵיהֶן אֶבֶן וְעָפָר הֵם חִילוּפִים דְּחִילוּפִים
כוּ' וּתְמוּרוֹת דִּתְמוּרוֹת כוּ' כַּנַּ"ל:

נִשְׁלַם חֵלֶק שֵׁנִי

בְּעֶזְ"ה יִתְבָּרֵךְ וְיִתְעַלֶּה

שֶׁהֵן תּוֹלְדוֹת וְהַמְשָׁכַת **caused derivatives/branches to flow and shine forth,**
הָאוֹר מֵהָאוֹתִיּוֹת — **which are derivatives of** diminished **flow from the letters,**
וְהֵן הֵן חִילוּפֵי אוֹתִיּוֹת וּתְמוּרוֹתֵיהֶן — the diminished flow being **nothing other**
than letters which were switched or exchanged, וּבָרָא בָּהֶן בְּרוּאִים פְּרָטִים שֶׁבְּכָל
עוֹלָם — **and through** the energy of **these** switched/exchanged letters, G-d **cre-**
ated the individual contents of each world and heaven.

The process of diminishment then continues.

וְכֵן הֵאִיר ה' עוֹד — **G-d then produced an increasingly** diminished **light,** וְהִמְשִׁיךְ
וְהוֹרִיד הֶאָרָה דְּהֶאָרָה דְּהֶאָרָה מֵהֶאָרוֹת הָאוֹתִיּוֹת — **downgrading the flow to a**
glimmer of a glimmer of a glimmer of the letters' light.

Lower, less vibrant creations require further energetic diminishment.

וְכֵן הִמְשִׁיךְ עוֹד וְהוֹרִיד — **Then** G-d **downgraded the** energetic **flow even fur-**
ther, עַד לְמַטָּה מַטָּה בִּבְחִינַת הִשְׁתַּלְשְׁלוּת — **through a chain of multiple down-**
grades, עַד שֶׁנִּבְרָא הַדּוֹמֵם מַמָּשׁ כָּאֲבָנִים וְעָפָר — **until** the least energetic forms
were created, motionless objects such as stones and dirt,

The *Tanya* reminds us of the letter exchange mentioned earlier which creates stones.

וּשְׁמוֹתֵיהֶן אֶבֶן וְעָפָר — **And their** Hebrew **names** *even* **("stone") and** *afar*
("dirt"), הֵם חִילוּפִים דְּחִילוּפִים כוּ' וּתְמוּרוֹת דִּתְמוּרוֹת — **have undergone mul-**
tiple switching and multiple exchanges, כַּנִּזְכָּר לְעֵיל — **as mentioned above**
(chapter 1, 7).

In early printings of the *Tanya* a note appeared here that the text was "in-
complete." Apparently, this is because the author "did not have enough time
to complete it to his satisfaction" (Rabbi Aharon Ha-Levi of Staroselye, *Sha'arei
Ha-Yichud ve-ha-Emunah* (Jerusalem, 2016), p. 8b; *Notes on Tanya*).

נִשְׁלַם חֵלֶק שֵׁנִי בְּעֶזְרַת ה' יִתְבָּרֵךְ וְיִתְעַלֶּה — **With G-d's help, may He be blessed**
and exalted, this concludes the second part of the *Tanya*.

GLOSSARY

Adam Kadmon. "Primordial man," the all-encompassing, general will to create the Universe which arose in the 'mind' of G-d prior to the entire creative process.

Amidah. "Standing prayer," also known as *Shmoneh Esrei*, the climax of each prayer service which is recited in silent devotion while standing.

Arizal. A Hebrew acronym for *Adonenu Rabbi Yitzchak Zichrono Livracha* "our master Rabbi Yitzchak of blessed memory," referring to Rabbi Yitzchak Luria (1534-1572), who founded the highly influential and authoritative school of Lurianic Kabbalah.

Asiyah. "Action," the lowest of the four supernal worlds, having both a spiritual and physical component.

Atzilus. "Emanation," the highest of the four supernal worlds, adjacent to the infinite source of creation.

Ba'al Shem Tov. "Master of the Good Name," an appellation given to Rabbi Yisrael ben Eliezer (1698-1760), the founder of Chasidism.

Ba'al Teshuvah (pl. *Ba'alei Teshuvah*). "Master of penitence," one who "returns" from a non-observant lifestyle to become a Torah observant Jew.

Beriah. "Creation," the second highest of the four supernal worlds.

Besht. Hebrew acronym for the *Ba'al Shem Tov.*

Binah. "Cognition," in the human soul, it is the power of precise, rational thought which forms the second stage of the intellectual process, following from *chochmah.* In its heavenly source, *binah* is the second of the ten *sefiros.*

Chabad. A Hebrew acronym of *chochmah, binah* and *da'as,* the three intellectual *sefiros.* It also refers to the school of Chasidic thought founded by Rabbi Shneur Zalman of Liadi, which emphasizes the role of mindful contemplation in worship.

Chasid (pl. *chasidim*). A devotee of the Chasidic movement.

Chasidism. A spiritual revivalist movement beginning in the southern Kingdom of Poland (today western Ukraine) in the 18th century, based on teachings of the *Ba'al Shem Tov.*

Chasidus. Chasidic teachings.

Chesed. "Kindness," a *sefirah* representing love, abundance, generosity and revelation. It stands in opposition to the *sefirah* of *gevurah.*

Chiluf. The "switching" of Hebrew letters that takes place during the creation process.

Chochmah. "Inquiry," in the human soul, it is the precognitive power of inspiration and creativity, which feeds *binah,* the second stage of the intellectual process. In its heavenly source, *chochmah* is the first of the ten *sefiros* which acts as a "window" to the Blessed Infinite Light.

Da'as. "Recognition," the third intellectual *sefirah,* following from *chochmah* and *binah. Da'as* does not add any new information; rather, it fosters an attachment to the existing idea, to render it "real" and relevant.

Din. Judgment energy which is the source of negative spiritual forces.

Elokim. Literally "judge," is one of G-d's names appearing extensively in the Bible, often denoting a Divine force of *gevurah* (see *gevurah*).

En-Sof. "Without end," a term in the Kabbalah used to refer to G-d.

Exodus Rabah. The section of *Midrash Rabah* on the Book of Exodus. (See "*Midrash Rabah*").

Gematria (pl. *Gematrios*). The numerical value assigned to Hebrew letters and words.

Genesis Rabah. The section of *Midrash Rabah* on the Book of Genesis. (See "*Midrash Rabah*").

Gevurah. "Severity," one of the ten *sefiros* signifying, fear, discipline, restraint and judgment. It stands in opposition to the *sefirah* of *chesed.*

Halachah. Jewish law.

Havayah. See Tetragrammaton.

Hishtalshelus. The unfolding "chain" of spiritual worlds through which G-d powers the universe.

Igeres Ha-Kodesh. Fourth section of *Tanya,* appended posthumously, containing letters by the author.

Igeres Ha-Teshuvah. Third section of *Tanya,* discussing the concept of repentence.

Is'hapcha: The approach of "transforming" negative forces completely.

Kabbalah. Jewish esoteric wisdom which has been received from a reliable source.

Kavanah (pl. *Kavanos*): "Intention," thoughts and feelings that accompany prayer and the performance of *mitzvos*.

Kelipah (pl. *Kelipos*). "Peel," a Kabbalistic term referring to negative and evil forces. *Kelipah* conceals the presence of G-d just as peel hides a fruit.

Kelipas Nogah. "Bright *kelipah*," a negative energy that contains some good and has the possibility of being transformed to holiness.

Keser. "Crown," the highest of the *sefiros*, acting as a medium between the Blessed Infinite Light and the other sefiros.

Kelos Ha-Nefesh. "Languishing of the soul," an intense passionate state, where the soul desires the extinction of its own separate identity, so as to merge with G-d.

Makif. "Surrounding [light]," a Divine energy which cannot be confined within limited, defined vessels and is only present in a disengaged fashion.

Malchus. "Sovereignty," the tenth and lowest of the *sefiros*, identified in Kabbalah with the feminine, *Shechinah*, the palpable presence of G-d on earth.

Ma'amarei Admor Ha-Zakein. Chasidic discourses by the author of Tanya, Rabbi Shneur Zalman of Liadi. 27 volumes.

Mechilta. Halachic Midrash of the Tannaic period to the Book of Exodus.

Midrash. Homilies and commentaries on the Torah by the *Talmudic* Rabbis.

Midrash Rabah. A major collection of homilies and commentaries on the Torah, ascribed to Rabbi Oshiah Rabah (c. 3rd century), perhaps assembled during the early Geonic period. First printed in Constantinople 1512.

Mishnah. Fundamental collection of the legal pronouncements and discussion of the *Tanna'im*, compiled by Rabbi Yehudah ha-Nassi early in the third century. The *Mishnah* is the basic text of the Oral Law.

Mishneh Torah. See *Rambam.*

Misnagdim. Hostile opponents to the Chasidic movement.

Mitzvah (pl. *mitzvos*). "Commandment," the Divine commandments articulated in the Torah.

Nefesh. Lowest of three levels of the soul, responsible for basic body intelligence.

Neshama. Highest of three levels of the soul, responsible for self-conscious intelligence.

Octogrammaton. An eight-lettered Divine name formed by alternating the letters of Havayah and Adonai.

Rabenu Bachaye. Rabbi Bachaye ben Asher (1263-1340) of Saragosa, Spain. Author of a popular Torah commentary which incorporates literal, allegorical and Kabbalistic interpretations, often cited in Chasidic discourses.

Ramak. Rabbi Moses Cordovero, Kabalist of 16th century Safed. Student of Rabbi Yosef Caro. Author of numerous works, including *Pardes Rimonim,* a classic work which explains fundamental concepts of Kabbalah.

Rambam. "Maimonides," acronym for Rabbi Moshe ben Maimon, (1135-1204) leading Torah scholar of the Middle Ages. His major works are *Sefer ha-Mitzvos, Commentary to the Mishnah, Mishneh Torah (Yad Ha-Chazakah)*, a comprehensive code of Jewish law, *Moreh Nevuchim,* "Guide for the Perplexed," a primary work of Jewish philosophy.

Rashbam. Acronym for Rabbi Shmuel ben Meir, *Talmud* and Torah Commentator, who supplemented *Rashi's* (his grandfather's) commentary on the *Talmud* (c. 1085-1174). Brother of Rabeinu Tam.

Rashi. Acronym for Rabbi Shlomo Yitzchaki (1040-1105), author of fundamental commentary to the Bible and Talmud.

Ratzon Ha-Elyon. "Higher will," the inner will of G-d.

Raya Mehemna. "The Faithful Shepherd," a section of the *Zohar* which discusses the Kabbalistic significance of the commandments.

Rebbe. Spiritual leader of a Chasidic group.

Ruach. Second of three levels of the soul, responsible for emotional intelligence.

Sefirah (pl. *Sefiros*). A network of ten "energies" or "potencies" in the human soul. These mirror the ten heavenly *sefiros*, the Divine forces through which G-d influences the universe.

Shaloh. Acronym for *Shnei Luchos Habris*, "The two tablets of the Covenant", an encyclopedic compilation of ritual, ethics, and mysticism by Rabbi Isaiah Horowitz (1560-1630).

Shechinah. The "Divine presence" which is palpable and manifest on earth.

Shulchan Aruch. Universally accepted Code of Jewish Law encompassing all areas of practical *halachah*, by Rabbi Yosef Caro (1488-1575).

Sifri. Halachic Midrash on the books of Numbers and Deuteronomy.

Sitra Achra. "Other side," that which does not belong to the side of holiness.

Sovev-Kol-Almin. "Encircles-all-worlds," a Divine light and energy that is incompatible with the created worlds because it is too intense to engage with the worlds and become enmeshed with them.

Talmud. Comprehensive term for the *Mishnah* and *Gemara* as joined in the two compilations known as *Babylonian Talmud* (6th century) and *Jerusalem Talmud* (5th century).

Temurah. The "exchanging" of Hebrew letters that takes place during the creation process.

Tetragrammaton. Sacred Divine Name which is never pronounced, consisting of four letters, *yud-hei-vav-hei.* Often referred to by spelling it in reverse as *Havayah.*

Tikunei Zohar. Section of the Zohar containing an extended commentary to the Torah portion of *Bereshis.*

Tiferes. "Beauty," the sixth of the *sefiros* which harmonizes the influences of *chesed* and *gevurah.*

Tohu. "Chaos," an intense, disorderly Divine energy which precedes *tikun,* the "corrected" heavenly system of interconnected *sefiros.*

Tzadik (pl. *tzadikim*). Literally, "a righteous person." In the *Tanya* the term refers to a person who has transformed their Animal Soul to good.

Tzimtzum. "Diminishment," a process described in Lurianic Kabbalah through which the Infinite Light of G-d was diminished to enable the creation of a finite universe.

Yalkut Shimoni. Comprehensive Midrashic anthology, covering the entire Bible, attributed to Rabbi Shimon Ha-Darshan of Frankfurt (13th century).

Yetzirah. "Formation," the third of four supernal worlds.

Yesod. "Foundation," the ninth *sefirah,* which connects the energies above it with the tenth *sefirah, malchus.*

Yichud Ha-Elyon. "Integration of Divine attributes," a harmonization of the channels through which G-d's influence flows down into the worlds.

Yichuda Ila'ah. "Upper Unification," a term used by the Zohar to describe the desired consciousness when reciting the first line of the *Shema.*

Yichuda Tata'a. "Lower Unification," a term used by the Zohar to describe the desired consciousness when reciting the second line of the *Shema.*

Zohar. Primary text of Kabbalah, containing the teachings of Rabbi Shimon ben Yochai and his disciples in the form of a commentary on the Torah. First published in the late 13th century by Rabbi Moshe de Leon (c. 1250–1305), in Spain.